'This book offers an original Islamic interpretation of formal and substantive equality as requiring Bangladeshi husbands to stop appropriating wives' earnings and to pay them maintenance and dower. Drawing on a deep understanding of national values, the author recommends Bangladesh criminalize income appropriation under existing anti-dowry legislation which does not apply to dower and could significantly improve the lives of working wives.'

Beverley Baines, Professor, Faculty of Law, Queen's University

'*Islam and Women's Income* provides a devastating critique of Bangladesh's dowry system, which both reinforces patriarchal power and reduces married women's control over their earned income. Indeed, Chowdhury develops a powerful argument for the importance of critically assessing the way cultural practices can interact with economic, political and legal forces to reinforce and legitimate gender inequality. This is a shocking and depressing story, but an essential read for scholars, development experts, policy makers and citizens concerned with developing a more gender equal world.'

Jane Parpart, Research Professor, University of Massachusetts Boston, Conflict Resolution, Human Security and Global Governance

Islam and Women's Income

This book examines the interrelationship between law, culture, patriarchy and religion in the context of contemporary Bangladesh. It explores the role of Islam in society and politics generally, and its influence on gender equality in particular. The work focuses on the situation of married women. Taking a socio-legal approach, it analyses the changing nature of the dowry practice and its relation to women's increasing paid labour force activity. Despite anti-dowry legislation, it is argued here that the dowry system continues in the form of the appropriation of wives' income. The work calls for legal recognition of this action and the amendment of the Dowry Prohibition Act 1980 as a result of the changing social realities that are taking place in the lives of Bangladeshi women. An Islamic approach is applied to equality between men and women in addressing and analysing these issues. The book includes international comparisons on gender equality and discusses the role of the Convention on the Elimination of All Forms of Discrimination Against Women (CEDAW), as well as the dowry system in South Asia.

The book will be of interest to academics and researchers working in the areas of law and religion, gender studies and international development.

Farah Deeba Chowdhury is a Scholar in Residence at the Global Labour Research Centre, York University, Canada. She has served as an Associate Professor in the Department of Political Science at the University of Rajshahi, Bangladesh and has also held a SSHRC Postdoctoral Fellowship in the Department of Gender Studies at Queen's University, Canada. She specializes in the areas of Islam, gender and law; gender and work; gender and politics; and gender and development. She has published widely on these topics.

ICLARS Series on Law and Religion

Series Editors: Silvio Ferrari, University of Milan, Italy, Russell Sandberg, Cardiff University, UK, Pieter Coertzen, University of Stellenbosch, South Africa, W. Cole Durham, Jr., Brigham Young University, USA and Tahir Mahmood, Amity International University, India

The *ICLARS Series on Law and Religion* is a new series designed to provide a forum for the rapidly expanding field of research in law and religion. The series is published in association with the International Consortium for Law and Religion Studies, an international network of scholars and experts of law and religion founded in 2007 with the aim of providing a place where information, data and opinions can easily be exchanged among members and made available to the broader scientific community. The series aims to become a primary source for students and scholars while presenting authors with a valuable means of reaching a wide and growing readership.

Other titles in this series

Religion and Equality
Edited by W. Cole Durham, Jr. and Donlu Thayer, Brigham Young University, USA

Church and State in Scotland
Francis Lyall, University of Aberdeen, UK

Religion as Empowerment
Edited by Kyriaki Topidi and Lauren Fielder, both at University of Lucerne, Switzerland

Religions and Constitutional Transitions in the Muslim Mediterranean
Edited by Alessandro Ferrari and James Toronto

Blasphemy, Islam and the State: Pluralism and Liberalism in Indonesia
Stuart Fenwick, Australian Catholic University and University of Melbourne, Australia

Islam and Women's Income

Dowry and Law in Bangladesh

Farah Deeba Chowdhury

Routledge
Taylor & Francis Group
LONDON AND NEW YORK

First published 2017
by Routledge

2 Park Square, Milton Park, Abingdon, Oxfordshire OX14 4RN
52 Vanderbilt Avenue, New York, NY 10017

Routledge is an imprint of the Taylor & Francis Group, an informa business

First issued in paperback 2020

British Library Cataloguing in Publication Data
A catalogue record for this book is available from the British Library

Library of Congress Cataloging-in-Publication Data
Names: Chowdhury, Farah Deeba, author.
Title: Islam and women's income : dowry and law in Bangladesh / Farah Deeba Chowdhury.
Description: Abingdon, Oxon ; New York, NY : Routledge, 2017. | Series: ICLARS series on law and religion | Includes bibliographical references and index.
Identifiers: LCCN 2016025688| ISBN 9781138228467 (hardback) | ISBN 9781315390697 (adobe reader) | ISBN 9781315390680 (epub) | ISBN 9781315390673 (mobipocket)
Subjects: LCSH: Marital property—Bangladesh. | Dowry—Bangladesh. | Women—Legal status, laws, etc.—Economic aspects—Bangladesh. | Muslim women—Legal status, laws, etc.—Bangladesh.
Classification: LCC KNG552.C46 2017 | DDC 346.549201/5—dc23
LC record available at https://lccn.loc.gov/2016025688

ISBN: 978-1-138-22846-7 (hbk)
ISBN: 978-0-367-59554-8 (pbk)

Typeset in Galliard
by Swales & Willis Ltd, Exeter, Devon, UK

Dedicated to the memory of my parents, Fabeha Chowdhury and Abdul Muttalib Chowdhury, for inspiring me to acquire knowledge

Contents

Acknowledgements

This book is a revised version of my PhD dissertation, which I completed at Osgoode Hall Law School, York University, Canada. First, I would like to express my deep and sincere gratitude to my supervisor, Professor Shelley Gavigan, for her guidance, inspiration and support. This book builds on my previous research on middle-class married women's income in Bangladesh, which I completed under the supervision of Professor Ann Porter for the MA programme in Political Science at York University. I am profoundly grateful to Professor Porter for her inspiration and insightful thoughts which greatly helped in the completion of this book. I am also grateful to Professor Craig Scott for his valuable comments on my dissertation as well as Professor Benjamin Berger and Professor Patricia McDermott for their constructive suggestions. During my time as a Postdoctoral Fellow at Queen's University, I conducted research on marriage transactions among South Asian Muslims in Canada, which was funded by the Social Sciences and Humanities Research Council of Canada (SSHRC). This research greatly helped me in revising my PhD dissertation and updating the information regarding the dowry system in South Asia as well as that pertaining to the current socio-economic, cultural and legal status of Bangladeshi women. I am indebted to Professor Beverley Baines, my postdoctoral supervisor, for her inspiration and constant support. A big 'Thank you' goes to all the staff members of the Osgoode library for their timely assistance.

I would also like to express my heartfelt appreciation to my parents. At a time when people were concerned about wealth, my parents taught me the value of education and intellect at a very young age. My parents, who are no longer with me, are still a big part of this journey. The confidence that they instilled in me helped me face all the obstacles while writing this book. Despite the geographical distance, my sisters, Helen and Darnee, were always with me. I am especially grateful to Helen for collecting from Bangladesh many valuable research materials used in this book. Without her assistance, this book would not have been completed. I am also grateful to my husband, Zaglul, for his support and for sharing our household activities in order to give me the time to work on this book. Finally, I would like to acknowledge my daughters, Mehran, Lubaba and Nashat, who are my constant sources of strength and inspiration in my writing on women's issues and Islam.

1 Introduction

This book is a study of the interrelationship between law, culture, patriarchy and religion in the context of contemporary Bangladesh. The particular focus of this book is the situation of married women in Bangladesh, where 90.39 per cent of the population is Muslim (Bangladesh Bureau of Statistics, 2013, p. 51) and Islam plays a very important role in society and politics. The legal status of Muslim women in Bangladesh is defined by the Muslim personal law along with the general law, which is secular in nature. The Muslim personal law covers the areas of marriage, divorce, maintenance, guardianship of children and inheritance. The general law deals with rights under the constitution, penal codes, civil and criminal procedure codes, evidence acts, etc. (Kamal, n.d, p. 4). This book argues that while Islam plays a vital role in Bangladeshi society and politics, many practices involve a misinterpretation of Islam that serves the interests of husbands who seek to control their wives' income and other financial resources and assets. In Bangladesh, most husbands, and in some cases in-laws, control women's income and assets either directly or indirectly. I characterize this appropriation of wives' income as a new form of dowry. This book builds on my previous research concerning middle-class married women's income in Bangladesh. For this research, I undertook interviews with 50 middle-class working women in Rajshahi, one of the divisional cities in Bangladesh, to determine the extent to which married women are able to control their own income, and was able to establish that most husbands, and in some cases mothers-in-law, do indeed control wives' income directly or indirectly (Chowdhury, 2007; Chowdhury, 2010b).

Bangladesh, which achieved independence in 1971, has been experiencing rapid socio-economic changes. Traditionally, women in Bangladesh are expected to take on child rearing and domestic activities. A central argument of this book is that Bangladeshi women are oppressed through misinterpretations of Islam by Bangladeshi men. Historically, women were prevented from being educated and joining the paid labour force through the misinterpretations of religion. Since independence, growing economic hardships, increasing opportunities for female employment and education, together with changing societal attitudes towards female employment and education have facilitated the entry of women into the paid labour force (Chaudhury, 1979, p. 162). Bangladeshi women, both urban and rural, are no longer hesitant about joining the paid labour force whenever opportunities arise (Khan, 1993, p. 3). Islam is no longer a barrier to women's paid work outside the home, but through the misinterpretations of Islam, married women are still expected to contribute their entire income exclusively to their husbands, children and in-laws' families. In Bangladesh, it is generally accepted that upon marriage women are transferred to their husbands' families (Chowdhury, 2004, p. 247). Most husbands consider their wives as property, and the patriarchal culture in Bangladesh falsely teaches girls that it is their religious duty to ensure the happiness of only their husbands and their husbands' families. Bangladesh's patriarchal society does not convey messages to women of their broader responsibilities set out by Islam (Chowdhury, 2009b, p. 610). Husbands, and in some cases fathers-in-law and mothers-in-law, control wives' income directly or indirectly (Rashid, 2006, p. 156; Chowdhury, 2010b). I find that husbands employ a number of strategies to control their wives' income, including: withdrawing their financial support; directly taking all of their wives' income; saving their own money while expecting their wives to meet family expenditures; threatening their wives by saying that they will not allow them to continue their jobs unless they hand over all of their income; buying land or flats in their own names by taking out loans and then repaying the loans with their income, thus compelling their wives to meet family expenditures; giving false information about loan commitments to their wives thereby trying to take all of their wives' income for personal expenditure; attempting to use their wives' income to invest in businesses; and appropriating their wives' income to maintain their parental family. Generally, however, wives are not allowed to look after their own parental families (Chowdhury, 2010b, pp. 1–30).

Despite these widespread practices by Bangladeshi husbands, Islamic law actually prohibits the appropriation or control of a wife's income by her husband or in-laws. Dower is an essential part of Muslim marriages. The distinction between dowry and dower is often misunderstood. Dower is religiously sanctioned and approved by the state and personal law; however, dowry is neither religiously sanctioned nor supported by state law in Bangladesh. The dower is paid by the husband to his wife as an honour and to show respect, and also to show that he seriously desires to marry her with a sense of responsibility and obligation (Monsoor, 2003). On the other hand, dowry refers to 'the transmission of large sums of money, jewelry, cash and other goods from the bride's family to the groom's family' (Monsoor, 2003). Maintenance is the lawful right of a wife to be provided at the husband's expense with food, clothing, accommodation and other necessities of life in Bangladesh. This law derives from the injunctions of the *Quran*, the Prophet's traditions and the consensus of jurists. In Bangladesh, a wife is entitled to maintenance whether she is economically solvent or not. In *Mst. Amena Khatun* v. *Sherajuddin*, (1965) the lower court took the view that the husband was absolved from the duty to maintain his wife because she was a woman of means. On appeal to the higher court, C. J. Murshed held that, legally, such a proposition is not tenable. The competence of a wife does not absolve the husband from his duty to maintain her (*Mst. Amena Khatun v. Sherajuddin*, 1965, p. 690). According to Islam, women have every right to spend their income independently and to control their own money. Badawi (n.d., p. 16) writes:

> No married woman is required to spend any amount at all from her property and income on the household. In special circumstances, however, such as when her husband is ill, disabled or jobless, she may find it necessary to spend from her earnings or savings to provide the necessities for her family. While this is not a legal obligation, it is consistent with the mutuality of care, love and cooperation among family members.

Formally, dowry has been abolished by law in Bangladesh (Government of the People's Republic of Bangladesh, 1980). Despite the anti-dowry legislation, the dowry system has continued and shifted as a result of women's increasing paid labour force activities. When women started participating in paid employment, men adopted various strategies to accumulate wealth from their wives. Their attitude is: 'We do not want dowry. We want working women.' Women's income is considered as 'sufficient compensation for waiving dowry demands' (Kabeer, 1997, p. 299). A woman worker said: 'How can they ask for dowry to marry us? We are the dowry' (Kabeer, 1997, p. 291).

I argue in this book that Bangladeshi law should be reformed to make the appropriation of wives' income into a punishable offence. I recognize that law alone cannot change Bangladeshi society. Social change has to be more than just legal reform, but the legal reforms that I am recommending for the Dowry Prohibition Act 1980 can be the first step to changing societal values. After the act came into being, many families changed their way of demanding dowry. Men now say that they do not want dowry, but they want working wives. In fact, their main intention is to appropriate wives' income. The legal reforms that I recommend will very likely have an impact on the people of Bangladesh. Women will be able to use this law, once reformed, as a bargaining tool within their marriages and divorced women will be able to take their husbands to court for violating the law.

In this book, I use an Islamic approach to equality between men and women in addressing and analysing this issue. Islam incorporates both formal and substantive equality regarding Muslim women. In my book, I demonstrate that Muslim women have every formal legal right to control what they earn and possess. Informed by an understanding of substantive equality, I argue that a wife's ability to earn does not absolve her husband from his duty to maintain her. Dower and maintenance, to be provided at the husband's expense, and encompassing food, clothing, accommodation and other necessities of life, is the lawful right of a wife in Bangladesh. The practice of appropriating or controlling wives' income should be considered a form of dowry and made a criminal offence because of the presence of Islamic dower and maintenance laws in Bangladesh.

Theoretical and conceptual issues

Equality debates in the West

The struggle for women's equality and the elimination of discrimination lies at the heart of contemporary feminism. However, from the very beginning, the definition of equality has been controversial and contested. In the early years of the twentieth century, the concept of formal equality was used in the West by feminists who began to struggle for universal suffrage. Feminists in the United States, the United Kingdom and Canada argued that they deserved the same rights and privileges as men and considered the issue of suffrage as the most important of their goals (Kealey, 1979, p. 10). Advocates for such formal equality are associated with liberal feminism. A liberal concept of equality calls for the elimination of laws and social practices that discriminate against women. This model is informed by the writings of John Stuart Mill (1869), who opposed laws and social practices that deprived women of equal civil rights. Diana Majury (2002) writes, 'Formal equality is premised on the understanding that equality means treating likes alike and posits same treatment as its defining feature' (p. 305). Using formal equality, women have officially achieved legal equality with men in the West. The recognition of formal equality between men and women was an essential step towards achieving legal and social equality. Sandra Fredman (1997, p. 11) writes:

> The extent of the contribution of liberal feminists to the emancipation of women should not be under-estimated. The slow but consistent movement towards removal of formal legal impediments against women was achieved partly because of the effective harnessing of liberal concepts to the cause of women's emancipation.

In the UK, full equality was not achieved until 1928 when the voting age for both men and women was set the same at twenty-one. However, formal equality was not realized and until 1963 women were prevented from entering the House of Lords. Furthermore, sex-based discrimination against women also continued legally until 1975 and political rights for women took decades to take effect fully (Fredman, 1997, p. 66). Formal equality has found expression in law reform in Canada. Canadian women achieved the right to vote in federal elections in 1918 (Hogg, 2009, p. 1059). In addition to the right to vote, they achieved the right to an education, to practise a profession, to earn money, to own property, to hold office and so on, just as men have. In the United States, equality has been shaped by the 'evolution of the equal protection doctrine', which is guaranteed by the constitution through the Fourteenth Amendment. However, the American Constitution offers a very broad guarantee of equal protection under the law (Weisberg, 1993, p. 123). The Supreme Court used constitutional equal protection analysis in the case of pregnancy in *Geduldig* v. *Aiello* and held that a state disability insurance programme's pregnancy-based categorization was not a violation of equal protection (*Geduldig* v. *Aiello*, 1974). As the Supreme Court identified this as a classification between women who are pregnant and people who are non-pregnant, this comparison based on pregnancy discrimination was not seen as discrimination based on gender. In the case of *General Electric Co.* v. *Gilbert*, the Supreme Court again upheld another disability plan where pregnancy-based discrimination was not considered sex discrimination in employment (*General Electric Co.* v. *Gilbert*, 1976).

However, due to feminist criticism, the Pregnancy Discrimination Act was passed in Congress in 1978 to prevent further discrimination based on pregnancy, childbirth and other related medical conditions (Weisberg, 1993, p. 123). Early cases in British courts also held a similar restrictive outlook of equality where likes were treated alike. As there are only pregnant women and no male equivalent, British courts completely excluded pregnancy from anti-discrimination law, and discrimination based on pregnancy was thus legally permitted (Fredman, 1997, p. 185). Later, in *Hayes* v. *Malleable Men's Working Club and Institute* (1985), the treatment of pregnant women was compared to that of ill men. However, even this argument is flawed, as Fredman (1997) points out that in order to find a male equivalent, pregnancy is being compared to an illness, which it is not and 'should not be stigmatized as unhealthy' (p. 186).

Martha Chamallas (2003) has argued that Western feminists placed an importance on women's similarity to men (p. 16). In her view, a formal concept of equality considers 'difference as a disadvantage', but the formal equality approach proved ineffective when biological differences such as pregnancy came before the court (Chamallas, 2003, p. 18). Stella Bliss, a pregnant woman in Canada, was fired and claimed unemployment insurance benefits after the birth of her child (*Bliss* v. *Attorney General of Canada*, 1979). She argued that she did not find any jobs despite her availability for work, so she was entitled to unemployment insurance benefits. The Unemployment Insurance Commission denied Bliss benefits on the ground that she was only entitled to maternity benefits, pursuant to section 46 of the Unemployment Insurance Act.[1] However, Bliss did not qualify for the maternity benefits, because under the act she had not worked long enough before the birth of her child. She only qualified for the regular benefits. In *Bliss* v. *Attorney General of Canada*, Stella Bliss argued that section 46 contravened the guarantee of equality before the law. The court held, 'Section 46 applies to women, it has no application to women who are not pregnant, and it has no application, of course, to men. If section 46 treats unemployed pregnant women differently from other unemployed persons, be they male or female, it is, it seems to me, because they are pregnant and not because they are women' (*Bliss* v. *Attorney General of Canada*, 1979).

The issue of pregnancy in the gender equality debate divided feminist theorists into two camps. The 'equal treatment' camp argued that identical treatment of both men and women is required without regard to pregnancy. In their view, pregnancy is a physical condition that affects the ability of an employee to work and pregnant women should not be treated differently from workers with other disabilities. The 'special treatment' camp rejects this formal equality model and argues for an equal opportunity model. This camp argues that 'positive pregnancy-specific benefits' should be introduced in the workplace to ensure equal opportunity for women, so that pregnant women are not disadvantaged due to biological differences (Weisberg, 1993, p. 124). For instance, Herma Hill Kay (1993) argues that biological reproductive sex differences should be considered and, as women's pregnancies are only for brief and self-contained periods, legal provisions should be provided against discrimination based on their sex or pregnancy (p. 187). Ann Scales (1981) argues that the law should recognize sex differences in a strictly limited way and recommends having rights different from men for pregnancy and breastfeeding (p. 435). For Anne Phillips (1987), 'Men and women are different; they are also unequal; feminists will continue to debate and disagree over how far the inequality stems from the difference, and how far the difference can or should be eliminated' (p. 22). Although formal equality is appropriate in some areas, for example voting rights, pay equity and property ownership, it is argued by many that it is not a perfect fit in areas of family law, such as alimony, child support, child custody and divorce (Jhappan, 1998, pp. 69–70). Sameness of treatment perpetuates inequality, especially in the context of family law (Fineman, 1991, p. 35; Fineman, 2009, p. 108). Despite the recognition of full citizenship, the benefits of citizenship are still distributed unevenly. Legal feminists are seeking other routes to equality for women due to problems with the formal equality approach. They argue for a 'substantive equality' approach that is concerned with the effect of legal rules and the inequalities that persist notwithstanding formal equality and gender neutrality. In the words of Canadian Chief Justice Beverley McLachlin (2001), 'Substantive equality is founded on the principle that all human beings are of equal worth and possessed of the same innate human dignity, which the law must uphold and protect, not just in form, but in substance' (p. 21). Advocates of substantive equality argue that equal treatment can cause unequal outcomes, because of the present social conditions and sex-based differences. They also argue that rules should consider these conditions and differences to remove unfair gender-related consequences (Bartlett, 1999, p. 6). Rosemary Hunter (2008, p. 4) writes:

> The concept of substantive equality has appeared more promising, as it involves taking into account gender-related differences in order to produce substantively fair results. This model is designed to deal with the phenomenon of structural discrimination rather than simply focusing on individual treatment. It acknowledges that treating people as if they were the same as a norm from which they actually differ in significant ways is just as discriminatory as penalizing them directly for their difference, and it suggests that dominant norms themselves need to be changed.

Elizabeth Archampong (2006, pp. 92–93) further explains the rationale of the substantive equality approach:

> It calls for acknowledging the differences in the way rules impact the sexes and seeks to eliminate unfair gender related outcome of rules. The shift to a substantive equality approach has led to theorizing about law with a focus on achieving equality that has a 'real' positive impact for women. Substantive equality has been manifested in laws that address women's differences from men, sometimes applying rules differently in order to eliminate particular disadvantages women experience in a male dominated society.

Archampong (2006) relies upon a substantive equality approach to analyse Ghana's matrimonial property legislation and cases concerning marriage breakdown. In her view, equality means, 'recognizing and giving similar significance to each spouse's contribution (whether by money or work or otherwise in the context of the matrimonial relationship) to the acquisition of property of the marriage' (Archampong, 2006, pp. 107–108).

The formal equal treatment approach can be useful for women who can conform to the male norm, who are less involved in child rearing activities and who have the financial resources to hire other women to work for them at home. It is also useful for those women who work in liberal institutions that accommodate their roles as mothers (Krieger and Cooney, 1983, p. 545). However, as Nancy Kim (1993) observes about the limitation of the liberal equality model, it 'ignores the needs of women as a class. It seeks gender neutrality, but in a world where "gender neutrality is simply the male standard" formal equality merely perpetuates the status quo (and consequently, the subordination of women)' (p. 97). Indeed, in the words of prominent United States feminist Catharine MacKinnon (1989), 'man has become the measure of all things' (p. 220). The notion of male as norm must be broken in order to establish equality (Miles, 1985, p. 67). The law in the United States, especially in the case of divorce, treats women more or less as equals of men despite custom, discrimination in the workplace and the traditional division of labour within the family, all of which combine to make women very unequal to men (Okin, 1989, p. 4). According to a liberal model of equality, 'once women are treated the same as men, equality will be achieved through individual competition in the societal marketplace' (Krieger and Cooney, 1983, p. 537). However, the idea of formal equality in family law reform does not consider the actual differences between men and women in employment and earning capacities or the problems of balancing child care with a full-time job, especially for women who have custody of children. In an early 'trilogy' of cases, the Supreme Court of Canada adopted the concept of formal equality for spouses at divorce (Mossman, 1994, p. 24). Later, the court moved to a substantive equality approach. In *Moge* v. *Moge* (1992), the court made the connection between women's poverty, spousal support and real equality, and ruled that Ms Moge was entitled to ongoing support from her husband.

Equality cannot be achieved by legislation where men and women are differently situated (Weitzman, 1985, p. 365). Formal equality masks real discrimination. Mary E. Becker (1993, p. 226) writes:

> treating women and men as though they are equal when, in fact, they are not has worsened the post-divorce economic position of women and children, especially those women (and their children) who are most in need because they are least like men.

Treating women the same way as men is not sufficient to achieve women's rights or equality. Different treatment is needed to achieve an equality of result (Eberts, 1985, p. 196). Thus, a combination of equal rights and differential or special rights are important for achieving equality (Wolgast, 1980, p. 42). Julia Abida Sohrab (1993, p. 159) does not totally reject either of the two approaches to equality: equal treatment or special treatment. She argues that we should not consider any specific right without examining the broader structure:

> The perceived necessity of making a choice between equal or special treatment is a false choice. In some areas equal rights are necessary, while in others it is gender-specific rights that are necessary, for instance in pregnancy. Neither approach is, nor should be, the exclusive 'answer' or strategy or claim, and arguing over substantive equality by opposing equal with special and vice-versa is at best redundant and at worst a costly distraction.

In my book, I use both the formal and substantive equality models within Islam.

Equality within Islam: formal and substantive

Having introduced equality debates within Western feminism, I now turn to the Islamic approach to equality, which I think is misunderstood in the West. Shaheen Sarder Ali (2000) analyses women's human rights in Islam by interpreting the basic texts of Islam from what she characterizes as a 'woman's perspective' (p. 5). She categorizes the verses of the *Quran* related to women into four categories: protective, corrective, non-discriminatory and discriminatory. She argues that protective and corrective categories of rights can be taken and turned into non-discriminatory categories because of the changing social condition (Ali, 2000, p. 57). However, in my view, the relationship between men and women and their roles in Islamic law are based on notions of both formal and substantive equality. The following verses of the *Quran* reveal that men and women are equal:

> And their Lord has accepted of them and answered them: 'Never will I suffer to be lost the work of any of you, be it male or female: you are members, one of another.' (3:195)
>
> If any do deeds of righteousness be they male or female and have faith, they will enter paradise and not the least injustice will be done to them. (4:124)
>
> For Muslim men and women and for believing men and women, for devout men and women, for true men and women, for men and women who are patient and constant, for men and women who humble themselves, for men and women who give in charity, for men and women who fast (and deny themselves), for men and women who guard their chastity, and for men and women who engage much in Allah's praise, for them Allah has prepared forgiveness and great reward. (33:35)
>
> The Believers, men and women, are protectors, one of another: they enjoin what is just and forbid what is evil. (9:71)

Islam adopts a formal equality approach in the context of full possession and control over women's wealth. Islam guarantees complete control by women over what they earn and possess. Ali (2000, p. 38) writes:

> She has been guaranteed complete control over what she earns and possesses. A woman is *sui juris* (legal person) and can make independent decisions as regards, entering into a contract, and the acquisition, disposal and alienation of property. The property laws of the Qur'an guarantee women the right to have full possession and control of their

> wealth including dower, during marriage and after divorce. In the area of family law too, certain provisions afford women complete equality. For example, the right to enter marriage of her own will, on attaining adulthood, without an intermediary (*wali*).

The following *Quranic* verses support full possession and control over their wealth:

> From what is left by parents and those nearest related there is a share for men and a share for women, whether the property be small or large, – a determinate share. (4:7)

> To men is allotted what they earn, and to women what they earn. (4:32)[2]

As I have demonstrated in the previous section, a substantive approach to equality recognizes differences (Wentholt, 1999, p. 55). Similarly, Islamic law recognizes physical and biological differences between men and women and it gives importance to the 'complementary but equally important roles of men and women' in the family (Venkatraman, 1995, p. 2004). Amina Wadud (1999) who interprets the *Quran* 'from within the female experience' argues, 'the *Quran* reveals a necessary and complimentary distinction between men and women . . . they have the same rights and obligations on the ethico-religious level, and have equally significant responsibilities on the social-functional level' (p. 102). Asma Barlas (2002) analyses the *Quran*, characterizing herself as a 'believing woman' (p. 19). She writes that she does not challenge its ontological status as Divine Speech, but challenges 'the legitimacy of its patriarchal readings' (Barlas, 2002, p. 19). She wants to understand the words of God and people's understanding of God's words (Barlas, 2002, p. 19). Barlas (2002, p. 204) argues:

> Not only does the *Quran* not employ the concept of sexual differences (or sameness) to discriminate against women, but it affirms the principle of the ontic equality of the sexes. This is why I believe that we can theorize radical sexual equality from the *Quran*'s teaching.

The *Quran* considers women and men 'as contraries ("A" and "B") and not as contradictories ("A" and "not A")' (Barlas, 2002, p. 136). The *Quran* considers women and men equally on some issues and differently on other issues, family and marriage, for example (Barlas, 2002, p. 197). Treating women and men identically does not necessarily mean treating them equally, and treating them differently does not necessarily result in inequality between them (Barlas, 2002, p. 5). Riffat Hassan (1999) sees the *Quran* 'through a nonpatriarchal lens' and finds that it does not discriminate against women. She argues, 'Women are exempted from the responsibility of being breadwinners in order that they may fulfill their function as child bearers. The two functions are separate but complementary, and neither is higher or lower than the other' (Hassan, 1999, p. 265).

Considering physical and biological differences, Islamic law imposes upon men the financial responsibility of the maintenance of their wives and children. Factual differences should not be concealed and legal distinctions should not always be avoided for establishing equality between men and women (Emon, 2013, p. 237). The right to maintenance and dower is intended to ensure women's economic security within marriage. Additionally, sexual violence against women also sometimes prevents them from entering certain forms of employment in many countries of the world. For these reasons, Allah did not make it mandatory for women to maintain themselves or their families. But it does not mean that within Islam women are considered inferior. The *Quran* considers women rational, because they have the same religious and moral duties and responsibilities as men. In fact, Islamic law acknowledges women's unpaid work, especially childbearing, child rearing and breastfeeding activities. Islam does not put double or triple burdens on women by making paid work mandatory for them. However, this does not mean that women do not have any rights to join the paid labour force. There is no decree in Islam that prevents women from seeking paid employment. There are no restrictions on the use of women's exceptional talents in any area of society, politics or the economy (Badawi, 1977, p. 141). However, working wives also have the right to maintenance and dower from their husbands.

Methodology

I use a socio-legal approach and have relied upon both primary and secondary sources. These include books, journal articles, dissertations, internet sites, reports, newspapers, government documents, cases and legislation as well as the *Quran*. In this book, I analyse the Dowry Prohibition Act 1980 and examine cases regarding Muslim family law in Bangladesh. I review the *Quran*, the Prophet's traditions and the opinions of Islamic scholars in order to analyse the status of women in Islam. I also use the interviews of 50 middle-class[3] working women in Bangladesh, which I undertook in 2006. The interviews were conducted in Rajshahi, one of the divisional cities in Bangladesh. As I wanted to interview middle-class working women from different professions, I went to schools, colleges, different departments of the University of Rajshahi, government offices and NGOs (non-governmental organizations). I approached women who were working at these different institutions for interviews and some of them volunteered to be interviewed. When showing them the questionnaire, I informed the women involved that the interviews would be informal discussions based on this. I started interviewing after obtaining informed consent from the women and getting them to sign the consent forms. Face-to-face interviews were conducted through open discussions. I asked the questions not in an interrogative way, but through informal discussions I had with the women; this meant that the interviews were more like conversations and that the whole process was very interactive. During the interviews, I took notes by hand. I used pseudonyms for maintaining the confidentiality and privacy of my respondents. I was also a middle-class working woman myself in Bangladesh at the time. Thus, my background helped me establish a rapport with the respondents. Out of the 50 working women I interviewed, most respondents (20 women) were employed in administrative jobs. Two were lawyers, two were doctors, eight worked in NGOs, six were bankers and twelve were teachers. Among the teachers, five were school teachers, four were college teachers and three were university teachers. Most (27 women) had master's degrees. Two had an SSC (Secondary School Certificate), four had an HSC (Higher Secondary School Certificate), twelve had bachelor's degrees and three had PhDs. Two women also had MBBS (Bachelor of Medicine and Bachelor of Surgery) degrees.

Overview of remaining chapters

Chapter 2 focuses on the important role of Islam in society and politics in Bangladesh. The majority of Bangladeshis do not tolerate even the slightest damaging or derogatory remark or criticism against Islam and the government and political parties are very careful about speaking on religious issues. Islam is recognized as the state religion in the Bangladeshi Constitution. Both the Bangladesh Awami League (AL) and the Bangladesh

Nationalist Party (BNP) use Islam to gain mass support in elections. Given the strength of the Bangladeshi population's commitment and devotion to Islam, the present prime minister, Sheikh Hasina, has pledged not to enact any laws or formulate any regulations that are inconsistent with the *Quran* and the *Sunnah* (Bangladesh Awami League, 2014). This chapter also focuses on women and Islam in Bangladeshi society. The ideology of Islam determines the relations between men and women in Bangladesh. Women are oppressed through the misinterpretations of Islam by Bangladeshi men and I analyse how Bangladeshi society uses these misinterpretations to make women seemingly inferior. Some popular books on Islam misinterpret the religion and reinforce husbands' supremacy over their wives due to women in Bangladesh lacking Islamic knowledge. It is generally accepted that women are transferred to their husbands' families through marriage. Therefore, husbands consider their wives as their own property and the patriarchal culture in Bangladesh teaches girls that their religious duty is to make only their husbands and husbands' families happy. On the contrary, women in Islam have other moral and religious responsibilities, including responsibilities towards their own parents. In the interests of men, Bangladeshi patriarchal society does not convey to women these messages of their broader responsibilities. Its dominant message is that women only have responsibilities towards their husbands, children and members of their in-laws' families.

Chapter 3 analyses Muslim family law in Bangladesh. I examine women's rights in Muslim family law in Bangladesh and I analyse the dower and maintenance laws in Bangladesh. I also explore polygamy, divorce, child custody and guardianship, and inheritance laws in Bangladesh. I argue that the reform of Muslim family law in Bangladesh can only be done within an Islamic framework. I also argue that existing law does not need any major reforms and has the potential to protect women from exploitation and violence.

Chapter 4 deals with the Convention on the Elimination of All Forms of Discrimination Against Women (CEDAW), Islam and women in Bangladesh. How does CEDAW conflict with Islamic law? Is the Bangladeshi government constrained in withdrawing the reservations on article 2 and article 16.1[c] of CEDAW? Does Islamic law contradict article 16.1[c] and article 16.1[d] of CEDAW that impose an obligation to ensure that men and women have the same responsibilities during marriage and its dissolution, and the same responsibilities as parents? How do these provisions affect Muslim women's lives if the same responsibilities during marriage and its dissolution and the same responsibilities as parents are ensured? Do these articles of CEDAW deprive women of their financial rights accorded by Islamic law? I address these questions in this chapter. I argue that in the name of equal responsibility, working women are taking on *more* than equal responsibility. CEDAW assumes that paid work is the key to women's liberation, but paid work cannot ensure equality between husbands and wives at home. CEDAW ignores the presence of conflicting human rights principles, such as equality between men and women on one hand and the right to freedom of religion, culture and custom on the other. If CEDAW is fully implemented it will deprive Muslim women of their maintenance and dower rights and the maintenance of children by their fathers. CEDAW ignores the vulnerable position of women, especially in developing countries, and in the name of formal equality it places the same responsibilities as men on women in the family. It encourages women to join the paid labour force at any cost, which perpetuates inequality.

Chapter 5 deals with dowry, women and law in Bangladesh. How does the dowry system work in South Asia? How did the dowry system emerge in Bangladesh? What are men's expectations from their wives or wives' families? I argue that dowry increased with the expansion of capitalist relations, which help men in Bangladesh to accumulate capital.

It has been turned into 'demand, extortion, material gain, and profit maximization' (Samuel, 2002, p. 205). The most common motives behind the dowry system are the grooms' and their families' greed, growing consumerism, excessive materialism, status seeking and rising expectations of a better and luxurious life.

Chapter 6 deals with women's income and dowry in Bangladesh. The general perception in Bangladesh is that women's power in the family increases when they earn money. How has the dowry system shifted as a result of women's increasing paid labour force activities? What are the limitations of the anti-dowry law in Bangladesh? This chapter examines these questions.

Chapter 7 concludes by bringing together the issues that I analyse throughout the book in order to make recommendations for amending the Dowry Prohibition Act 1980. In sum, this book argues that despite women's participation in the paid labour force, we cannot expect any major changes in the status of women if appropriation of wives' income by their husbands or in-laws continues. If Bangladeshi women are not able to control their own income, then paid employment will only give them a double burden instead of benefit and this will further strengthen patriarchy.

Notes

1 Unemployment Insurance Act 1971, S.C 1970–1971, c. 48, s. 46 stated: 'Subject to section 30 [the pregnancy benefits section], a claimant is not entitled to receive benefit during the period that commences eight weeks before the week in which her confinement for pregnancy is expected and terminates six weeks after the week in which her confinement occurs.'
2 This may refer to shares of inheritance, wages and reward in the Hereafter.
3 One must have some educational and cultural attainment to belong to the middle class in Bangladesh (Karim, 1980, p. 235). Here, middle class is also considered a middle-income group.

2 Women and Islam in Bangladesh

One highly educated Bangladeshi woman asked me, 'Is it mandatory for a man to divorce his wife, if his mother asks him to divorce her?' Her husband said that a son must divorce his wife if his mother wants him to divorce her. She was extremely shocked to hear this, but did not say anything. When she heard that I was working on Islamic family law, she asked me about it, saying, 'If Islam allows this, how can I protest?' I said that marriage in Islam only requires the consent of a husband and a wife; divorce in Islam also only requires the decision of a husband or a wife. No other person can decide whether a husband or a wife should initiate divorce and it is a great sin to instruct anyone to divorce, because divorce is the last resort in Islam. It is not encouraged, although it is permitted. The woman was relieved after hearing this from me. Her question and comment suggest that Islam is powerful in Bangladesh, yet Bangladeshi men and women lack proper Islamic knowledge and the religion is often misinterpreted by men.

As a result, Bangladeshi women are oppressed and made to feel inferior. Benazir Bhutto, the former prime minister of Pakistan and the first woman to lead the government of a Muslim country writes, 'We learned at an early age that it was men's interpretation of our religion that restricted women's opportunities, not our religion itself' (Bhutto, 1988, p. 31). Boys are regarded as assets in Bangladeshi patriarchal society, while girls are considered to be liabilities.

The birth of a son is welcomed because not only will he be a future earning member of the family, he will contribute to the 'continuity of the lineage and old age security' (Maloney et al., 1981, p. 107). A daughter is considered to be a burden to the family and she is always treated as a temporary family member, because she is given away to another family through marriage and her children belong to the other family (Maloney et al., 1981, p. 107). Parents who do not have sons feel insecure in the absence of security provided by the state. Kotalova (1996) did some research on a Bangladeshi village. In the village a young mother exclaimed to her after giving birth to a girl, 'A girl? What for? She will leave one day. Here she will stay like a guest fed for others' (Kotalova, 1996, p. 65).

What is the role of Islam in Bangladeshi society and politics? Does Islam consider women inferior to men? How are women being portrayed in the popular books on Islam in Bangladesh? How does patriarchy work in a husband–wife relationship in the name of Islam? I will address these questions in this chapter. I argue that Islam is very powerful in Bangladesh and Bangladeshi society misinterprets Islam in order to make women inferior. Some popular books on Islam, whether intentionally or unintentionally, misinterpret Islam and in doing so reinforce husbands' supremacy over their wives given the lack of Islamic knowledge in Bangladesh. It is believed that women are transferred to their husbands' families through marriage. Husbands consider their wives as their property and the patriarchal culture in Bangladesh teaches girls that their religious duty is to ensure only the happiness of their husbands and husbands' families. On the contrary, women in Islam have other moral and religious responsibilities, including responsibilities towards their own parents. In the interests of men, Bangladeshi patriarchal society does not convey to women these messages of their broader responsibilities. Its dominant message is that women only have responsibilities towards their husbands, children and members of their in-laws' families.

The politics of Islam in Bangladeshi society

After a nine-month-long bloody struggle, Bangladesh achieved its independence on 16 December 1971 and on 16 December 1972 the country instituted a fully fledged constitution. This constitution incorporated four basic principles of the state: nationalism, socialism, democracy and secularism. The ruling party, the Bangladesh Awami League (AL), never articulated what it meant by a socialist economy. It seemed that by socialism it meant a policy of nationalization. Despite having socialism as one of the state principles, the AL continued to depend on the surplus of farmers in villages who made up its old power base. In urban areas it depended on lawyers, businessmen and educated professionals (Jahan, 1987, p. 101). Secularism was adopted as the state ideology and, in the beginning, this meant the non-use of religious symbols in state activities. Secular slogans such as *Joy Bangla* (Victory of Bengal) were used in public meetings and on radio and television. Religious slogans such as *Allahu Akbar* (God is Great) were dropped. However, the Bangladeshi population considered the non-use of religious symbols as an anti-Muslim and pro-Indian ideology. Under pressure from the people, the government began defining secularism as giving equal status to all religions in public life (Jahan, 1987, pp. 115–116). While Islam was not expressed strongly for the time being, it was never dead and re-emerged in Bangladeshi politics (Maniruzzaman, 1990, p. 64). In 1975, General Ziaur Rahman (popularly known as Zia) came to power through coups and countercoups. Zaglul Haider (2006) argues, 'The Zia regime substantially shifted from the Mujib regime and at first changed the constitution giving increasing attention to Islam' (p. 203). Zia included *Bismillah-ar-Rahman-ar-Rahim* (in the name of Allah, the Beneficent, the Merciful) at the beginning of the constitution and substituted 'secularism' with 'absolute trust and faith in the Almighty Allah'. He discarded the socialist economic policy of Sheikh Mujibur Rahman and introduced special measures for privatization. Zia reintroduced a multi-party system in Bangladesh and also allowed and legitimized Islamic politics, which were banned under the Sheikh Mujibur government on the grounds of communalism (Haider, 1999, p. 73).[1] After the country's independence in 1971, the *Morning News* reported:

> The government of the peoples' republic of Bangla Desh (Bangladesh) has banned four communal parties with immediate effect. These four political parties are Muslim League and all its factions, Pakistan Democratic Party, Nezam-e-Islam and Jamat-e-Islami. In addition to these, the government has also banned the Pakistan People's Party. The announcement was made by the Bangla Desh government in a radio broadcast.
>
> (Manik, 2009)

The Zia government amended the constitution through proclamation orders issued at different times between August 1975 and April 1979 and the amendments were ratified through the Fifth Amendment (Hakim and Hauqe, 1995, p. 262). Zia was killed in an abortive military coup. On 24 March 1982 General H. M. Ershad came to power through a bloodless coup. Ershad also followed a market-oriented economic policy, which was prescribed by the International Monetary Fund (IMF), the World Bank and donors (Kabir, 1995, p. 553). Ershad emphasized Islamic values and in an apparent attempt to gain popularity he made Islam the state religion of Bangladesh. Both Sheikh Hasina[2] and Khaleda Zia[3] played major roles in the 1990 mass upheaval against Ershad and he was forced to resign. Ershad handed over power to the Chief Justice of the Supreme Court, Justice Shahabuddin Ahmed, who was a consensus candidate of all opposition political parties, on 6 December 1990. All opposition political parties gave a mandate to hold free and fair parliamentary elections within three months of him assuming office. The fifth parliamentary election was held under Justice Shahabuddin Ahmed on 27 February 1991.

In the 1991 election, secularism versus 'absolute trust and faith in the Almighty Allah' was one of the most debated issues. The AL declared that it would re-establish secularism as it was stated in the original 1972 constitution. The BNP declared that it would not return to the 1972 constitution. Khaleda Zia said, 'We do not want to establish impiousness in the name of secularism. We want to ensure the equal rights of people of all religions.'[4] An eight-party alliance led by the AL declared that it did not oppose keeping *Bismillah-ar-Rahman-ar-Rahim* in the constitution.[5] In a meeting, Sheikh Hasina said, 'There is no hostility between secularism and *Bismillah*. Secularism does not mean impiousness; rather it is the essence of Islam. In Islam the principle of secularism is against ultra-communalism. We are God fearing people, but not fanatic.'[6] The BNP headed by Khaleda Zia formed the government with the support of the Jamaat-e-Islami, Bangladesh (Jamaat). The government continued a free-market economic policy (Baxter, 1992, pp. 166–167). In the 1996 parliamentary elections the AL won and formed the government. Although ideologically the AL believed in socialism, it changed its manifesto and has adopted a free-market economic policy since 1992 (Ahmed, 2003, p. 60). In the 2001 parliamentary elections the BNP and its three coalition partners[7] secured a two-thirds majority and Khaleda Zia again formed the government. Although Islamic parties were the coalition partners of the Khaleda Zia government, Islamic militancy was not observed in the election. Rather, the performance of the AL government over the preceding five years was the main issue in the election. People did not see any do-or-die Islamic agenda (Rashiduzzaman, 2002, p. 187). In the 2001 parliamentary elections the Islamists and the BNP fought in the election against the AL, but Khaleda Zia did not share the same manifesto with the Islamic parties (Rashiduzzaman, 2002, p. 188).

Although the AL claims to be a secular political party, it always uses religion to secure mass support. It signed a memorandum of understanding (MoU) with the Bangladesh Khelafat Majlish, a fundamentalist Islamic party, before the ninth parliamentary elections, which were scheduled to be held on 22 January 2007. The accord stated that, if voted to power, the alliance would not enact any laws which would contradict the values of the *Quran*, the *Sunnah* and the *Sharia*. The accord also stipulated that the alliance would 'reserve the right' of a certain category of Islamic clerics 'to issue fatwa', that criticism of prophets and their associates would be considered a criminal offence and that steps would be taken to ensure government recognition of certificates awarded by the Qaumi madrassah.[8] Sheikh Hasina defended the agreement with the Khelafat on a 'tactical ground' to ensure its victory in the parliamentary elections against the BNP-led four-party alliance.[9] The elections scheduled for 22 January were cancelled and the president declared a state of emergency in the wake of the AL-led grand alliance's boycott of parliamentary elections and its series of siege and *hartal* (total shutdown) programmes to resist the polls.[10] Again, both the AL and the BNP used Islam to secure mass support in the ninth parliamentary elections that were held on 29 December 2008. Khaleda Zia and Sheikh Hasina both launched their election campaigns with a visit to the holy shrine of Shah Jalal in Sylhet. Khaleda Zia urged people, 'Save the country and Islam by voting for the BNP and its alliance and don't cast your vote for those who defamed the religion.'[11] Hasina pledged not to enact any laws or formulate any regulations that would go against the *Quran* and the *Sunnah*.[12] The AL's election manifesto in the ninth parliamentary elections 2008 also mentioned, 'Laws repugnant to the *Quran* and the *Sunnah* shall not be made' (Bangladesh Awami League, 2008).

A Bangladeshi newspaper, which supports secularism, published the following report on election day to demonstrate that Sheikh Hasina was a devout Muslim:[13]

> Awami League (AL) President Sheikh Hasina spent most of yesterday reciting from the Holy Quran, praying and holding indoor meetings with foreign election observers . . . After offering Fazr prayers and reciting from the Holy Quran, Hasina met the election observing delegation of International Republican Institute around 7:30 am at her Sudha Sadan home in Dhanmondi. . . . She recited from the Holy Quran for several hours and offered Esha and especial prayers for the salvation of her departed family members who were killed on August 15, 1975.

In the elections, the AL alone won 230 seats with an absolute majority out of the 262 seats won by the entire AL-led alliance. The alliance led by the BNP faced a sudden disaster in the elections, wining only 32 seats. Both Sheikh Hasina and Khaleda Zia won the highest number of seats, with three each. The AL received 49.02 per cent of votes in the ninth parliamentary elections. On the other hand, the number of popular votes cast for the BNP was 32.74 per cent.[14] A majority of the Bangladeshi population do not want any legislation which is inconsistent with Islamic law, which is why in the ninth parliamentary elections the AL had to promise that 'laws repugnant to the *Quran* and the *Sunnah* shall not be made'. The AL was planning to ban religion-based political parties. However, fearing a strong public backlash, the AL government was not able to do this and could not remove the phrase *Bismillah-ar-Rahman-ar-Rahim* and the declaration of Islam as being the state religion from the constitution.[15] The High Court rejected a 1988 writ petition challenging Islam as the state religion according to the Eighth Amendment in the constitution.[16]

Considering the strong role of Islam in Bangladeshi society and politics, the AL chooses to use religion in politics. Prime Minister Sheikh Hasina said, 'The words "Bismillah-Ar-Rahman-Ar-Rahim" in the preamble to the constitution and declaration of Islam as the state religion will remain as they are, since they reflect the beliefs of the people.'[17] Hasina also said the decision on whether a political party would be banned rested with the Election Commission, not with the government.[18] The Bangladeshi parliament passed the Fifteenth Amendment, where Islam's status as the state religion was retained in the constitution as well as the phrase *Bismillah-ar-Rahman-ar-Rahim*. The amendment allowed religion-based politics, which had been banned on paper after the cancellation of the Fifth Amendment, but it also restored two of the four basic principles of the 1972 constitution – socialism and secularism. Secularism was restored by dropping the phrase 'absolute faith in Allah' from the constitution. Basic provisions of the constitution were then made non-amendable.[19] The AL reintroduced secularism in Bangladesh and yet again promised in the tenth national parliamentary elections, 'No law contradicting the *Quran* and the *Sunnah* will be passed' (Bangladesh Awami League, 2014). Terming Bangladesh as a Muslim-majority country, Prime Minister Sheikh Hasina said that the country would be run as per the Madinah Charter and the last sermon and directives of Prophet Muhammad (PBUH).

She said, 'There will be no law against the Holy Quran and Sunnah here ever.' Hasina also mentioned that the government stated clearly in the Women Development Policy that if any international laws had anything against the *Quran* and the *Sunnah*, they would not be applicable in Bangladesh.[20] Several bloggers were killed by Islamist militants for their anti-Islamic writings. Although Sheikh Hasina does not support the killings of bloggers who write against Islam, in an effort to satisfy the Muslim-majority Bangladeshi population she warned bloggers:[21]

> Dirtiness and porn story writings aren't called free thinking. A few people are writing abusive and porn stories regarding religions . . . Hitting the emotions of believers in religions is not expected and acceptable. Currently, dirty thinking takes place of free thinking.

Huque and Akhter (1987, p. 200) argue:

> Generally, the people of Bangladesh have strong attachments to Islam, and no one among the rulers and the ruled would risk retribution by opposing or criticizing religious customs, practices and beliefs. A large number of Bangladeshis do not perform the mandatory religious practices, but most display their devotion to Islam in public. [Casting] [t]he slightest aspersion on Islam results in hostile public reaction, which is why neither the government nor the opposition political parties of Bangladesh speak out against Islam.

In Bangladesh, people want to see the use of religious symbols at state level. Sheikh Hasina and Khaleda Zia frequently perform Hajj (pilgrimage) and attend religious functions so that people accept they are practising Muslims. They have to follow the Islamic dress code by covering their heads with a sari. Many women in Bangladesh, especially in rural areas, observe purdah by covering themselves with a burkha or chador. Some women use scarves, ornas or saris to cover their heads. Although many people from the East and the West believe that purdah enhances women's subordination, a British anthropologist, Katy Gardner (1994, p. 1), finds that a pious, purdah-observing village woman is one of the most powerful women in her community:

> She owns a large amount of land, and runs her family with a will of iron. She, rather than her sons is indisputably head of the household; there is no question that, as popular Western images of purdah frequently suggest, she is passive and subordinate.

Another study shows that the burkha actually enhanced the mobility of Muslim women and it also increased their participation and visibility in social activity (Feldmann and McCarthy, 1983, p. 953.). Sheikh Hasina and Khaleda Zia also ensured their participation and visibility in the politics of Bangladesh by showing that they followed the Islamic dress code (Chowdhury, 2009a, p. 557). White (2010, pp. 336–337) also observes that the visibility of Islam is increasing in Bangladeshi society:

> The number of mosques has grown, and they are more elaborate, with more people attending . . . There is also increased observance of core Islamic practice, such as prayer and fasting, including amongst the young and a marked increase in women wearing maxis, burqas and shawls over their saris.

Women, Islam and society in Bangladesh

I have three daughters and I am very proud to have three daughters. My husband also feels the same way, but many people in Bangladesh think that we must be unhappy and disappointed because we don't have any sons. They console us and say, 'Oh, you don't have any sons. What can you do? You have no control over it. It will be good if you raise your daughters as sons.' By this they mean that if we provide a good education for our daughters, they will be established in life like men. Geetiara Safia Choudhury, a former advisor of the interim caretaker government in Bangladesh and the chief executive of the advertising firm Adcom, who is recognized as an icon in the communications and advertising industry in Bangladesh, stated in an interview that her father raised her as a son.[22] Shakhina, a village girl who is now studying at the Asian University for Women, Bangladesh, was encouraged by her parents to get an education. Her father used to tell her, 'You are not my daughter, you are my son' (Ismail, n.d.). After the death of Syed Mohsin Ali, the Social Welfare Minister of Bangladesh, his daughter Sabrina Sharmin wrote on Facebook:[23]

> I could not show him that I was really my dad's son. I am the youngest of three sisters, but my dad used to say that I was his son. He introduced me as his son to everyone. He asked me to perform many duties. I had to take on responsibility for my sisters' weddings, the medical treatment of my parents and family members at home and abroad, my dad's social and political activities, our family business, etc . . . I promise . . . I will dedicate my life to the welfare of the people and I will really prove that I am your son.

These comments reflect the views of many Bangladeshis who subconsciously believe that girls must be treated as boys in order to receive equal opportunities in education and paid employment. It is as if girls do not inherently have these rights simply because they are born into the world as girls. However, education is not only a right, but a responsibility of all Muslim males and females. Prophet Muhammad (PBUH) said, 'Seeking knowledge is mandatory for every Muslim' (Badawi, n.d., p. 22). Here, the term Muslim is used to refer to both males and females. It is believed that investing in a daughter who will be transferred to another family through marriage is a waste of resources. There is an old Bengali saying, 'Caring for a daughter is like watering a neighbor's tree' (Raynor, 2005, p. 83). As such, in rural areas of Bangladesh only a few girls were sent to school. Rounaq Jahan (1975, p. 4) writes:

> According to the 1961 census only 21.9 percent of rural females (as compared to 46.7 percent of males) were enrolled in school between the ages 5 to 14. Girls are given some schooling only by economically and socially established families. And that schooling usually consists of learning how to read and recite the Quran (the holy Book) and four or five years of formal school attendance. The major purpose of formal schooling is very similar to that of the girl's informal learning at home, i.e. training her to be a good wife and a mother. A girl's stock in the marriage market goes up if she has some formal schooling. Educated men prefer wives who can at least read and write letters and keep basic accounts. 'Respectable' families in rural areas therefore give their daughters some formal schooling so that they can be married to educated men employed in urban areas.

At the time of independence in 1971, the number of boys being enrolled in primary schools was twice as high as that of girls. This gender gap in primary schools started to close during the 1980s and 1990s. Gender parity in enrollment in primary schools was noticeable by 2005 (Amin and Chandrasekhar, 2009, p. 5). Girls' gross enrollment in secondary school was 13.6 per cent in the 1990s and it increased to 46.9 per cent in 2000. The female to male ratio of gross enrollment was 0.39 in 1970, but it increased to 1.05 in 2005 (Amin and Chandrasekhar, 2009, p. 5). Free tuition for girls and monetary incentive programs are offered in Bangladesh to reward families for sending girls to secondary school. These incentive programs have been introduced especially to raise the age of marriage through facilitating continued education and thus encouraging later marriages and lower fertility (Amin and Huq, 2008, p. 3). Girls' enrollment in secondary school is increasing; however, the dropout rate of girls is still higher than that of boys. Boys' enrollment in primary school was 54.7 per cent, while girls' enrollment was 45.3 per cent in 1995. In 2015, it increased to 97.1 per cent for boys and 98.8 per cent for girls. Boys' enrollment in secondary school was 53.03 per cent in 1995 while that of girls was 46.91 per cent. In 2015, this increased to 62.16 per cent for boys and 71.85 per cent for girls. On the other hand, boys' dropout rate from secondary school in 1995 was 51.69 per cent and for girls it was 48.31 per cent, while in 2015 the dropout rate for boys was 33.72 per cent and that of girls was 45.92 per cent. Girls are dropping out before completing secondary education because of poverty and a lack of security and these in turn lead to child marriages.[24]

I observed that in the 1970s many people in Bangladesh believed that female education should only be up to class five, so that women can keep basic accounts and write letters. That is why many girls were only educated up to that point. However, educated girls were increasing and I observed that after the mid 1970s parents who wanted highly educated grooms had problems finding them, as the demands of grooms changed. Grooms started to demand girls who had passed at least the SSC or the HSC. In the 1980s, I observed that it was not easy to find an educated groom if girls did not have bachelor's degrees from colleges or if they were not studying at universities. As a result, parents changed their minds about providing education to girls at higher levels. At present, parents are interested in educating their daughters, but their intentions are to find better grooms. Female students in Bangladesh study to get certificates and degrees, not to acquire knowledge. Their certificates and degrees ensure better marriages (Chowdhury, 2002, p. 190). One respondent in Arends-Kuenning and Amin's (2001) study on women's capabilities and education in Bangladesh said, 'If I educate my son, then he will be able to get a job and survive. If I educate my daughter, I will be able to get her married well. Or she can get a job and survive' (p. 134). Male–female relationships in Bangladesh are determined by Islam, but women in Bangladesh do not know what their rights and responsibilities are in Islam, because the objective of educating daughters is only for marriage or getting a job, not for acquiring knowledge. It is generally thought that only Islamic scholars can understand and interpret the *Quran*. This is clearly in conflict with the *Quran*, which gives importance to actually understanding it. The *Quran* says: 'Verily, We have made this (Quran) easy, in your tongue, in order that they may give heed' (44:58). The instruction in the *Quran* is to apply one's intellect in understanding it. It warns those who do not apply the faculty of their reasoning. It is obligatory for a Muslim to believe, read, understand, apply and share the *Quran*. The *Quran* says:

> Read! In the Name of your Lord Who has created (all that exists). (96:1)
>
> Say: Are those equal, those who know and those who do not know? (39:9)
>
> We explain in detail the signs for a people who give thought. (10:24)

Bangladeshi women only read the *Quran* in Arabic; they do not bother to read the Bengali translations of the *Quran* and think about what the *Quran* actually says. The patriarchal society in Bangladesh does not encourage women to acquire knowledge and develop their thinking abilities. The Bangladeshi education system is based on memorizing and girls are not encouraged to acquire deeper or broader knowledge or to apply reasoning in understanding the *Quran*. Women are thus oppressed and exploited in Bangladesh because of the misinterpretations of Islam by Bangladeshi men as well as their own lack of understanding of Islam.

Bangladeshi society has made men superior through the misinterpretation of Islam. Sultana (2010) writes about preferences for sons in the rural areas of Bangladesh: 'In my community, I observed some of fathers refused to see a new born baby if the baby is a daughter. Sometimes a mother was blamed and tormented by her husband or relatives if she delivers a daughter' (p. 33). I also observed at the university where I worked in Bangladesh that many highly educated women prefer sons because they see their own position in their families as inferior compared to their brothers or husbands. In addition, they are socially conditioned to think and believe that they are inferior to men. Many women in Bangladesh welcome their female children with tears. When a woman does not have a son, everybody consoles her, 'Allah (God) did not give you, what will you do?' It is as if God punished that woman by not giving her a son. The *Quran* does not condone the unwelcoming attitudes among some parents upon hearing the news of the birth of a baby girl instead of a baby boy. The *Quran* (16:58–59) states:

> When the news is brought to one of them of (the birth of) a female (child) his face darkens and he is filled with inward grief! With shame does he hide himself from his people because of the bad news he has had! Shall he retain her on (sufferance and) contempt or bury her in the dust? Ah! what an evil (choice) they decide on!

The *Quran* abolished the practice of female infanticide and warned that the crime of infanticide against innocent girls would be revealed and questioned on the Day of Judgment: 'When the female (infant), buried alive, is questioned – For what crime she was killed' (81:8–9). Parents must support their daughters and show kindness and justice to them. Prophet Muhammad (PBUH) said:

> Whosever has a daughter and he does not bury her alive, does not insult her, and does not favor his son over her, Allah will enter him into paradise.
>
> Whosever supports two daughters till they mature, he and I will come in the day of Judgment as this (and he pointed with his two fingers held together).
>
> (Badawi, n.d., p. 22)

The birth of a boy or a girl is completely determined by Allah and women should not be blamed for this. The *Quran* (42:49–50) states:

> He creates what He wills. He gives to whom He wills female (children), and He gives to whom He wills males. Or He makes them [both] males and females, and He renders whom He wills barren. Indeed, He is Knowing and Competent.

Women and men in Bangladesh do not know that the *Quran* does not state anywhere that one gender is superior to the other. Badawi says, 'The Quran makes it clear that the sole basis for superiority of any person over another is piety and righteousness not gender, color, or nationality' (Badawi, n.d., p. 13).

The *Quran* (49:13) states:

> O mankind! We created you from a single (pair) of a male and a female and made you into nations and tribes that you know each other. Verily the most honoured of you in the sight of Allah is (one who is) the most righteous of you. And Allah has full knowledge and is well acquainted (with all things).

Although Bangladeshi men claim that they are devout Muslims, when the question of women arises, they misinterpret Islam and discriminate against women. Schuler et al. (1996, p. 1730) argue:

> Discrimination against women and girls in everyday life is rationalized by the fact that they are seen as an economic burden. Girls learn to accept dependence and deprivation relative to male family members. In extremely poor families where frequently there is not enough for everyone, this means that women and girls are most likely to go without a meal, to eat inadequate meals, to go without warm clothing in the winter and to receive minimal health care and education.

Women in the popular books on Islam in Bangladesh

Instead of trying to understanding the *Quran*, many Bangladeshi women turn to popular textbooks to learn about Islam. It is thus important to know what these publications present in order to understand attitudes about women in Bangladesh. It is common for many Bangladeshi households to carry a copy of popular Islamic books, such as *Maksudul Momeneen* (Rahman, 1984), *Maksudul Mumin* (Anwari, 2002) and *Bahishti Zewar* (Thanwi, n.d.). As such, I also had a copy of all of these books at home in Bangladesh. In my teen years I found these books, especially *Bahishti Zewar*, to be very helpful in learning prayers and understanding basic principles of Islam. To this day, I find *Bahishti Zewar* to be a very useful introductory book about basic Islamic principles and prayers. Metcalf (1990, p. 13) points out that:

> The *Bihishti Zewar* differs in significant ways from the advice books for women that proliferated in nineteenth-century America and England – or in Bengal . . . Unlike them, however, this work did not attempt to enhance gender differences, making women's unique self-sacrifice and dependence the key to a guardianship of morality. That guardianship was entrusted to anyone, woman or man, who honed his or her essential character to Islamic standards through knowledge and through relentless discipline and self-control.

However, as I read and began to understand the sections of these books relating to women, I found that these specific interpretations were actually misinterpreted from the *Quran* and the *Hadith*. In my view, the misinterpretations in these books regarding women may, in fact, serve to legitimize and justify both male supremacy and the subjugation of women in the name of Islam (Hashmi, 2000, pp. 71–90). For example, *Maksudul Momeneen* (Rahman, 1984, p. 327) and *Maksudul Mumin* (Anwari, 2002, p. 487) both mentioned that the Prophet said, 'A wife's heaven lies under the feet of her husband.' Bangladeshi men try to impose male supremacy and try to control and oppress women with this message; however, there is no validity of this in the *Hadith* (Shehabuddin, 2008a, p. 594). In *Maksudul Momeneen* (Rahman, 1984), Mohammad Golam Rahman sets out thirty-five commandments for becoming the ideal woman (pp. 343–356) and his advice seems to promote a husband's supremacy over his wife. One of the representations of an ideal woman would be for her to accede to the following: 'If your husband asks you to stand beside him with your hands tied up the entire night, obey him, because then Allah and the Prophet will be happy with you' (Rahman, 1984, p. 347). In *Bakishti Zewar*, Maulana Ashraf Ali Thanwi also instructs women to do the same (p. 54). Moreover, Thanwi adds (p. 53), the Prophet said:

> If the husband orders his wife to carry the boulders of one mountain to the next mountain and the boulders of the next mountain to another mountain, then the wife should be ready to do this difficult and meaningless command then and there.

Women are advised that men are angry by nature and wives should accept this and have patience. Women should not argue with their husbands, even if they disagree. Even if women are right, they should not tell their husbands straightaway. Instead, they should first listen to their husbands and then explain to them later, slowly and steadily with patience and a smile (Rahman, 1984, p. 349). These books state that men have the right to beat their wives and swear at them using vulgar language (Thanwi, n.d., p. 54; Rahman, 1984, p. 350). The authors state that women should always try to understand their husbands' moods. If women see that their husbands are in a joyful mood, then they should talk to them nicely with a smile. If women see that their husbands are not in a good mood, then they should never giggle in front of them. Husbands may become angry with their wives and they may beat their wives or swear at them, which is why women should behave carefully (Thanwi, n.d., p. 56; Rahman, 1984, p. 350). The books also advise women not to be angry with their husbands if they beat them or swear at them when they find that something was their fault and wives should not hide themselves away from their husbands. Rather, wives should admit that it was their fault and apologize politely by touching their husbands' hands and feet (Thanwi, n.d., p. 56; Rahman, 1984, p. 351). Women should not stop serving their husbands, even if their husbands are bad people. Women should not compete with their husbands or show anger to correct them, because men's anger is like the tiger's. When a tiger gets angry, its prey is torn apart and eaten (Thanwi, n.d., p. 59). The patriarchal society in Bangladesh spreads a message that men should express anger to show masculinity and they must show it to their wives to control them. This message contradicts the *Quran*. The *Quran* (3:133–134) states:

> Be quick in the race for forgiveness from your Lord, and for a Garden whose width is that (of the whole) of the heavens and of the earth, prepared for the righteous, Those who spend (freely), whether in prosperity, or in adversity; who restrain anger, and pardon (all) men; for Allah loves those who do good.

Islam does not allow husbands' cruelty towards their wives. Prophet Muhammad (PBUH) taught men to be kind to women and he said 'the best of you is the best to his family (wife)' (Badawi, n.d., p. 24). The *Quran* asks husbands to be kind and considerate to their wives, even if they do not like them, but patriarchy in Bangladesh hides this message and gives men the authority to oppress their wives. The *Quran* (4:19) states:

> O you who believe! You are forbidden to inherit women against their will. Nor should you treat them with harshness that you may take away part of the marital gift you have given them except where they have been guilty of open lewdness; on the contrary live with them on a footing of kindness and equity. If you take a dislike to them it may be that you dislike a thing and Allah brings about through it a great deal of good.

Contrary to the teachings of the *Quran*, these books are legitimizing men's cruel and oppressive behaviour towards women so that patriarchal domination is maintained in Bangladesh. Thanwi (n.d.) advised women, 'Do not disagree with your husbands' opinions or do not do anything that they do not like, even if your husband says that it is day when it is actually night, do not protest' (p. 54). The *Quran* says, 'The Believers, men and women, are protectors, one of another: they enjoin what is just, and forbid what is evil' (9:71). So, why can Bangladeshi women not correct their husbands and have a say in what is right and what is wrong? Women in Bangladesh are considered inferior due to some misinterpretations in popular books that justify wife-beating. Thanwi (n.d., p. 54) also justifies wife-beating. He writes:

> One of the rights of the husband is that a wife should not remain in an untidy and sloppy state. Instead she should always remain clean and beautiful for her husband. In fact, if she remains untidy and sloppy despite her husband ordering her to remain clean, he has the right to beat her.

Golam Rahman (1984, p. 378) also justified wife-beating for four reasons:

1 If a husband calls his wife to come beautifully, but the wife disobeys him;
2 If a husband calls his wife for sexual intercourse, but the wife does not come without any valid reason under *Sharia*;
3 If the wife gives up praying and taking baths for purity;
4 If the wife goes to another person's house without her husband's permission.

One verse in the *Quran* (4:34–35) is misused by many Bangladeshi men to justify wife-beating. That particular verse is:

> Men are the protectors and maintainers of women, because Allah has given the one more (strength) than the other, and because they support them from their means. Therefore the righteous women are devoutly obedient, and guard in (the husband's) absence what Allah would have them guard. As to those women on whose part you fear disloyalty and ill conduct, admonish them (first), (next), refuse to share their beds, (and last) beat them (lightly) [darb]. But if they return to obedience, do not seek against them means (of annoyance): for Allah is most High, Great (above you all). If you fear a breach between them twain, appoint (two) arbiters, one from his family, and the other from hers; if they wish for peace, Allah will cause their reconciliation: for Allah has full knowledge, and is acquainted with all things.

Azizah Y. al-Hibri (2003) argues that the *Quran* completely changed beating into a non-violent symbolic act (p. 208). The *Quran* says that beating should be an act of last resort. Beating a wife is prohibited for Muslim men for any reason other than disobedience, which is mentioned in the *Quran* (al-Hibri, 2003, p. 209). The husband must establish that the wife is disobedient and disobedient women are those who do not honour marital contracts and thus disobey Allah. The focus of obedience here is Allah, not the husband and this obedience is not obedience to the husband's arbitrary rule (al-Hibri, 2003, pp. 214–215). The husband must undergo numerous steps of anger management and conflict resolution and, if all of these steps fail, he can then think of maybe hitting his wife symbolically, perhaps with a bunch of basil or a handkerchief (al-Hibri, 2003, p. 209). The *Quran*'s permission for hitting is limited only to disobedient women and hitting can only be symbolic (al-Hibri, 2003, p. 212). The *Quran* states, 'the parties should either hold together on equitable terms, or separate with kindness' (2:229). It was clear in the last speech of Prophet Muhammad (PBUH) that adultery is the act of a disobedient woman. The Prophet said:[25]

> O People, it is true that you have certain rights with regard to your women, but they also have rights over you. Remember that you have taken them as your wives only under Allah's trust and with his permission. If they abide by your right then to them belongs the right to be fed and clothed in kindness. Do treat your women well and be kind to them for they are your partners and committed helpers. And it is your right that they do not make friends with any one of whom you do not approve, as well as never to be unchaste.

Abusulayman (2003) points out that the word *daraba* has approximately 17 different meanings in the *Quran*. Some of the meanings are: 'to isolate, to separate, to depart, to distance, to exclude, to move away' (p. 19). He argues (p. 20):

> the purpose of this verse is reconciliation in a dignified manner and without coercion or intimidation as each spouse has the ability and the right to dissolve the relationship. Therefore, the meaning of *daraba* cannot imply the infliction of injury, pain, or disgrace. The most straightforward interpretation is hence that of departure, separation or seclusion. This arrangement where the estranged husband deserts his wife altogether for some time, helps to bring the situation to a possible resolution because it is the final step beyond admonishing her and refusing to share her bed. Now, as the husband is away, the wife has ample opportunity to rethink the whole situation, to ponder the eventual consequences, and to realize the inevitable outcome of disobedience and rejection, namely divorce. At this point she must carefully decide if she would prefer to be separated permanently from her husband or be returned to the marital state. It is the moment of the truth and if she is the party in the wrong, she has the choice to see reason and win back her estranged husband before it is too late. Therefore, *daraba* in the context of improving a difficult marital relationship and resorting harmony, should be construed as to 'leave' the marital home, to 'move away' or 'separate' from her. This is the last resort before seeking the mediation of arbiters from their respective families.

Abusulayman (2003) also argues that the above interpretation is consistent with the tradition of the Prophet. The Prophet never beat his wives. If wife-beating was allowed in Islam, then he would have practised it first (p. 21). However, the majority of Muslim scholars came to the conclusion that while the act of 'beating' (non-violent and symbolic with a bunch of basil or a handkerchief) is permissible in Islam, not doing it at all is preferable and more graceful (al-Hibri, 2003, p. 222). They also agreed that a woman has the right to divorce her husband if she is physically and verbally abused by him (al-Hibri, 2003, p. 222). Forced sexual relationships are also justified in the name of Islam. The objective of marriage in Islam is to have mutual support, mutual comfort and mutual protection between a husband and a wife. How will forced sexual relationships create love, affection and mercy? When marital sexual relationships are reciprocal, then both the husband and the wife can enjoy their sex life. The *Quran* (30:21) says:

> And of His signs is that He created for you from yourselves mates that you may find tranquility in them; and He placed between you affection and mercy. Indeed in that are signs for a people who give thought.

The following verses of the *Quran* (2:222–223) are used to justify the fact that forced sexual intercourse is allowed in Islam:

> They ask you concerning women's courses. Say: They are a hurt and a pollution,[26] so keep away from women in their courses, and do not approach them until they are clean. But when they have purified themselves, you may approach them in any manner, time, or place ordained for you by Allah. For Allah loves those who turn to Him constantly and He loves those who keep themselves pure and clean. Your wives are a tilth unto you; so approach your tilth when and how you will; but do some good act for your souls beforehand; and fear Allah, and know that you are to meet Him (in the Hereafter), and give (these) good tidings to those who believe.

Sexual intercourse is prohibited during menstruation to prevent the wife's discomfort. It may hurt women and the restriction is limited only to intercourse, not other types of permitted sexual intimacy (Barlas, 2002, p. 161). Muslims are also not allowed to have sex during fasting when Muslims abstain from food or drink. When the *Quran* says, 'when they have purified themselves, you may approach them in any manner, time, or place ordained for you by Allah', it means that men should always follow whatever Allah orders them to do. Asma Barlas (2002) argues, 'The permission to husbands to go into their wives, then, is not as open ended as it seems; if anything, it is clear that men cannot have sex with their wives as, when, and how they please' (p. 162). Lindsey E. Blenkhorn (2002, pp. 196–197) writes:

> Although Muslim women are routinely characterized as sexually oppressed, women enjoy equal access to sex, which is viewed as neither sinful nor taboo, albeit only in the context of marriage. The Quran recognizes and even fears the normal human sexual urges of both men and women, and thus encourages marriage in the belief that such a union is the only way to safely express and satisfy those urges. Sex is thus very important to marriage; in fact, the full legal consequences of marriage are not realized until sexual intercourse consummates it. Evidence of equal access to sex is indicated by the law that, once a woman moves in with her husband, she has the right to demand sex from him, and if he does not perform, she may either request a divorce or receive additional monetary compensation.

Popular books in Bangladesh also spread a message that the wife's parents' status is lower than the husband's parents' status; the status of the wife's parents is even considered lower than the status of the husband. These books advised women not to allow their husbands to massage their arms and legs, even if they wanted to do it out of love and affection, because women never let their parents touch their feet and the status of their husbands is higher than that of their parents (Thanwi, n.d., p. 56; Rahman, 1984, p. 351). *Maksudul Momeneen* provides an example of a good wife who did not get to see her dying father because she did not have permission to leave the house (Rahman, 1984, p. 331). How is it that women are not allowed to see their dying parents or visit their parents when the *Quran* clearly states:

> And We have enjoined on the person (to be good) to his/her parents: in travail upon travail did his/her mother bear his/her and in years twain was his/her weaning: (hear the command) 'show gratitude to Me and to your parents: to Me is (your final) Goal'. (31:14)

> We have enjoined on the person kindness to his/her parents: in pain did his/her mother bear him/her and in pain did she give him/her birth. The carrying of the (child) to his/her weaning is (a period of) thirty months. (46:15)

Why are women not allowed to perform their religious duty of looking after their parents? Do husbands have the authority to prevent women from taking care of their parents? Why do wives need permission from their husbands? On the contrary, the advice regarding husbands' parents in these popular books ensures their superior position over the status of wives' parents. These books advised women:

> If your husband gives you money, take it happily. And if he gives his money to his parents, be happy. It is better to tell him to give the money to his parents instead of you. This will enhance your position with your in-laws and other members of your husbands' families.
>
> (Thanwi, n.d., p. 57; Rahman, 1984, p. 352)

Women are also advised, 'Serve your parents-in-law happily as long as they are alive. Never argue with them and never hurt their feelings. If your mother-in-law and sister-in-law hurt your feelings, tolerate it' (Thanwi, n.d., p. 57; Rahman, 1984, p. 352). Thanwi (n.d.) writes, 'a wife should think that her husband's mother brought him up with difficulties and hoped that in her old age her daughter-in-law would look after her. A wife should remember this' (p. 57). Thanwi (n.d., p. 49) also writes about wives' visits to their parents:

> A wife can visit her parents once a week. She can visit other relatives (with whom marriage is prohibited) once a year. She cannot demand more than this. Her parents can visit her once a week and the husband has the authority to prevent them from coming more than that. Other relatives also cannot visit more than once a year. Husbands also have the right to prevent them from visiting more than that.

He also wrote (p. 49):

> if the father is ill and there is no one to take care of him, then the wife can go daily and look after her father and her husband cannot prevent her. Even if her father is a non-believer, the same rule applies. If her husband stops her, she should still go. But if she goes without his permission, then she cannot claim her maintenance.

Bahishti Zewar and *Maksudul Momeneen* both also advised women not to visit neighbours and relatives without their husbands' permission (Thanwi, n.d., p. 54; Rahman, 1984, p. 348).

The relationship between a husband and a wife is based on love, cooperation, understanding and mutual advice. My understanding is that it is the duty of both a husband and a wife to know each other's whereabouts and to not engage in extramarital relationships. However, many men in Bangladesh do not feel the need to explain their whereabouts to their wives, while still expecting to know their wives' whereabouts. Many men in Bangladesh often tell their wives, 'Why should I tell you where I am going?' Using the word 'permission', the authors of these popular books ensure male supremacy, when in fact this is about mutually informing each other. These popular books assume that the negative attitudes of men towards women are inherently natural and will never change, which is maybe why they put forward these recommendations for women as a way to possibly ensure their security against the cruel nature of men in their households. However, it was revealed in the *Quran* that all forms of oppression and injustice were to be abolished, which these books neglect to see and, rather than challenging the negative and oppressive attitudes of men, they reinforce patriarchy and male cruelty towards women.

Misinterpretation of Islam and husband–wife relationships in Bangladesh

Islam governs and shapes the relationships of husbands and wives in Bangladesh. Popular books on Islam about husband–wife relationships have a greater influence and impact on Bangladeshi women because they do not have knowledge of Islam and they do not know their rights and responsibilities as set out in the *Quran*. Bangladeshi men misinterpret religion for their own interests and maintain patriarchy. Islam recognizes the difference between men and women and it adopts a substantive equality approach regarding family law. This substantive approach to equality recognizes differences (Wentholt, 1999, p. 55) and Islamic law recognizes the physical and biological differences between men and women, giving importance to the 'complementary but equally important roles of men and women' in the family (Venkatraman, 1995, p. 2004). Dower (*mahr*) and maintenance are the financial rights of Muslim women, which they are entitled to receive from their husbands through marriage contracts. The objective of dower and maintenance laws is to safeguard women's economic position within marriage. Bangladeshi culture forces women to waive their dower on the night of the wedding, thus depriving women of their right of receiving it. A wife is entitled to maintenance whether she is economically solvent or not. The *Quran* instructs men to provide full maintenance to their wives, even if their wives are independently wealthy (Doi, 1984, p. 204). Working wives also have the right to maintenance and dower, but this does not in any way mean that women are considered inferior and passively dependent within Islam.

It is Bangladeshi society that considers women as being passively dependent on men. Bangladeshi people ignore the fact that men are also dependent on women. A wife satisfies her husband's sexual and emotional needs, gives birth to legitimate children, breastfeeds and raises children and these services in turn help a man to work in paid employment. Although men earn money, they depend on women for their survival. Bangladeshi patriarchal society fails to recognize unpaid work done by women, which strengthens patriarchy (Chowdhury, 2009b, p. 613). Even Bangladeshi women themselves do not consider their household activities as work. If someone asks a housewife, 'what do you do?', she replies, 'I do nothing.' One village leader commented on women's work, 'Our women do not work; they only eat and sleep' (Zaman, 1996, p. 3). These patriarchal expressions make women and their unpaid labour inferior to men and their labour outside the home (Chowdhury, 2009b, p. 612). Constructing men as independent and women as dependent masks the dual dependency between men and women, where men (and children) are dependent on women's domestic and reproductive labour while women (and children) are dependent on men for the provision of income (Olmsted, 2005, p. 117). Pregnancy and childbirth receive the following treatment in the *Quran*:

> And We have enjoined on (every) person (to be good) to his/her parents: in travail upon travail did his/her mother bear him/her and in years twain was his/her weaning: (hear the command) 'show gratitude to Me and to your parents: to Me is (your final) Goal'. (31:14)

> We have enjoined on (every) person kindness to his/her parents: in pain did his/her mother bear him/her and in pain did she give him/her birth. The carrying of the (child) to his/her weaning is (a period of) thirty months. At length, when he/she reaches the age of full strength and attains forty years, he/she says, 'O my Lord! Grant that I may be grateful for Your favor which You have bestowed upon me and upon both my parents and that I may work righteousness such as You may approve; and be gracious to me in my issue. Truly have I turned to You and truly do I bow (to you) in Islam (submission).' (46:15)

The *Quran* considers women rational and they have the same religious and moral duties and responsibilities as men (3:195; 4:124; 33:35). Most Bangladeshi men believe that their greater physical strength is a reflection of their superiority. A college principal advised his female students:[27]

> Don't rule over men. See (raising his right hand) I have more strength in one of my hands than five of yours combined. So, men have more strength than women. Women are born weak. Husbands have authority over wives. Women are under men's control.

However, Muslim men in Bangladesh forget that the *Quran* says, 'The Believers, men and women, are protectors, one of another: they enjoin what is just, and forbid what is evil' (9:71). Here the *Quran* assumes that women are also rational and they can also protect men by advising them to do what is just and preventing them from doing what is evil. The *Quran* (103:1–3) says:

> By time,
> Indeed, mankind is in loss,
> Except for those who have believed and done righteous deeds and advised each other to truth and advised each other to patience.

Bangladeshi men ignore the statement in the *Quran* that a 'husband and wife are each other's garments' (2:187), which means that the relationship between a husband and a wife is based on mutual support, mutual comfort and mutual protection (*Quran* 30:21).

In Bangladesh, women are transferred to their husbands' families through marriage (Chowdhury, 2004, p. 247). Husbands consider their wives as their property and Bangladeshi patriarchal culture teaches girls that it is their religious duty to only make their husbands and husbands' families happy. Bangladeshi society teaches that Islam promises paradise for women in return for their complete submission to their husbands. Bangladeshi patriarchal society misuses religion to support this argument and teaches that a wife's heaven lies under her husband's feet; however, this statement is not found in the *Quran* or in the words of the Prophet. Bangladeshi patriarchal society spreads this message in the name of Islam and allows men to exploit women. Due to a lack of proper religious education, women believe this and thus patriarchy is maintained through the misinterpretation of religion (Chowdhury, 2009b, p. 609). Husbands consider their wives as their property and it is believed that a woman's only responsibility is to look after her husband, children and in-laws' families. As such, daughters cannot look after their parents from their in-laws' home. Kabir et al. (1998, p. 362) point out:

> Daughters are considered to be 'temporary guests to the family' who will be married off when they reach the appropriate age. Even if a daughter wants to, according to social norms she is not expected to directly look after her parents or have her parents live with her.

Married women who want to look after their parents are criticized by their husbands and in-laws. The husbands and in-laws always put pressure psychologically on them by saying something like, 'You are so poor and helpless that you do not have anybody to look after your parents.' On the other hand, according to social norms, women must take care of their in-laws. Sometimes husbands and husbands' families sever the relationship with their daughter-in-laws' natal families so that their daughter-in-law cannot look after her parents. When the *Quran* instructs about the responsibilities towards parents, it does not only instruct men, but also women (31:14; 46:15).

The patriarchal society in Bangladesh does not teach women about this instruction in the interests of the husband and husband's family. For this reason, girls are considered liabilities in their natal family. Parents who do not have sons feel insecure in the absence of a welfare system provided by the state. In 2013 the government passed the Parents Maintenance Act. Under the act, every child, both male and female, is responsible for ensuring the maintenance of his or her parents (Parents Maintenance Act 2013). However, in the light of this, I have observed that society has still not changed its attitude towards women's parents. In Bangladesh, married working women are expected to contribute financially only to their husbands and children. Chaudhury points out that a deviation from this norm may cause tensions in the family, an issue that deserves further investigation (Chaudhury, 1979, p. 161). Parents feel ashamed to take their daughters' money because they think that this income belongs to their husbands. A professor who has gained a PhD in the United States thinks that it is inappropriate to take her daughter's money. It seems to her that it is similar to begging or taking another person's resources.

In my study, out of 50 respondents only 9 women reported that they helped their parental families financially after their marriages. Among them, only one woman was able to have her parents live with her without her husband objecting to it. Another respondent's mother lived with her and her husband did not seem happy about it, although he did not explicitly say anything. Two respondents regularly gave money to their parents and two paid for the educational expenses of their brothers. One woman reported that she was only able to give her parents Tk. 400 out of her monthly income of Tk. 9,500. Three respondents said that they sent money to their parents, but not on a regular basis. Nine women indicated that they wanted to help their parents financially, but could not because of their husbands. In two cases, husbands and mothers-in-law did not allow women to help their parents. It was observed that sometimes husbands allowed their wives to spend their income independently when they were absolutely certain that their wives would not spend it on their parents or other people. Ten women spent their money according to joint decisions with their husbands and it was found that in these cases wives did not look after their parental families; husbands knew that they would benefit fully from their wives' income. Thirty-two respondents in total said that they did not help their parental families. Among them, many women believed that it was not their responsibility to look after their parents. One lawyer said, 'I do not look after my parents. I have brothers. If I did not have any brothers, it would be the responsibility of my maternal and paternal uncles to look after my parents.' Husbands become angry when their wives give regular payments to their parents. They say, 'You are wasting your money. You don't save.' Many Bangladeshi women thus do not help or look after their parents in order to make their husbands happy. I found that four working women took care of their mothers-in-law who were unable to move or function independently. However, they said that they cannot look after their own parents and their husbands will never take care of their (wife's) parents in the same way that they (wife) take care of their in-laws. Shonali said:

> I know that my husband will not allow me to give money or look after my parents. He is not nice with my parents and relatives. His attitudes show that they are his enemies. He does not even always allow me to visit my parents. He says, 'They are OK. Why do you need to visit them? My sister is a doctor. She does not give money to my parents.' But her husband who is a doctor always hurts her by saying, 'You are saying that you don't give money. I don't believe that. They are getting at least two taka.'

Monjura earns Tk. 12,000 a month and her father wanted Tk. 500 a month from her, but her husband did not allow her to give it to him. She managed to find a job for her brother. However, her husband always hurts her feelings by saying, 'You are giving your life for your brother. You even managed a job for your brother.' Monika is a government officer and her mother lives with her. She said, 'My husband does not respect her that much. When she needs to go to the doctor, I have to take her. He never says that today I will take her. If this happened to his mum, I would have definitely taken care of her.'

Reba is a college teacher. She cannot look after her parents and relatives because of her mother-in-law. Her mother-in-law does not allow her to visit them when she wants to. However, she takes care of her mother-in-law, because the lady is unable to move on her own. Rekha works in an autonomous institution. She said:

> My husband is not good to my parental family. He does not spend any money for my family, but he takes my salary. He just gives gifts to my relatives when he goes to a birthday party or wedding, but those gifts are not very expensive. But he wants to spend Tk. 50,000 for his niece's wedding.

Rupa is a university teacher. She said:

> My husband takes care of his parental family. His sister did a master's from the University of Rajshahi. He provided all of his sister's educational expenses and paid for all her wedding expenses. He also gives money to his parents every month, but I cannot spend money for my parental family. I can only give them some gifts occasionally and he does not even want me to give gifts to my family members.

On the other hand, many parents who have daughters feel that it is a shame to take money from their sons-in-law. Moushumi and her husband are doctors. She said, 'My parents do not want me to look after them. My husband is very kind. Once he gave Tk. 5,000 as a gift to my mum. She did not take it, because it is her son-in-law's money.' Shahana is a college teacher. She spends a lot of her own money on family expenditures. Once, Shahana's mother came to visit her and stayed for two months. She wanted to stay with Shahana for one more month, but Shahana's husband was always saying to her, 'Your mum doesn't have any shame. She is staying in Jamai's (son-in-law's) house.' Shahana did not understand how it became Jamai's house when she was sharing the costs and paying for many of her household expenses. Some women help their parents, but they cannot do it publicly. Sarah said, 'If I give gifts to my parents or relatives I do not let my in-laws know. If they know, they will say that I am a beggar's daughter.' Rahima earns Tk. 11,000 per month and she only gives Tk. 2,000 to her mother. She said:

> I give, but nobody knows it. One day I gave the money in front of my husband and my mother was so embarrassed. She asked me not to give it any more in front of my husband. My relatives, neighbours, nobody knows. My husband earns only Tk. 6,000 as a teacher at a private college and he is happy that he found an educated officer like me. My mother is always ashamed of even drinking one cup of tea in my house. My brothers and sisters also feel shy when they stay at my house.

Sometimes, husbands take their wives' income to maintain their big parental families, but at the same time they do not want their wives to look after their own parental families. Sometimes husbands and in-laws force women to sever ties with their own parental families. They believe that if women maintain their relationship with their families, they may give them money. Sometimes husbands and in-laws want to sever women's relationships with their parental families to continue their oppression. Nora's husband severed all relations with Nora's parental family so that they would not be able to give her advice on financial matters. Moreover, he wanted to keep Nora isolated from her family so that she would feel helpless and give him all her money. Salway et al. (2005) also find that in-laws limit women's contact with their natal family to exercise their control over them (p. 322). Ranu's parents are not allowed to visit her. Ranu said:

> I cannot argue with my mother-in-law. I have to take care of her, because my husband said that she did a lot for him. I think that my mum also did a lot to have me educated, why does my mum not even have the right to visit me?

Nipu is a banker and she gives money every month to her husband for day-to-day expenses. She also sends money to her parents, and Nipu's husband and in-laws are very unhappy about this. If guests from Nipu's parental family or any of her friends come to her house, she has to give extra money to her husband for their visits, including costs for food. Nipu's husband does not want to maintain good relations with her family and friends. Every time they quarrel, Nipu asks, 'Why did you marry me? I did not ask you to marry me.' He replies by saying, 'I did not know that you are a beggar's child.' Nipu asked her husband to give her gifts for Eid and her husband replied, 'You earn money, why do you need gifts from me?'

Women also have responsibilities to kinfolk, orphans, those in need, neighbours and friends but, in the interests of men, the patriarchal society in Bangladesh never gives women these messages about their broader responsibilities. It only spreads the message that women have responsibilities exclusively towards their husbands, children and in-laws. In Bangladesh, husbands want to appropriate all the income of their working wives and do not even allow their wives to give their own money to charity. When women pay their *zakat* (money for charity),[28] it is their husbands who determine where and to whom the money should go and instruct accordingly. Many women in Bangladesh have no choice as to where their *zakat* goes. Women are expected not to think beyond their husbands, children and husbands' families. Moreover, Muslim men in Bangladesh demand dowry from their poor in-laws, which they are not allowed to do under the law or Islam. The dowry system indicates the superiority of men and is a way to establish patriarchal norms. Muslims should help their in-laws when they are in need, whether rich or poor (even rich people can be helpless when they have nobody to look after them). However, Bangladeshi men are appropriating their in-laws' resources in the name of marrying their daughters, acting as if they are saving the girls' lives. How do men in Bangladesh claim to be practising Muslims while carrying out this unethical practice? The Prophet said, 'A woman is married for four things, i.e. her wealth, her family status, her beauty and her religion. You should marry the religious woman (otherwise) you will be losers.'[29] As things stand at the moment in Bangladesh, wealth, family status and beauty are important factors in selecting brides, but the question of how religious a woman is does not seem to matter (Chowdhury, 2010a, pp. 203–209).

How do Muslim men claim to be good Muslims when they forbid their wives to take care of their own parents and consider taking care of their wives' parental families as a waste of money? How do Bangladeshi men encourage or force women to sever ties with their parents and blood relations? Why should women only look after their in-laws and not their own parents? These are the main reasons why parents prefer having sons. The Prophet said, 'One who disregards blood ties of kinship will not enter Paradise.' Do Bangladeshi men not violate Islamic law by forcing or encouraging their wives to sever all relations with their families? A governing assumption of Bangladeshi society is that men are always right and women are always wrong and that is why the responsibility of men is to correct women. Men want to keep women under their control so that they can rule over them. Even many highly educated women in Bangladesh always have to hear things like, 'You don't know anything. Who gave you the highest degree? I don't understand. Your degree is nothing, because you don't know anything' from their husbands and husbands' families.[30] Husbands and in-laws psychologically abuse women so that women lose their confidence and eventually come to think that they are inferior. Many men in Bangladesh swear at their wives using vulgar language, always talk angrily and even beat their wives to express male superiority. In Bangladesh, 87 per cent of married women currently experience different forms of violence at the hands of their husbands.[31] Villagers in Bangladesh believe that men who do not beat their wives are spineless (Ameen, 2005, p. 35). Ameen states, 'In rural areas there is a saying that, "My son keeps his wife at the end of a stick"' (Ameen, 2005, p. 35). In villages, wife-beating is justified if women do not conform to traditional role expectations:

> a man might beat his wife if he comes home from work and finds that his meal is not ready, or she serves him reheated rice from the morning meal rather than freshly cooked rice in the evening, she forgets to do something, like washing a shirt, or she does not respond quickly enough when he asks her to do something, or he thinks she is neglectful in caring for the children. Talking back when reprimanded, leaving home without permission, and failing to obey the in-laws (according to the in-laws) are other common examples of women's behavior that provokes their husbands to beat them.
>
> (Schuler et al., 1996, p. 1732)

Even in urban areas, the husbands of many highly educated women beat them. Many men in urban areas were born and raised in villages and migrated to urban areas for education and jobs. When they migrated to urban areas, they also brought along with them their abusive attitudes towards women. When they beat their wives they justify the beatings through the misinterpretations of Islam and when children observe this, boys especially start to feel that they also have the right to beat their wives and girls feel that they have to endure beatings from their husbands. A highly educated woman in Bangladesh expressed her experience:

> My husband often beats me. My mother complained to my father-in-law that my husband beats me. My father-in-law replied, 'A good wife does not say to other people that her husband beats her. Your daughter is not a good girl. So she informed you. It is the personal matter of a husband and a wife.'
>
> (Chowdhury, 2009b, p. 611)

From childhood, girls are taught to have patience and to remain in abusive marriages. A doctor remarked, 'For the sake of society women have to marry and remain married. The marriage sign is like a label which gives women a status in Bangladeshi society. Therefore, even when the marriage is abusive, women have to endure it' (Ameen, 2005, p. 36). Lower-income women with less education are more vocal and leave abusive marriages without hesitation more than women with a higher income and a better standard of education (Ameen, 2005, p. 88). Bangladeshi men misinterpret and distort Islam and justify wife-beating in the name of Islam. As Schuler et al. (1996) note, 'Women learn from religious sermons that the parts of their bodies beaten by their husbands will go to heaven, that they should endure their husbands' beatings without protest, that they should not complain to each other about this' (p. 1733).

Conclusion

It appears from the above discussion that Islam plays a very important role in society and politics in Bangladesh. The Bangladeshi population does not tolerate the slightest criticism of Islam and the government and political parties are very careful when speaking on religious issues. The government in Bangladesh cannot make any laws that contradict Islam. Although Sheikh Hasina reintroduced secularism, she does not have the courage to remove *Bismillah-ar-Rahman-ar-Rahim* and the state religion, Islam, from the constitution and ban religious political parties because of the strong role of Islam in society and politics in Bangladesh. A majority of the Bangladeshi population does not want any legislation that is inconsistent with Islamic law and so the ruling party, the AL, had to promise, 'Laws repugnant to the *Quran* and the *Sunnah* shall not be made.'

Islam is a very powerful force in the everyday lives of Muslim men and women in Bangladesh. Male–female relationships in Bangladesh are governed by Islam, but I have argued that women in Bangladesh do not know what their rights and responsibilities are in Islam. Bangladeshi patriarchal society does not encourage women to acquire knowledge and develop critical or analytical abilities. Women are not encouraged to acquire knowledge and apply reasoning in understanding the *Quran*. Although Bangladeshi men claim to be devout Muslims, when the question of women arises they misinterpret Islam and oppress women. Women do not know that in Islam 'the sole basis for superiority of any person over another is piety and righteousness not gender, color, or nationality'. Instead of trying to understand the *Quran*, many Bangladeshi women refer only to popular books to understand Islam. These books help legitimize and justify both male supremacy and the subjugation of women in the name of Islam. However, it was revealed in the *Quran* that all forms of oppression and injustice were to be abolished, which these books ignore and, rather than challenging the oppressive attitudes of men, they reinforce patriarchy and male cruelty towards women.

The patriarchal society in Bangladesh creates a situation where it is a great shame to get help from sons-in-law. As practising Muslims, men should be kind towards their wives and their wives' parental families. Instead of showing kindness, they prevent their wives from performing their religious responsibilities towards their parents and relatives as well as other people. They oppress their wives physically and psychologically, demand dowry, appropriate their wives' income and remove women from their parental families to continue their oppression and exploitation. When Bangladeshi women are aware of their rights and responsibilities in Islam, only then will they resist the oppression and exploitation against them. Women must have knowledge of Islam in order to protest and to protect them from the oppression of men that is carried out in the name of Islam.

Notes

1 Here, communalism means strong allegiance to the Muslim population, rather than to society as a whole.
2 Sheikh Hasina is the current prime minister of Bangladesh. She is the daughter of Sheikh Mujibur Rahman under whose leadership Bangladesh got its independence. On 15 August 1975, when Sheikh Mujib and all his family members were brutally killed in Bangladesh, Sheikh Hasina was a housewife, living in West Germany with her husband. Her sister, Sheikh Rehana, was in West Germany visiting them. Thus, the two sisters of the Mujib family escaped the conspiracy to eliminate their entire family. When the AL was about to disintegrate in 1981, Sheikh Hasina emerged as the leader of her father's political party. It was assumed by the AL that, as a daughter of Sheikh Mujibur Rahman, Hasina could be the symbol of unity and take the party to power by using her family's legacy. Sheikh Hasina became the prime minister in 1996 and served until 2001 and in 2009 she again became the prime minister.
3 Khaleda Zia is the opposition leader in Bangladesh. She is the widow of the late President Ziaur Rahman and emerged as the leader of the BNP as a symbol of unity for the party. In March 1983 Khaleda Zia was appointed vice-chairman of the BNP. In February 1984 she became the chairperson. She became Bangladesh's prime minister in 1991 and served until 1996 and again from 2001 to 2006.
4 *Daily Ittefaq*, 4 January 1991.
5 *Daily Ittefaq*, 8 January 1991.
6 *Daily Ittefaq*, 9 February 1991.
7 The three coalition partners of the BNP are the Jamaat-i-Islami, Bangladesh, the Bangladesh Jatiya Party led by Naziur Rahman and the Islami Oikya Jote (IOJ).
8 *New Age*, 26 December 2006.
9 *New Age*, 26 December 2006
10 *Daily Star*, 12 January 2007.
11 *Daily Star*, 23 December 2008.
12 *New Age*, 16 December 2008.
13 *Daily Star*, 29 December 2008, 'Religious rituals mark her day Hasina to vote at City College'.
14 *Daily Star*, 1 January 2009.
15 *Daily Star*, 5 January 2010.
16 *Daily Star*, 29 March 2016, 'HC rejects writ over Islam as state religion'.
17 *Daily Star*, 6 January 2010.
18 *Daily Star*, 19 October 2010.
19 Constitution of the People's Republic of Bangladesh (1972). Article 7 B.
20 *Daily Star*, 22 March 2014. 'Country to be run as per Madinah Charter: PM'.
21 *Abnews24.com*. 'Dirtiness and porn not free thinking: Sheikh Hasina' 18 April 2016, available at www.abnews24.com/english/2016/04/18/276 [accessed 11 July 2016].

22 Tea with Tootli, Geetiara Safia Chowdhury, available at www.youtube.com/watch?v=lhOe7Z757PE [accessed 11 July 2016].
23 *amadershomoy.com*. 'Babar Shopno Bastobion Korte Chai' (I Want to Implement My Dad's Dream) 20 September 2015, available at www.amadershomoys.com/newsite/2015/09/20/401775.htm#.V4R4S2grLIU [accessed 12 July 2016).
24 BBC Bangla Report. 'Why Are Girls Dropping Out Before Completing Secondary School?' 4 March 2016, available at www.bbc.com/bengali/multimedia/2016/03/160304_bbcbangla_probahotv_secondary_dropout_girls [accessed 11 July 2016].
25 Prophet Muhammad's Last Sermon, available at www.themodernreligion.com/prophet/prophet_lastsermon.htm [accessed 11 July 2016].
26 Pollution applies to menstrual blood, not to women (Barlas, 2002, p. 161).
27 *Daily Ittefaq*, 25 July 2009.
28 It is an obligation for Muslims to pay 2.5 per cent of their wealth to specified categories in society when their annual wealth exceeds a minimum level.
29 *Sahih Bukhari*, available at www.sahih-bukhari.com/Pages/Bukhari_7_62.php [accessed 11 July 2016].
30 This information is based on the conversations I had with 50 working women in Bangladesh during my interviews with them.
31 *Daily Star*, 20 October 2015. 'Gender Based Violence: Current Situations and Ways Forward'.

3 Muslim family law in Bangladesh

Bangladesh's personal status laws continued to be the legislation enacted by Pakistan prior to Bangladeshi independence. The *Hanafi* school is the predominant *madhhab* in Bangladesh. The legal status of Muslim women in Bangladesh is defined by the Muslim personal law along with the general law, which is secular in nature. The Muslim personal law covers the areas of marriage, divorce, maintenance, guardianship of children and inheritance. The general law deals with rights under the constitution, penal codes, the civil and criminal procedure codes, evidence act, etc. (Kamal, n.d.). The substantive equality approach recognizes differences (Wentholt, 1999, p. 55) and in the areas of marriage, divorce, maintenance, guardianship of children and inheritance in Bangladesh, Muslim family law is mostly based on this approach.

Monsoor (1999) argues that existing law in Bangladesh does not need any major reform and it has the potential to protect women from economic deprivation and violence (pp. 258–259). She advocates for reform in Bangladesh within an Islamic framework. Monsoor (1999) argues that it is patriarchal society that did not grant women rights under Islamic law. In this context, radical change outside the Islamic framework will give rise to more conservatism (p. 125). Women's organizations are agitating for the introduction of a Uniform Family Code following a secular approach. However, Monsoor (1999) doubts the possibility of introducing uniform family law (p. 134). She points out that the family law of Bangladesh is based on religion and does not operate on the basis of absolute equality for men and women. She argues that gender equity rather than fully fledged gender equality can be meaningfully developed in the family law of Bangladesh through implementation of the existing law (p. 3).

On the other hand, Bhuiyan (2010) argues that Muslim personal law on marriage and divorce is discriminatory to women and needs substantive legal reform and this should be guided by 'welfare principles and human right considerations', which she believes is encouraged by Islam (p. 244, 289). She seems to support secular demands in legal reform, but prefers to use Islamic rational reinterpretation. However, she is aware that legal reform in family law requires the support of a majority of people (p. 290).

Pereira (2002) adopts a secular approach with regard to family law reform in Bangladesh and argues that the Uniform Personal Code is the instrument through which a more egalitarian and universal system can be created and that it would be a viable option for Bangladesh (p. xxii). Pereira (2002) argues that the idea of a uniform system of laws for all citizens of the state, irrespective of religious belief, gender and place of origin or birth goes against discriminatory treatment on the basis of gender and religion. Women are discriminated against in varying degrees because of the personal law system (p. 59).

Tamanna (2008) also argues for a uniform and secular personal code, although she is doubtful of achieving this because of the present socio-political situation in Bangladesh (p. 335). The Law Commission of Bangladesh rejected the idea of the framing of a Uniform Family Code. The commission states:

> To take up a position that these laws should be suitably changed so as to fit in with a Common Family Code of all faiths and denominations is not merely an intellectual decision, but basically a decision as to whether the Muslims of Bangladesh should give up [the] Quran as a revealed Book or not. The Law Commission has no hesitation to say that the Muslims of Bangladesh would rise in revolt as one man if they are asked to give up a basic tenet of their faith.
>
> (Government of the People's Republic of Bangladesh, 2005)

Considering the strong role of Islam in Bangladeshi society, Tamanna (2008) suggests pursuing different strategies to achieve 'a uniform and equality-based personal law' (p. 336). She argues, 'while the ultimate objective of legal reform should be to ensure a uniform and equality-based personal law, different strategies can be pursued to achieve the same goal'. She suggests that reform can be made through 'progressive interpretations of religious sources and doctrines' (p. 336). Tamanna (2013) argues that the two approaches – 'protectionist' and 'corrective' – are relevant for understanding gender differences in Islam. In the protectionist approach, women need protection as they are constructed as subordinate to men, and gender difference and special protections are considered natural and essential. On the other hand, the corrective approach seems more in line with the substantive approach to equality, because it focuses on the impact of differential treatment rather than considering difference as natural and essential (p. 334). Substantive equality adopts a contextual analysis which considers 'relevant socio-legal and economic contexts while judging disadvantage' (Tamanna, 2013, p. 339). She argues that some of the provisions can be interpreted in an alternative way using the 'corrective approach', i.e. substantive equality (Tamanna, 2013, p. 337). She also argues that recognizing difference, which is interpreted and understood in a corrective way, opens the door for 'dialogue, compromise and flexibility' in Bangladesh where any reform initiative is seen with suspicion, blamed on Westernization and causes violent resistance (Tamanna, 2013, p. 339). In my view, her way of reinterpretation of the *Quran* will not be accepted by the majority of people in Bangladesh, because they believe that the difference between men and women is divine and natural. In fact, Islamic law recognizes physical and biological differences between men and women and it gives importance to the 'complementary but equally important roles of men and women' in the family (Venkatraman, 1995, p. 2004). Treating women and men identically does not necessarily mean treating them equally and treating them differently does not necessarily mean treating them unequally (Barlas, 2002, p. 5). In order to introduce a Uniform Family Code, a coalition of women's organizations used the media as a tool for promoting their cause. Workshops were held in different divisional and district towns and there was extensive media coverage. However, these strategies failed to reach the grassroots level (Nazneen, 2013, pp. 112–113).

Esposito and DeLong-Bas (2001) point out, 'The true effectiveness of existing reforms is dependent upon their acceptance not simply by those who legislate but by the entire Muslim community' (p. 127). Azizah al-Hibri (1997) argues that a secular approach will not work for the advancement of Muslim women. She offers a Muslim feminist solution to the advancement of women's rights in Muslim countries. She argues, 'The majority of Muslim women who are attached to their religion will not be liberated through the use of a secular approach imposed from the outside by international bodies or from above by undemocratic governments' (p. 3). In this chapter, I argue that existing law does not need any major reform as it has the potential to protect women's rights. The effectiveness of family law reform in Bangladesh depends on its acceptance by the people of Bangladesh. Although the Islamic revival movement in Bangladesh is not so strong, Bangladeshis have strong attachments to Islam. No one wants to take the risk of criticizing religious customs, practices and beliefs (Huque and Akhter, 1987, p. 200). Again, as noted earlier, while many Bangladeshis do not perform mandatory religious practices, most express their devotion to Islam in public (Huque and Akhter, 1987, p. 200). In my view, if reform is done within an Islamic framework, there is a stronger likelihood that it will be accepted by the people of Bangladesh.

Dower and maintenance in Bangladesh

Marriage is a civil contract that legalizes a sexual relationship between a man and a woman in Islamic law. Esposito and DeLong-Bas (2001) argue, 'The contractual nature of marriage in Islam makes the woman a party to the marriage agreement, rather than an object of sale' (p. 15). Dower (*mahr*) and maintenance are the financial rights of Muslim women, which the wife is entitled to receive from her husband through a marriage contract. Dower, which is known by several names (*mahr*, *sadaq*, *oqr*, *nehra*, *ajr* and *fareeda-portion*) is defined by Nasir as 'a sum of money or other property which becomes payable by the husband to the wife as an effect of marriage' (Nasir, 1990, p. 83). Baillie (1965, p. 91) argues:

> Dower is not the exchange or consideration given by the man to the woman for entering into the contract; but an effect of the contract, imposed by the law on the husband as a token of respect for its respect, the woman.

The *Quran* states about dower:

> And give the women (on marriage) their dower as a free gift. (4:4)

> O prophet! We have made lawful to you your wives to whom you have paid their dowers. (33:50)

Nasir (1990, p. 97) defines maintenance as:

> The lawful right of the wife under a valid marriage contract on certain conditions. It is the right of the wife to be provided at the husband's expense, and at a scale suitable to his means, with food, clothing, housing, toilet necessities, medicine, doctors' and surgeons' fees, baths, and also the necessary servants where the wife is of a social position which does not permit her to dispense with such services, or when she is sick.

The law of maintenance derives from the injunctions of the *Quran*, the Prophet's traditions and the consensus of jurists. The *Quran* states:

> Men are protectors and maintainers of women, because *Allah* has given the one more (strength) than the other, and because they support them from their means. (4:34)

> The mothers shall give suck to their offspring for two whole years, if the father desires to complete the term. But he shall bear the cost of their food and clothing on equitable terms. (2:233)[1]

> Let the women live (in *iddat*) in the same style as you live, according to your means. (65:6)

> Let the man of means spend according to His means; and the man whose resources are restricted, let him spend according to what Allah has given him. Allah puts no burden on any person beyond what He has given him. (65:7)

The Prophet said in his last speech:[2]

> O People! It is true that you have certain rights with regard to your women but they also have rights over you. Remember that you have taken them as your wives only under Allah's trust and with His permission. If they abide by your right then to them belongs the right to be fed and clothed in kindness. Do treat your women well and be kind to them for they are your partners and committed helpers.

The objective of dower and maintenance laws is to safeguard women's economic position within marriage. In pre-Islamic Arabia, *mahr* was paid to the bride's father. Esposito and DeLong-Bas (2001, p. 23) argue:

> Islamic law made dower payable not to the bride's father, but only to the bride herself. Like the contract itself, this action also made the woman a party to the contract and so the marriage agreement could not be considered a sale.

The *Quran* instructs men to provide full maintenance for the wife, even if the wife is a rich woman (Doi, 1984, p. 204). Shaheen Sarder Ali (2000) thinks that the provision of wives' maintenance cannot be used to achieve non-discriminatory status for women. Although she assumes that if women achieve economic independence they would get the same status as men, she recommends further research on this issue (p. 65). Similar to Shaheen Sarder Ali, a number of scholars argue that in Islamic law men are considered as the maintainers and protectors and this makes women dependent on them (Rahman, 1982, p. 295; al-Hibri, 1997, p. 30; Esposito and DeLong-Bas, 2001, p. 134; Ali, 2003, pp. 163–164). Kecia Ali (2003), who considers herself a progressive Muslim, observes that most progressive Muslims 'follow the key elements of classical marriage in the wedding, but may reduce the dower to a symbolic amount due to discomfort with its "commercial" connotations' (pp. 163–164). Patriarchal society believes that dower and maintenance grant husbands a type of ownership over their wives. This view ignores the statement of the *Quran* that 'husband and wife are each other's garments' (2:187). This means the relationship between a husband and a wife is based on mutual support, mutual comfort and mutual protection. These laws are very useful for women, because many women in the Islamic countries go to the courts for realizing dower and maintenance after divorce or separation to have some relief from economic constraints. Even some working women in Islamic countries use these laws as a weapon to punish their husbands financially when they divorce them without any valid reason. The substantive approach to equality recognizes differences (Wentholt, 1999, p. 55). Considering the physical and biological differences, Islamic law gives the financial responsibility for wives and children to men in order to ensure women's economic security within marriage. Dower is an essential part of Muslim marriage in Bangladesh and it is divided into two forms: prompt dower and deferred dower. Prompt dower is payable to the wife at any time before or after consummation. Deferred dower is payable upon divorce or death (Bhuiyan, 2007, p. 115). Section 6(5) of the Muslim Family Laws Ordinance 1961[3] states:

> Any man who contracts another marriage without the permission of the Arbitration Council shall:
>
> (a) pay immediately the entire amount of the dower, whether prompt or deferred, due to the existing wife or wives, which amount, if not so paid, shall be recoverable as arrears of land revenue.

Section 10 of the Muslim Family Laws Ordinance 1961[4] states:

> Where no details about the mode of payment of dower are specified in the *nikah nama* or the marriage contract, the entire amount of the dower shall be prescribed to be payable on demand.

The amount of dower is reduced through the custom of *usool* (paid) and thus a woman's right has been curtailed. In the marriage contract, jewellery or other items which are given to the bride at the wedding ceremony are written as paid dower. The bride's party does not usually bargain with the groom's party at the time of the marriage, because they want the ceremony to proceed without any interruptions (Monsoor, 1999, p. 200). Bangladeshi culture forces women to waive dower on the wedding night and thus they are deprived of the right of dower. In Bangladesh, although dower is a legal obligation, the question of its payment arises only for divorce cases (Monsoor, 1999, pp. 202–205). Monsoor (1999) mentions that in Bangladesh 88 per cent of Muslim wives do not receive any dower and she argues, 'This is a proof of the patriarchal arbitrariness of Bangladeshi society which regards women's claim to dower as challenging the existence of the patriarchal system itself, despite the fact that it is an Islamic obligation' (p. 206). Most women in rural Bangladesh do not know the actual amount of *mahr* that they are supposed to receive in their own marriage and even if they know the amount, they are scared to demand their *mahr* from their husbands as it will create bad feeling (Shehabuddin, 2008b, p. 86).

In Bangladesh a wife is entitled to maintenance whether she is economically solvent or not. In *Mst. Amena Khatun* v. *Sherajuddin* the lower court took the view that the husband was absolved from the duty to maintain the wife, because she was a woman of means. C. J. Murshed held that, legally, such a proposition is not tenable. The competence of the wife does not absolve the husband from his duty to maintain her (*Mst. Amena Khatun* v. *Sherajuddin*, 1965). A wife is entitled to a separate house and maintenance, even if she refuses to live with her husband because of his cruelty or for any valid reason. In *Begum Hamida* v. *Abdul Hamid* (1974), the wife alleged that her life became miserable after her husband's second marriage. She could not live there honourably because of the ill-treatment by her husband and his second wife and was compelled to take up a separate residence for her and her children. The court held:

> In view of the circumstances which made it impossible for her to live with her husband and compelled her to have a separate residence for her and her children, her claim for maintenance cannot be refused if the claim is otherwise not unsustainable.

In *Hosne Ara Begum* v. *Rezaul Karim* (1991), the High Court Division of the Supreme Court ordered the husband to pay maintenance even if the wife was not residing at the husband's house on the grounds of cruelty.

The courts in Bangladesh used to refuse the Muslim women's right to past maintenance unless stipulated in the marriage contract. In *Rustom Ali* v. *Jamila Khatun* (1991), the High Court Division of the Supreme Court did not grant the past maintenance allowed by the lower court. Later in *Jamila Khatun* v. *Rustom Ali* (1996) the Appellate Division of the Supreme Court held that the wife is entitled to past maintenance even if there is no prior agreement. There is no provision for post-divorce alimony in Bangladesh. In *Hefzur Rahman* v. *Shamsunahar Begum* (1995), the High Court Division of the Supreme Court of Bangladesh held that a divorced wife is entitled to maintenance beyond the waiting period (*iddat*) for an indefinite period until her remarriage. The Appellate Division overruled the decision on the basis that a wife is not entitled to maintenance after the waiting period according to *Sharia* (*Hefzur Rahman v. Shamsunahar Begum*, 1999). Divorced women in Bangladesh are generally deprived of the rights of dower and maintenance. Complicated, expensive and lengthy court procedures prevent poor and middle-class women from claiming their dower and maintenance rights. Bhuiyan (2007, p. 135) writes:

> Under Muslim law, a man is obligated to pay dower money, maintenance during the continuation of marriage, and at the time of divorce, during *iddat,* as well as to provide maintenance for minor child. These obligations are not voluntarily followed by most husbands, and the wives have to go to the court for relief. In rural areas, many husbands, on trifling reasons treat their wives most inhumanly, drive them out of their home, and abandon them at their poor parents' or relatives' houses without any maintenance. When the wife sues for maintenance, most husbands either send letters of divorce or blame them that they were disobedient or unfaithful, then divorce them and marry again. Marriage and divorce is easy for men, because they don't have to pay any maintenance to the existing wife or children at the time of divorce. They know that it will be very difficult for their ex-wives to go to court and realize their dues.

Divorce

Section 7 of the Muslim Family Laws Ordinance 1961[5] seeks to curb unilateral divorces by Muslim men and requires the intervention of the Arbitration Council. It states:

> Any man who wishes to divorce his wife shall, as soon as may be after the pronouncement of *talaq* in any form whatsoever, give the chairman notice in writing of his having done so, and shall supply a copy thereof to the wife.

The divorce will not be effective until 90 days have expired and the days will be counted from the day on which notice is sent to the chairman. The chairman will then convene the Arbitration Council for bringing about reconciliation between the parties within 30 days of the receipt of the notice and the council will take all necessary steps to bring about reconciliation. If the wife is pregnant, divorce will not be effective until the pregnancy is over or until 90 days have expired. Any person who does not comply with these provisions is liable to be punished with 'simple imprisonment for a term which may extend to one year or with a fine which may extend to ten thousand taka or with both'.

The *talaq* is better than any other type of divorce because it preserves the wife's entitlement to her dower. In fact, in Bangladesh when a husband gives notice to the chairman, he does not pay the dower and maintenance for the *iddat*. A lawyer suggested that the dower and maintenance for the *iddat* must be sent with the divorce notice. This would protect a woman's economic right which was granted by the *Quran*. There should be a law that the chairman would not accept notices of divorce without receiving the dower money and the maintenance for *iddat* (Monsoor, 1999, p. 186). Sometimes, men in Bangladesh persuade their wives to *khula* divorces. A *khula* divorce is 'an agreement between the parties to dissolve the marriage by the wife's foregoing of dower' (Monsoor, 1999, p. 186). Monsoor (1999) notes, 'The "judicial *khul*" has abolished the husband's consent criteria. But the compensation paid by the wife, usually by restoration of her dower, has remained intact' (p. 186). Judicial divorce under the Dissolution of Muslim Marriages Act 1939[6] proved to be a better solution for a wife than *khul*, because in this method she can claim dower money and maintenance (Bhuiyan, 2007, p. 217). Section 2 of the act provides grounds for divorce.

> A woman married under Muslim law shall be entitled to obtain a decree for the dissolution of her marriage on any one or more of the following grounds, namely:
>
> (i) that the whereabouts of the husband have not been known for a period of four years;
> (ii) that the husband has neglected or has failed to provide for her maintenance for a period of two years;
>
> (iia)[7] that the husband has taken an additional wife in contravention of the provisions of the Muslim Family Laws Ordinance 1961;[8]
>
> (iii) that the husband has been sentenced to imprisonment for a period of seven years or upwards;
> (iv) that the husband has failed to perform, without reasonable cause, his marital obligations for a period of three years;
> (v) that the husband was impotent at the time of the marriage and continues to be so;
> (vi) that the husband has been insane for a period of two years or is suffering from leprosy or a virulent venereal disease;
> (vii) that she, having been given in marriage by her father or other guardian before she attained the age of [eighteen years],[9] repudiated the marriage before attaining the age of [nineteen years][10]: provided that the marriage has not been consummated;
> (viii) that the husband treats her with cruelty, that is to say
>
> (a) habitually assaults her or makes her life miserable by cruelty of conduct even if such conduct does not amount to physical ill-treatment, or
> (b) associates with women of evil repute or leads an infamous life, or
> (c) attempts to force her to lead an immoral life, or
> (d) disposes of her property or prevents her exercising her legal rights over it, or
> (e) obstructs her in the observance of her religious profession or practice, or
> (f) if he has more wives than one, does not treat her equitably in accordance with the injunctions of the Quran;
>
> (ix) on any other ground which is recognized as valid for the dissolution of marriage under Muslim law, provided that
>
> (a) no decree shall be passed on ground (iii) until the sentence has become final;

(b) a decree passed on ground (i) shall not take effect for a period of six months from the date of such decree, and if the husband appears either in person or through an authorised agent within that period and satisfies the Court that he is prepared to perform his conjugal duties, the Court shall set aside the said decree; and
(c) before passing a decree on ground (v) the Court shall, on application by the husband, make an order requiring the husband to satisfy the Court within a period of one year from the date of such order that he has ceased to be impotent, and if the husband so satisfies the Court within such period, no decree shall be passed on the said ground.

Rabiya Bhuiyan (2007, p. 219) writes:

> the wife needs strong evidence to prove her case. The grounds for dissolution of marriage are fault based and for a Muslim wife, living a secluded life in her husband's house, to prove cruelty and torture by her husband and in-laws is an extremely difficult task.

Clause 8 of The Muslim Family Laws Ordinance 1961[11] provides the husband with the option to delegate the right to divorce in the form of the *kabinnama* (marriage contract). If it is delegated to the wife, then she can divorce herself extra-judicially (Bhuiyan, 2007, p. 211). Both the *Hanafi* and the *Maliki* schools agree that a wife can include any condition in her marriage contract, including her right to divorce, which will ensure her security and protect her from her husband's domination (Bhuiyan, 2007, p. 210). Monsoor (1999) suggested that the marriage contract or *kabinnama* should automatically provide for delegated divorce (p. 262). Bhuiyan (2007, p. 135) writes:

> Marriage and divorce is easy for men, because they don't have to pay any maintenance to the existing wife or children at the time of divorce. They know that it will be very difficult for their ex-wives to go to court and realize their dues.

To ensure women's economic security the divorce law should be changed. It should be framed in such a way that divorce would not be effective unless the payments of dower and maintenance were made.

There can be legal provision for compensation for a divorced wife if she is not at fault. This legal reform will not go against Islam, because 'divorce is a last resort, permissible but not encouraged'. However, Islam does not approve any divorce without a valid and significant reason. The Prophet Muhammad (PBUH) said, 'Of all the permitted things divorce is the most abominable by God' and also 'Marry and do not divorce, undoubtedly the throne of the beneficent Lord shakes due to divorce' (Sultan, n.d.).

Polygamy

Polygamy in Islam is neither mandatory, nor encouraged, but merely permitted. Dealing justly with a wife is an obligation for a husband. This applies to dower, maintenance, kind treatment, etc. for which the husband is fully responsible. If a man is not sure of being able to deal justly with his wives, the *Quran* says, 'then (marry) only one' (4:3). Another verse shows some discouragement of such plural marriages. The verse states: 'You are never able to be fair and just as between women even if it is your ardent desire' (4:129). The question is, why does Islamic law not allow women to have more than one husband at a time? The objective of marriage is to fulfil the sexual needs of both men and women legally. If a woman is pregnant by a husband, then the other husband or husbands will be deprived of sexual relations, because during pregnancy women are not always able to maintain them. It is important in Islam to know who the fathers and mothers of children are. If a woman maintains sexual relationships with more than one person, then it is difficult to know who the father is. Identifying the father is important, because the father should take financial responsibility for the children.

Under the Dissolution of Muslim Marriages Act 1939[12] a woman is entitled to obtain a decree for the dissolution of her marriage on the grounds that her husband has taken an additional wife, so violating the provisions of the Muslim Family Laws Ordinance 1961.[13] A woman who does not want to stay within a polygamous marriage can divorce her husband. Section 6 of The Muslim Family Laws Ordinance 1961[14] imposes some restrictions on polygamy:

1 No man, during the subsistence of an existing marriage, shall except with the previous permission in writing of the Arbitration Council, contract another marriage, nor shall any such marriage contracted without such permission be registered [under the Muslim Marriages and Divorces (Registration) Act, 1974 (LII of 1974)]
2 An application for permission under sub-section (1) shall be submitted to the Chairman in the prescribed manner, together with the prescribed fee, and shall state the reasons for the proposed marriage, and whether the consent of the existing wife or wives has been obtained thereto.
3 On receipt of the application under sub-section (2) the Chairman shall ask the applicant and his existing wife or wives each to nominate a representative, and the Arbitration Council so constituted may, if satisfied that the proposed marriage is necessary and just, grant, subject to such conditions if any, as may be deemed fit, the permission applied for.
4 In deciding the application the Arbitration Council shall record its reasons for the decision, and any party may, in the prescribed manner, within the prescribed period, and on payment of the prescribed fee, prefer an application for revision to the Assistant Judge concerned and his decision shall be final and shall not be called in question in any court.
5 Any man who contracts another marriage, without the permission of the Arbitration Council shall:
   (a) pay immediately the entire amount of dower, whether prompt or deferred, due to the existing wife or wives, which amount, if not so paid, shall be recoverable as arrears of land revenue; and
   (b) on conviction upon complaint be punishable with simple imprisonment which may extend to one year, or with fine which may extend to ten thousand taka,[15] or with both.

A few women commit suicide in response to their husbands' second marriage. In some cases they kill themselves and their children.[16] Although women in Bangladesh are not happy with their husbands' new marriages, even if they know their legal rights, they often accept the remarriages of their husbands. Most of them do not have time and money and they cannot face the difficulties of filing cases (Shehabuddin, 2008b, p. 91). Shehabuddin (2008b, p. 91) points out:

> they don't want to be deprived of what security they are afforded by having a husband. A woman may prefer to put up with an abusive husband or a co wife than risk the financial, social, and sexual vulnerability to which his absence would subject her. With her husband in jail, a woman's financial situation is likely to deteriorate further, and, living alone, she is also likely to be harassed by male relatives and neighbours. Cognizant of the realities of poor rural women's lives and the limited options available to them, some NGOs often encourage women to accept a co wife.

Despite the restriction, many men in Bangladesh remarry without the consent of the first wives. In most of the cases wives' consent is extorted. If the wife does not consent to her husband's remarriage, the husband divorces her and remarries (Serajuddin, 2001, p. 182). Serajuddin (2001, p. 182) writes:

> To avoid being divorced and socially disgraced and left a destitute, a wife would readily consent to her husband marrying a second time, at whatever cost to her feelings. For the same reason, where the husband has married a second wife without the permission of the Arbitration Council, the first wife who is given the right to seek dissolution of her marriage in such cases, would prefer to ensure being a co-wife rather than ask for dissolution of the marriage and left without financial support and protection. For these reasons, it has been forcefully argued that to prohibit polygamy or to severely restrict it without severely curbing the husband's power to divorce his wife unilaterally may do more harm than good to the first wife. In such cases, a man determined to marry a second wife would feel compelled to divorce the first wife, thus creating the problem of successive monogamy instead of simultaneous polygamy.

To this, I want to add that if maintenance and dower laws are implemented properly then polygamy will decrease and it will only take place under special circumstances.

Child custody and guardianship

In Muslim law, the mother is not entitled to the guardianship of her children, but a mother is always entitled to the care and custody of her young children. A mother can keep her sons until they are seven, and her daughters until puberty, but the father is responsible for their maintenance during that period. If a mother remarries a stranger, someone who is not barred to the children by the rule of consanguinity, she may lose custody of her children, particularly her daughters (Kamal, n.d.). The age limit with regard to custody of children is not mentioned in the *Quran* and there is no record of evidence from the practice of the Prophet (Monsoor, 1999, p. 104). In recent years, the High Court of Bangladesh delivered a number of judgments regarding custody and guardianship using the 'welfare of child' doctrine (Tamanna, 2014, p. 290). In a number of child custody cases, the court showed sensitivity to the unfortunate situations of women and children by interpreting Islamic law liberally or drawing inspirations from it (Hoque and Khan, 2007, p. 217). The cases of custody reveal that the judiciary in Bangladesh is seriously considering the welfare of the minor (Monsoor, 1999, p. 194). In *Md. Abu Bakar Siddique* v. *S. M. A. Bakar and others* (1986) the Appellate Division of the Supreme Court upheld the mother's right to custody of her eight-year-old son. The court said:

> It is true that, according to the *Hanafi* school, the father is entitled to the *hizanat* or custody of the son over 7 years of age. Indisputably, this rule is the recognition of the prima facie claim of the father to the custody of the son who has reached 7 years of age. But this rule which is found neither in the Quran nor *sunnah* would not seem to have any claim to immutability so that it cannot be departed from, even if circumstances justified such departure.
>
> (*Md. Abu Bakar Siddique* v. *S. M. A. Bakar and others*, 1986, p. 114)

In the above case the mother was a doctor and because of the illness of the minor she was considered to be better suited than the father to take care of the child. As the rule of child custody is not found in the *Quran* or *Sunnah*, the state can make a law stating that the best interest of a child will be the determining factor regarding child custody and guardianship.

Inheritance law

According to prevailing inheritance legislation, a daughter's share is half that of a son's. In Islam, women have no financial obligation to support their husbands and children, and they have the right to independent control over their personal assets. Although the constitution of Bangladesh allows every citizen to 'have the right to acquire, hold, transfer or dispose of property' in most cases women do not receive their legal share of any inherited property.[17] In 2008, when the caretaker government announced the Women Development Policy, which made some radical recommendations to ensure equality in personal rights, as well as property, land and at work, etc., some religious political parties started staging demonstrations against it. The *ulemas* protested because they thought that the government would change the inheritance law on the basis of this policy. However, the AL election manifesto of the ninth parliamentary elections 2008 said, 'Laws repugnant to the *Quran* and *Sunnah* shall not be made' (Bangladesh Awami League, 2008). Sheikh Hasina announced that she believed that women should have equal rights to property and that her government would repeal the laws discriminatory to women.[18]

In 2011, the cabinet approved the Women Development Policy. Section 23.5 of this stipulates that women should have equal opportunities with regard to, and shares in, property and employment, and be able to invest in the stock market. The concept of property has a number of dimensions: moveable property, fixed property, earned property or inherited property (Urmee, 2011). The *ulemas* of Bangladesh considered that the government had tactfully avoided referring to inherited property.[19] The law minister and state minister for women declared that there was nothing contradictory between the policy and Muslim inheritance law. In this policy, equal shares in inherited property are not mentioned.[20] However, the majority of Muslims in Bangladesh are not convinced by their arguments. The Islamic Law Implementation Committee, a group consisting of a number of Islamist parties and a group linked to a faction of the Islami Oikya Jote (IOJ), led by Fazlul Huq Aminee, called a dawn-to-dusk nationwide general strike on 4 April 2011 to protest against the newly introduced Women Development Policy. On 2 April 2011, a madrassah student was shot dead and 30 others, including 10 policemen, were injured when they clashed in the city of Jessore after police had intercepted a procession in support of a general strike.[21] The general strike enforced by Islamic activists ended in violence leaving over 250 people injured, including 16 policemen, and 200 people were detained. The protesters wore white clothes, which symbolized shrouds, and carried copies of the *Quran*. The activists belonging to Islamist groups carried the *Quran* during the general strike and this was the first time the holy book was used during a demonstration.[22] In my view, if the government changes the inheritance law following a secular approach, then the law cannot be implemented. Most Bangladeshi women do not claim the property they inherit from their parents because they want to maintain good relations with their brothers. Sometimes, Bangladeshi women return to their natal home after widowhood or divorce. Adnan (1989) points out that if a married woman claims her inherited property, it is usually operated and controlled by her husband. Practically, it is men (brothers or husbands) who 'take over *de facto* control' of property inherited by women' (p. 5). A study of two villages in Bangladesh found that 77 per cent of women whose family had land did not want to claim their legal share in their parental property in order to maintain the relationship with their natal families (Monsoor, 2008, p. 112). Jenneke Arens

(2014) finds that in rural Bangladesh only a few women had control over their own land and most of it was controlled by their brothers, husbands or sons (p. 277). How on earth will women obtain an equal share with their brothers when at present they are not receiving even a half share of what their brothers own as granted by Islamic law? I have observed that even many devout Muslims in Bangladesh deprive women from their due share in the parental property. Most married women in Bangladesh cannot control their income although they have every right to control it. Husbands, and in some cases fathers-in-law and mothers-in-law, control wives' income directly or indirectly (Rashid, 2006, p. 156; Chowdhury, 2010b, pp. 1–10). I think that an ability to control their resources, whatever they may have, is important for the empowerment of women, and Bangladeshi women can achieve this through the use of Islamic law (Chowdhury, 2013a, p. 268). Some scholars argue that a half share in inheritance rights for women cannot be justified because of the changing socio-economic realities; millions of women in the world are taking full financial responsibility for the family (Rahman, 1982; Ali, 2000, p. 73; Shah, 2006, p. 898; Haddad, 2007; Ramadan, 2009). Rahman (1982) argues that, considering the gender roles in traditional society, unequal inheritance shares and economic obligations assigned to sexes were revealed in the *Quran*. He also points out, 'There is nothing inherently unchangeable about these roles – indeed, when justice so demands, change is Islamically imperative.' Tariq Ramadan (2009) argues that inheritance law in Islam is justified and logical for the different responsibilities and roles of men and women within family and society. However, he points out (p. 228):

> what should be done when, in contemporary families and societies, the logic of solidarity no longer works, when men have (willingly or not) abdicated their financial responsibilities and women find themselves alone, sometimes without an extended family, with several dependent children? Is it enough to repeat the 'final incontrovertible norm', without paying attention to context, and thus support obvious injustice? Or should we, on the contrary, revise the implementation of the texts or suspend their application, or ask for clear compensation from the community – whether the State or local authorities – as I have been suggesting for years?

In my view, Ramadan's suggestion will give men the opportunity to easily ignore their legal financial duty towards their families, wives and children and it will help strengthen patriarchy. In the case of asking for compensation from the community, men will take further advantage of this to neglect their Islamic duties. Instead of revising or suspending Islamic inheritance law, the state should strictly enforce Islamic maintenance and dower laws.

Conclusion

Existing law in Bangladesh has the potential to protect women from exploitation and violence and it does not need any major reform. The effectiveness of family law reform in Bangladesh depends on its acceptance by the people of Bangladesh. Although the Islamic revival movement in Bangladesh is not that strong, Bangladeshis have a strong attachment to Islam. In my view, if reform is done within an Islamic framework, then people will accept it. The substantive approach to equality recognizes differences and in the areas of marriage, divorce, maintenance, guardianship of children and inheritance in Bangladesh, Muslim family law is mostly based on this approach.

Islamic law recognizes physical and biological differences between men and women and it gives importance to the 'complementary but equally important roles of men and women' in the family (Venkatraman, 1995, p. 2004). Considering physical and biological differences, Islamic law gives the financial responsibility for wives and children to men to ensure women's economic security within marriage. To ensure women's economic security the divorce law should be changed and should be framed in such a way that divorce would not be effective unless the payments of dower and maintenance were made. The marriage contract or *kabin-nama* should automatically provide for delegated divorce. There can be legal provision for compensation for a divorced wife if she is not at fault. This legal reform will not go against Islam, because 'divorce is a last resort, permissible but not encouraged'.

Under the Dissolution of Muslim Marriages Act 1939 [23] a woman is entitled to obtain a decree for the dissolution of her marriage on the grounds that her husband has taken an additional wife, so violating the provisions of the Muslim Family Laws Ordinance 1961.[24] A woman who does not want to stay within a polygamous marriage can divorce her husband. Although women in Bangladesh may not be happy with their husbands' new marriages, even if they know their legal rights, they often accept their husbands' remarriages. Many women in Bangladesh prefer to live with abusive husbands or co-wives due to the financial, social and sexual vulnerabilities they would be exposed to if they were left on their own. Considering this reality, restrictions imposed on polygamy are logical. Prohibiting polygamy is unrealistic for Bangladeshi society. It will create 'the problem of successive monogamy instead of simultaneous polygamy'. If maintenance and dower laws are implemented properly then polygamy will decrease and it will only take place under special circumstances.

Bangladesh could enact a law making the best interest of a child the determining factor with regard to child custody and guardianship because there is no rule for child custody in the *Quran* or the *Sunnah*. According to prevailing inheritance legislation, a daughter's share is half that of a son's. In Islam, women have no financial obligation to support their husbands and children, and they have the right to independent control over their personal assets. In most cases, women are deprived of their legal share of any inherited property. Married women's property is usually operated and controlled by men (brothers or husbands). If equal rights with regard to inheritance law are introduced, then how will women obtain an equal share with their brothers when at present they are not receiving even a half share of what their brothers own as granted by Islamic law? I think that an ability to control their resources, whatever they may have, is important for the empowerment of women and Bangladeshi women can achieve it through the use of Islamic law.

Notes

1 It refers to maintenance when the wife is divorced.
2 The Last Sermon of Prophet Muhammad. This speech was delivered on the Ninth Day of Dhul Hijjah, 10 A.H. (632 CE) in the Uranah valley of Mount Arafat in Makkah at the pilgrimage. It is also known as the Farewell Pilgrimage, available at www.cyberistan.org/islamic/sermon.html [accessed 16 July 2015].
3 *Muslim Family Laws Ordinance 1961* (Ordinance No. VII of 1961), available at http://bdlaws.minlaw.gov.bd/print_sections_all.php?id=305 [accessed 16 July 2016].
4 *Muslim Family Laws Ordinance 1961* (Ordinance No. VII of 1961), available at http://bdlaws.minlaw.gov.bd/print_sections_all.php?id=305 [accessed 16 July 2016].
5 *Muslim Family Laws Ordinance 1961* (Ordinance No. VII of 1961), available at http://bdlaws.minlaw.gov.bd/print_sections_all.php?id=305 [accessed 16 July 2016].
6 *Dissolution of Muslim Marriages Act 1939* (Act No. VIII of 1939), available at http://bdlaws.minlaw.gov.bd/print_sections.php?id=180&vol=&sections_id=4813 [accessed 16 July 2016].
7 Clause (iia) was inserted by section 13 of the Muslim Family Laws Ordinance 1961 (Act No. VIII of 1961).

8 *Muslim Family Laws Ordinance 1961* (Ordinance No. VII of 1961), available at http://bdlaws.minlaw.gov.bd/print_sections_all.php?id=305 [accessed 16 July 2016].

9 The words 'eighteen years' were substituted for the words 'sixteen years' by section 2 of the Dissolution of Muslim Marriages (Amendment) Ordinance 1986 (Ordinance No. XXV of 1986).

10 The words 'nineteen years' were substituted for the words 'eighteen years' by section 2 of the Dissolution of Muslim Marriages (Amendment) Ordinance 1986 (Ordinance No. XXV of 1986).

11 *Muslim Family Laws Ordinance 1961* (Ordinance No. VII of 1961), available at http://bdlaws.minlaw.gov.bd/print_sections_all.php?id=305 [accessed 16 July 2016].

12 *Dissolution of Muslim Marriages Act 1939* (Act No. VIII of 1939), available at http://bdlaws.minlaw.gov.bd/print_sections.php?id=180&vol=&sections_id=4813 [accessed 16 July 2016].

13 *Muslim Family Laws Ordinance 1961* (Ordinance No. VII of 1961), available at http://bdlaws.minlaw.gov.bd/print_sections_all.php?id=305 [accessed 16 July 2016].

14 *Muslim Family Laws Ordinance 1961* (Ordinance No. VII of 1961), available at http://bdlaws.minlaw.gov.bd/print_sections_all.php?id=305 [accessed 16 July 2016].

15 The words 'ten thousand taka' have been substituted for 'five thousand rupees' vide amendment Section 4 of Ordinance No. 21 of 1982.

16 *Daily Star*, 10 August 2010.

17 Article 42(1) of the Bangladeshi Constitution states: 'Subject to any restrictions imposed by laws, every citizen shall have the right to acquire, hold, transfer or otherwise dispose of property, and no property shall be compulsorily acquired, nationalized or requisitioned save by authority of law'; see Constitution of the People's Republic of Bangladesh, available at http://bdlaws.minlaw.gov.bd/print_sections_all.php?id=367 [accessed 16 July 2016].

18 *Daily Star*, 9 March 2010.

19 *Amardesh*, 4 April 2011.

20 *Amardesh*, 4 April 2011.

21 *Daily Star*, 3 April 2011.

22 *Daily Star*, 5 April 2011.

23 *Dissolution of Muslim Marriages Act 1939* (Act No. VIII of 1939), available at http://bdlaws.minlaw.gov.bd/print_sections.php?id=180&vol=&sections_id=4813 [accessed 16 July 2016].

24 *Muslim Family Laws Ordinance 1961* (Ordinance No. VII of 1961), available at http://bdlaws.minlaw.gov.bd/print_sections_all.php?id=305 [accessed 16 July 2016].

4 CEDAW, Islamic law and women in Bangladesh

In Bangladesh, 90.39 per cent of the population is Muslim (Bangladesh Bureau of Statistics, 2013, p. 51) and, as I have demonstrated in earlier chapters, Islam plays a very important role in society and politics. It governs the relations between men and women in Bangladesh. As a result, there are difficulties with the implementation of secular human rights standards in Muslim-majority countries where most people believe that international human rights instruments reflect 'Western' values and norms, so they consider these as both 'culturally and religiously alien' (Ali, 2000, p. 246). As I noted in Chapter 3, al-Hibri (1997) argues that a secular approach will not work for the advancement of Muslim women (p. 3). She writes, 'The majority of Muslim women who are attached to their religion will not be liberated through the use of a secular approach imposed from the outside by international bodies or from above by undemocratic governments' (al-Hibri, 1997, p. 3). Monsoor (1999, p. 2) argues that Bangladeshi women are not demanding sexual equality, freedom and liberation like some Western women:

> Rather they see their roles within social contexts and would prefer gender equity within the traditional framework. Although there is some influence of idealized feminist thinking about sexual equality, women's proper place is seen to be within the family in the wider context of Bangladeshi society.

At present, CEDAW is perceived as the 'magic remedy' for women's liberation by the women's organizations in Bangladesh.[1] Bangladesh ratified CEDAW with reservations on articles 2, 13[a], 16.1[c] and [f] as they conflict with '*Sharia* law based on the Holy *Quran* and *Sunnah*'.[2] Later, Bangladesh withdrew its reservations from articles 13[a] and 16.1[f]. It still has reservations on articles 2 and 16.1[c].[3] Women's organizations in Bangladesh are demanding complete ratification of CEDAW.[4] In contrast, Werner Menski (2002, p. 6) has argued forcefully:

> I no longer believe that a global legal order can be one in which only Western norms dressed up as universal values have validity . . . This Convention, pushed by a certain class of Western women, above all (and their non-Western assistants, who will incidentally never achieve equality of status, however hard they try, because of plain racism) claims that the ideal is that the law should accept that men and women are simply equal, full stop. That approach of course expresses another 'ought' or 'should' an ideal, which I find wonderful too, but do not see manifesting itself in reality . . I argue that CEDAW does perhaps a good job in highlighting the need for the elimination of unjustified

> discrimination against women, but it totally misses the target when it comes to safeguarding for little local women anywhere in the world a form of equitable treatment that allows them to survive in dignity and to the best of their ability in their particular circumstances. For a Bangladeshi village woman, arguing for absolute equality rather than fair treatment in her local circumstances seems more than a bit unrealistic. I do not see the scope for that even in the West, so that this clamouring for absolute equality is an excellent 'ought' ideal, but not a strategy that we can recommend to Bangladeshi and other South Asian women.

Is Menski's criticism well founded? Does CEDAW really 'miss the target' for Bangladeshi women in their particular circumstances and, importantly, in their family relations? Is CEDAW actually ineffective with regard to family relations in the advancement of women in Bangladesh? Does CEDAW conflict with Islamic law? Does Islamic law contradict articles 16[c] and 16[d] of CEDAW that impose an obligation to ensure the same rights and responsibilities for both men and women during marriage and its dissolution and the same responsibilities as parents? How does CEDAW affect Muslim women's lives if the same responsibilities during marriage and its dissolution and the same responsibilities as parents are ensured? I address these questions in this chapter.

I argue that in the name of equal responsibility working women are taking *more* than equal responsibility. CEDAW assumes that paid work (any work for pay or profit) is in fact the key to women's liberation, but paid work cannot ensure equality between a husband and wife at home. CEDAW ignores the presence of conflicting human rights principles, such as equality between men and women on one hand and the right to freedom of religion, culture and custom on the other. I argue that if CEDAW is fully implemented, it will deprive Muslim women of their maintenance and dower rights as well as the maintenance of children by their fathers. I also argue that CEDAW ignores the vulnerable position of women, especially in developing countries and in the name of formal equality it puts the same responsibilities that men have on women in the family too. It encourages women to join the paid labour force at any cost, which actually perpetuates inequality.

CEDAW and Islamic law

Some scholars argue that there is no conflict between CEDAW and Islamic law. By Islamic law I mean the law which is based on the *Quran* and the *Sunnah* of the Prophet. Mir-Hossaini (2009, p. 47) argues:

> In the twenty-first century, the provisions of CEDAW – which stands for justice and equality for women in the family and in society – are more in line with the *sharia* than are the provisions of family laws in many contemporary Muslim countries.

In the context of CEDAW, Ali and Mullally (1992) also argue that the concept of equality between men and women is not in conflict with *Sharia*, but with its interpretation and application (p. 113). Ali (2000) thinks that there is a possibility of compatibility of women's human rights in Islam with the international norms of non-discrimination on the basis of sex (p. 281). An-Na'im (1987) argues that Islam is so powerful a political and cultural force that the best way to challenge fundamentalists is to show that the rights of women are 'Islamic and not alien western notions' (p. 501). He writes (p. 515):

> International standards are meaningless to Muslim women unless they are reflected in the concrete realities of the Muslim environment. Like members of other cultural traditions, Muslims tend to be suspicious and unreceptive towards what they perceive to be an attempt to impose alien standards. To obtain their cooperation in implementing international standards on the rights of women, we need to show the Muslims in general that these standards are not alien at all. They are, in fact, quite compatible with the fundamental values of Islam. In other words, we need to provide Islamic legitimacy for the international standards on the rights of women.

An-Na'im (2000) assumes that there is no 'immediate compatibility or permanent contradiction' between human rights and Islam (p. 95). He argues that *Sharia* was not concerned with achieving complete legal equality between men and women. Fundamental reform of *Sharia* is a must to achieve complete legal equality between men and women (An-Na'im, 1987, p. 500). An-Na'im (1990a) supports the evolutionary approach to Islamic law reform prescribed by the late Sudanese author, Ustadh Mahmoud Muhammad Taha. He believes that there are two levels of the message of Islam. One was revealed in the earlier Mecca period and the other was in the Medina period. The earlier message of the Mecca period stressed the importance of the inherent dignity of all human beings. Here, nobody is discriminated against on the basis of gender, religion, race and so forth (p. 52). The Medina verses differentiate between men and women, Muslim and non-Muslim in their legal status and rights (An-Na'im, 1990a, p. 54). An-Na'im (1990a, p. 56) argues:

> the evolutionary principle of interpretation is nothing more than reversing the process of *nskh* or abrogation so that those texts which were abrogated in the past can be enacted into law now, with the consequent abrogation of texts that used to be enacted as *sharia*. Verses that used to be enacted as *sharia* shall be repealed, and verses that used to be repealed shall be enacted as modern Islamic law.

Are the Meccan verses really abrogated? In fact, this method of reform is very difficult to apply in Islamic countries, because Muslims in general believe that the *Quran* is eternal and complete. Muslims do not have any authority to repeal any verse of the *Quran*. An-Na'im (1990a) suggests that this evolutionary approach will not violate 'the Islamic authenticity of the law' (p. 60). However, it is not clear how the Islamic authenticity of the law can be maintained if most of the Muslims do not accept this as an Islamic approach. Shah (2006) writes, 'repealing or changing a Koranic verse is solely the right of God, and there is no room for human involvement as An-Na'im suggests' (p. 880). This evolutionary approach may encourage extremism in many Muslim countries like Bangladesh.

In Krivenko's (2009) view, equality between men and women can be achieved through a new understanding and interpretation of Islam developed by modernist Muslim scholars, and she thinks that modernist Muslims should work to convince or remind ordinary Muslims that 'diversity of opinions, new interpretations and constant change' are essential in Islamic tradition, so new perception with regard to the status of women can come from within the Islamic tradition itself (pp. 212–213). In Malaysia, Sisters in Islam, a feminist organization, has been working to establish women's rights within an Islamic framework. Zainah Anwar (2005), the executive director of Sisters in Islam argues, 'Rejecting religion is not an option for most Muslim women. We are believers, and as such we want to find liberation, truth and justice within our own faith' (p. 231). Musawah, an initiative of Sisters in Islam, is a global movement of women and men who believe in equality and justice in the Muslim family. Musawah (2011) published a research report on CEDAW and Muslim family laws. Musawah (2011) argues that full implementation of CEDAW is possible, because CEDAW and Islam are compatible (p. 2). Shah (2006, p. 882) argues:

> if the Koranic verses, which are the basis of state practiced gender discriminatory legal principles, are interpreted in their proper context and if gender-biased laws are reformed according to that interpretation, then gender equality may be achieved that will be compatible with international human rights law.

Are the provisions of CEDAW and Islamic law really compatible? Connors (1996) points out, 'It is undeniable that a number of provisions of CEDAW are inconsistent with Islamic law and it is not possible for state parties to accept these provisions which apply Islamic law' (p. 365). Hamid (2006) also believes that CEDAW and Islamic law are incompatible in some areas in family law (p. 130). He writes:

> It would be extremely difficult even for a moderate Islamic country to go against the most fundamental precepts of *sharia*, which are founded on clear and unambiguous Qur'anic injunctions . . . Even if Governments of Islamic countries, for political or other reasons, made new legislation to reform or amend certain provisions of the Islamic family law, which are based on clear and unambiguous Qur'anic injunctions, those reformed or amended laws would be purely man-made, like other ordinary domestic law, and would definitely be at odds with true believers of the Islamic faith.

CEDAW incorporates both formal and substantive equality approaches (Merry, 2006, p. 74; Cook and Howard, 2007, p. 1043). The committee's General Recommendation on Temporary Special Measures explains the approach taken:

> a purely formal legal or programmatic approach is not sufficient to achieve women's de facto equality with men, which the Committee interprets as substantive equality. In addition, the Convention requires that women be given an equal start and that they be empowered by an enabling environment to achieve equality of results. It is not enough to guarantee women treatment that is identical to that of men. Rather, biological as well as socially and culturally constructed differences between women and men must be taken into account. Under certain circumstances, non-identical treatment of women and men will be required in order to address such differences. Pursuit of the goal of substantive equality also calls for an effective strategy aimed at overcoming underrepresentation of women and a redistribution of resources and power between men and women.[5]

In my view, CEDAW adopts a transitional approach to substantive equality as apparent from the passage below from the committee's General Recommendation on Temporary Special Measures:

> As steps are being taken to eliminate discrimination against women, women's needs may change or disappear, or become the needs of both women and men. *Thus, continuous monitoring of laws, programmes and practices directed at the achievement of women's de facto or substantive equality is needed so as to avoid a perpetuation of non-identical treatment that may no longer be warranted.* [emphasis added][6]

Although CEDAW goes beyond equality of opportunity and deals with the concept of equality of result, and provides affirmative action programmes and protection against indirect discrimination, Hilary Charlesworth et al. (1991) point out, 'the underlying assumption of its definition of discrimination is that women and men are the same' (p. 631). The term 'discrimination against women' is defined as:

> any distinction, exclusion or restriction made on the basis of sex which has the effect or purpose of impairing or nullifying the recognition, enjoyment or exercise by women, irrespective of their marital status, on a basis of equality of men and women, of human rights and fundamental freedoms in the political, economic, social, cultural, civil or any other field.[7]

In CEDAW, 'equality is defined as being like a man' except in special circumstances, such as pregnancy (Hilary Charlesworth et al., 1991, p. 632). The provision of affirmative action programmes in article 4 of CEDAW assumes that these measures will be used temporarily in order to enable women to perform exactly like men (Charlesworth, 1994, p. 64). Article 4(1) of CEDAW states:

> Adoption by state parties of temporary special measures aimed at accelerating de facto equality between men and women shall not be considered discrimination as defined in the present convention, but shall in no way entail as a consequence the maintenance of unequal or separate standards; these measures shall be discontinued when the objectives of equality of opportunity and treatment have been achieved.

Ratna Kapur (2012) also writes about article 4(1), 'The clause can be read treating special measures as an exception to equality rather than as integral to equality. It also stresses the "temporariness" of these measures, which again implies that the preferable standard is "sameness in treatment"' (p. 271).

CEDAW focuses on public life, the economy, the legal system and education, and little recognition is given to oppression in the family that contributes to the unequal position of women (Charlesworth and Chinkin, 2000, p. 231). As Krivenko (2009) points out, 'CEDAW does not go far enough in defining and protecting women's rights in the private sphere' (p. 42). Later, the committee adopted general recommendations on violence against women (Krivenko, 2009, p. 42).[8] The committee's General Recommendation on Equality in Marriage and Family Relations recognizes women's unpaid work and recommends women's equal right to the marital property:

> There are countries that do not acknowledge that right of women to own an equal share of the property with the husband during a marriage or de facto relationship and when that marriage or relationship ends. Many countries recognize that right, but the practical ability of women to exercise it may be limited by legal precedent or custom . . . In some countries, on division of marital property, greater emphasis is placed on financial contributions to property acquired during a marriage, and other contributions, such as raising children, caring for elderly relatives and discharging household duties are diminished. Often, such contributions of a non-financial nature by the wife enable the husband to earn an income and increase the assets. Financial and non-financial contributions should be accorded the same weight.[9]

Although the committee recognizes differences between men's work and women's work, CEDAW adopts mostly a formal equality approach in the area of family law.[10]

The CEDAW committee recommends banning polygamy, ensuring equal inheritance right and imposes an obligation on state parties to ensure the same rights and responsibilities of men and women during marriage and its dissolution and the same responsibilities as parents.[11] Some feminists argue that polygamy is not always harmful or discriminatory against women (Griffiths, 2001, p. 114; Baines, 2007, p. 28). As I noted in Chapter 3, in Bangladesh, under the Dissolution of Muslim Marriages Act 1939, a woman is entitled to obtain a decree for the dissolution of her marriage on the grounds that her husband has taken an additional wife, thus violating the provisions of the Muslim Family Laws Ordinance 1961. A woman who does not want to stay within a polygamous marriage can divorce her husband. Although women in Bangladesh are not happy with their husbands' new marriages, even if they know their legal rights, they often accept the remarriages of their husbands. Many women in Bangladesh prefer to live with abusive husbands or co-wives due to the financial, social and sexual vulnerabilities that would ensue if they left the marital home. Considering this reality, restrictions imposed on polygamy are logical. However, prohibiting polygamy is unrealistic for Bangladeshi society. It would create 'the problem of successive monogamy instead of simultaneous polygamy' (Serajuddin, 2001, p. 182). If maintenance and dower laws are implemented properly then polygamy will decrease, but this will only happen under certain circumstances.

Regarding inheritance law, some scholars argue that a half-share in inheritance rights for women cannot be justified because of changing socio-economic realities; millions of women in the world are taking full financial responsibility for the family (Rahman, 1982, p. 297; Ali, 2000, p. 73; Shah, 2006, p. 898; Haddad, 2007; Ramadan, 2009, p. 228). Musawah (2011) follows a holistic framework that incorporates 'Islamic teachings, universal human rights, national constitutional guarantees of equality, and lived realities' of women and men (p. 22) and argues that, currently, Muslim women are economically active and are engaged in the public sphere, are sharing the financial responsibilities in the household and looking after their parents. On the other hand, some irresponsible sons do not look after their parents and the responsibilities of husbands are also reduced due to their wives' income (Musawah, 2011, p. 27). The report says, 'The specific legal rules of the Quran, be they on maintenance or inheritance, are conditioned by the socio-historical background of their enactment. Given a different time and context, what was once considered just may today be considered unjust' (Musawah, 2011, p. 28). The question is, how many Muslim women are engaged in the public sphere? In fact, female labour force participation is 49.6 per cent (International Labour Organization, 2016). Musawah's report (2011) ignores the fact that in the name of equal responsibility working women are taking *more* than equal responsibility because of childbearing and child rearing activities. Even when there are maintenance and dower laws in effect in Bangladesh, husbands, and in some cases fathers-in-law and mothers-in-law, control wives' income directly or indirectly (Rashid, 2006, p. 156; Chowdhury, 2010b, pp. 1–10). If laws are reformed to give men and women equal financial responsibility then husbands and in-laws will in turn get more opportunities to appropriate their wives' income and resources in the name of equal financial responsibility. As I discussed in Chapter 3, in Bangladesh most women are deprived of their legal share of their inherited property. In many cases, women's inherited property is usually operated and controlled by their husbands, brothers or sons (Adnan, 1989, p. 5; Monsoor, 2008, p. 112; Arens, 2014, p. 277). How will women obtain equal share with their brothers when currently they are not receiving even half of their brothers' share as granted by Islamic law?

I think that the ability to control resources, whatever they may have, is important for the empowerment of women, and Muslim women can achieve this through the use of Islamic law (Chowdhury, 2013a).

Equality is presented in CEDAW in a way that suggests either that women be treated in the same way as men or that women have the same opportunity to be treated like men, but it does not consider whether male standards are appropriate for women, especially in the area of family law (Charlesworth and Chinkin, 2000, p. 23; Brooks, 2002, p. 351). In my view, CEDAW is based on Western liberal feminist discourse that gives importance to women's individual rights and ignores the multiplicity of their identities. It is a 'combination of law, modernization theory and western liberal feminist jurisprudence' (Ali, n.d., p. 87). The liberal concept of equality deals with the elimination of laws and social practices that treat women differently from men. The liberal model was found in the writings of John Stuart Mill (1869), who opposed laws and social practices that deprived women of equal civil rights. Krieger and Cooney (1983) write, 'The liberal view addresses the problem of disparate treatment, and advances the proposition that once women are treated the same as men, equality will be achieved through individual competition in the societal marketplace' (p. 537). This model is relatively useful for those women who can conform to the male norm, who are less involved in child rearing activities and/or who have the financial resources to hire other women to work for them at home. It is also useful for those women who work in liberal organizations that accommodate their roles as mothers (Krieger and Cooney, 1983, p. 545). Kim (1993) also identifies the limitations of this liberal model: 'it ignores the needs of women as a class. It seeks gender neutrality, but in a world where "gender neutrality is simply the male standard"' (p. 97).

The concept of equality between men and women in Islamic law is different from CEDAW's concept of equality. Both CEDAW and Islamic law incorporate formal and substantive notions of equality. However, with regard to family law, CEDAW mostly adopts a formal equality approach and Islamic law mostly adopts a substantive equality approach (detailed discussion on the concept of equality in Chapter 1). Islam adopts the substantive equality approach through recognizing the physical and biological differences between men and women and it gives importance to the 'complementary but equally important roles of men and women' in the family (Venkatraman, 1995, p. 2004). Therefore, some provisions of CEDAW are clearly inconsistent with Islamic law. For example, article 1 states: 'The term "discrimination against women" shall mean any distinction, exclusion or restriction made on the basis of sex.' This definition of discrimination extends to both public and private lives. Here, the words 'any distinction' are inconsistent with Islamic law, because Islam recognizes differences between men and women, but these differences do not mean unequal.

Article 2 obliges state parties to take measures to eliminate all forms of discrimination against women especially by introducing legislation. Article 2[f] states: 'to take all appropriate measures, including legislation, to modify or abolish existing laws, regulations, customs and practices which constitute discrimination against women'. As the meaning of 'discrimination against women' is different in Islamic law, it is difficult for Muslim-majority countries to modify or abolish all the existing laws, regulations, customs and practices which are considered as discrimination against women according to the definition of CEDAW.

Article 6 obligates state parties to 'take all appropriate measures, including legislation, to suppress all forms of traffic in women and exploitation of prostitution of women'. Islamic law also does not allow any form of traffic in women, and it prohibits any kind of sexual relations outside marriage for both men and women. As a result, prostitution is itself illegal in Islamic law. The *Quran* (24:30–31; 17: 32) says:

> Say to the believing men that they should lower their gaze and guard their modesty: that will make for greater purity for them: and Allah is well acquainted with all that they do. And say to the believing women that they should lower their gaze and guard their modesty. (24:30–31)

> Nor come near to adultery: for it is a shameful (deed) and an evil, opening the road (to other evils). (17:32)

Article 13[a] of CEDAW suggests that state parties take all appropriate measures to ensure, on a basis of equality of men and women, the same rights, in particular, the right to family benefits. This article goes against Islamic law because, according to this, a daughter's share is half that of a son (*Quran* 4:11). Here CEDAW adopts a gender-neutral formal equality approach and Islamic law adopts the substantive equality approach. This inheritance law is not discriminatory for two reasons: in Islam women have no financial obligation to support their husbands and children, and they have the right to independent control over their personal assets.

The provision with regard to co-education[12] is culturally insensitive. This provision ignores the possibility that compulsory co-education could have a negative impact on women's equality. Some parents may decide not to send their daughters to a co-educational establishment because of strict purdah (separation of the sexes and veiling of women). As Venkatraman (1995) argues, 'The coeducation recommendation illustrates that neglecting the varying cultural and religious circumstances of women may be a self-defeating feature of the convention' (p. 2004). Venkatraman (1995, p. 2005) continues:

> a certain amount of cultural relativity is appropriate in enforcement of the women's Convention. While some language in the convention may potentially defeat the purpose of women's equality if unmodified and enforced, other provisions simply fail to consider the diversity of the culture-specific or culturally favored definition of equality, and the practicability or even desirability of implementation.

Articles 16[c] and [d] of CEDAW, which deal with the family law, are not consistent with Islamic law. Article 16.1[c] imposes an obligation on state parties to ensure the 'same rights and responsibilities between men and women during marriage and its dissolution' and article 16.1[d] obligates state parties to ensure the same responsibilities as parents. CEDAW adopts a gender-neutral formal equality approach in these articles and Islamic law adopts a substantive equality approach.

It is very difficult for Muslim-majority countries to modify their entire social and cultural patterns of men and women with regards to behaviour or all the stereotyped roles for men and women because of these inconsistencies between CEDAW and Islamic law.[13] Most women in Muslim-majority countries want to lead their private lives within an Islamic framework. Although the majority of Muslim women want gender parity, they 'want it on their terms and within their own cultural context' (Esposito and Dalia Mogahed, 2008, p. 107). If articles of CEDAW that are inconsistent with Islamic law are imposed in the name of women's liberation, then they will become a form of oppression for the majority of Muslim women. Asifa Quraishi (2011, pp. 217–218) argues:

> there is a lot of women-empowering material in the uncontroversial, un-reformed, established *fiqh* rules that do have persuasive weight with the vast majority of practicing Muslims. For example, established *fiqh* not only insists on the spiritual equality of women and men but it also affords women several significant specific legal rights, most of which went unrecognized in Western societies until quite recently.

CEDAW and Muslim countries

All 57 OIC (Organization of the Islamic Conference) member countries approach CEDAW in different ways and there is no uniform stance with respect to reservations on CEDAW articles. Not all states entered reservations and not all made reservations to maintain Islamic laws and practices (Krivenko, 2009, p. 115) (Table 1). Iran, Sudan and Somalia did not ratify CEDAW (Musawah, 2011, p. 5). The government of Algeria has declared that it is prepared to apply article 2 on condition that it does not conflict with the provisions of the Algerian Family Code. It has expressed its reservation on article 9(2) due to the incompatibility with the provisions of the Code of Algerian Nationality and the Algerian Family Code. It also has reservations on articles 15(4) and 16 which contradict the Algerian Family Code.[14] The government of Niger has declared its reservations on articles 2[d] and [f], 5[a] and [b], 15(4) and 16(1)[c], [e] and [g], as 'they are contrary to existing customs and practices'.[15] The reasons for Tunisian reservations were the Tunisian constitution, the Tunisian Nationality Code and the Tunisian Code of Personal Status. The reason for Turkish reservations was that some articles were not compatible with the Turkish civil code. Turkey removed all its reservations by 2008.[16]

Article 16 of CEDAW, which is related to marriage and family relations, has been reserved by most states. Most of the Muslim-majority states also reserved article 2 which deals with the general measures on the elimination of discrimination against women. Malaysia withdrew its reservation on article 2[f]. It still has reservations on articles 5[a], 7[b], 9(2), 16(1)[a] and 16(2) because they are in conflict with the provisions of Islamic *Sharia* law and the Federal Constitution of Malaysia.[17] Article 2[f] says, 'To take all appropriate measures, including legislation, to modify or abolish existing laws, regulations, customs and practices which constitute discrimination against women.'[18] There is no point in withdrawing the reservation on article 2[f] without withdrawing the reservations on other articles. Sixteen Muslim states entered a reservation on article 9 which covers nationality issues.

A significant number of Muslim states also have reservations on article 15(4), which is related to the freedom to choose one's residence and domicile. The United Arab Emirates (UAE) only reserved the second paragraph of article 15 (Krivenko, 2009, p. 121). This states:

> State parties shall accord to women, in civil matters, a legal capacity identical to that of men and the same opportunities to exercise that capacity. In particular, they shall give women equal rights to conclude contracts and to administer property and shall treat them equally in all stages of procedure in courts and tribunals.[19]

Qatar has a reservation on article 15(1), which states that 'State parties shall accord to women equality with men before the law.'[20]

Article 7, which deals with political and public life, has been reserved by Malaysia, Maldives and Kuwait, but Kuwait withdrew its reservation in 2005.[21,22] Article 11, which deals with employment, has been reserved by Malaysia, and article 5[a], which is related to sex role stereotyping and prejudice, was only reserved by Malaysia and Niger.[23,24]

CEDAW, Islam and politics in Bangladesh

Islam plays a very important role in society and politics (see detail in Chapter 2). Both the AL and the BNP used Islam to elicit mass support in the ninth parliamentary elections, held on 29 December 2008. Khaleda Zia and Sheikh Hasina both launched their election campaigns

Table 1 CEDAW and Muslim countries

No.	*Country*	*Year ratified*	*Articles affected*	*Modification*	*Conflicting with*
1	Afghanistan	2003	No reservations		
2	Albania	1994	No reservations		
3	Algeria	1996	Art. 2 Art. 9(2) Art. 15(4) Art. 16 and Art. 29.1		Code of Algerian Nationality; Algerian Family Code
4	Azerbaijan	1995	No reservations		
5	Bahrain	2002	Art. 2 Art. 9(2) Art. 15(4) Art. 16 and Art. 29.1		Islamic *Sharia*
6	Bangladesh	1984	Art. 2 Art. 13[a] Art. 16(1)[c] Art. 16[f]	Modified on 23 July 1997 Art. 2 Art. 16(1)[c]	*Sharia* law based on the *Quran* and the *Sunnah*
7	Benin	1992	No reservations		
8	Brunei	2006	General; Art. 9(2) and Art. 29.1		Constitution; Beliefs and principles of Islam
9	Burkina Faso	1987	No reservations		
10	Cameroon	1994	No reservations		
11	Chad	1995	No reservations		
12	Comoros	1994	No reservations		
13	Côte d'Ivoire	1995	No reservations		
14	Djibouti	1998	No reservations		
15	Egypt	1981	Art. 2 Art. 9(2) Art. 16 and Art. 29.1		General reservation for Islamic *Sharia* custom
16	Gabon	1983	No reservations		
17	Gambia	1994	No reservations		
18	Guinea	1982	No reservations		
19	Guinea Bissau	1985	No reservations		
20	Guyana	1980	No reservations		
21	Indonesia	1984	No reservations		
22	Iran		Not a signatory		
23	Iraq	1986	Art. 2[f] [g] Art. 9(1) Art. 9(2) Art. 16 and Art. 29.1		Islamic *Sharia*
24	Jordan	1992	Art. 9(2) Art. 15(4) Art. 16(1)[c] [d] [g]		Islamic law*
25	Kazakhstan	1998	No reservations		
26	Kuwait	1994	Art. 7[a] Art. 9(2) Art. 16[f] and Art. 29.1	Modification on 9 Dec. 2005 Art. 9(2) Art. 16[f]	Kuwaiti nationality law; Islamic *Sharia*
27	Kyrgyzstan	1997	No reservations		

28	Lebanon	1997	Art. 9(2) Art. 16(1)[c] [d] [f] [g] and Art. 29.1		
29	Libya	1989	General	Modification on 5 July 1995 Art. 2 Art. 16[c] [d]	Personal status derived from Islamic *Sharia*
30	Malaysia	1995	Art. 2[f] Art. 5[a] Art. 7[b] Art. 9 Art. 16	Modification in Feb. 1998 2[f], 9(1), 16[b] [d] [e] [h]	Islamic *Sharia* law; Federal Constitution of Malaysia
31	Maldives	1993	General	Modification on 29 Jan. 1999 Art. 7[a] Art. 16	The Constitution of the Republic of Maldives; Islamic *Sharia*
32	Mali	1985	No reservations		
33	Mauritania	2001	General		Islamic *Sharia*; Constitution
34	Morocco	1993	Art. 2 Art. 9(2) Art. 15(4) Art. 16 and Art. 29.1		Islamic *Sharia*; Moroccan Code of Personal Status; Moroccan nationality law
35	Mozambique	1997	No reservations		
36	Niger	1999	Art. 2[d] [f] Art. 5[a] [b] Art. 15(4) Art. 16 1[c] [e] [g] and Art. 29.1		Existing customs and practices
37	Nigeria	1985	No reservations		
38	Oman	2006	General; Art. 9(2) Art. 15(4) Art. 16[a] [c] [f] in particular and Art. 29.1		Islamic *Sharia*; Existing legislation
39	Palestine Authority				
40	Pakistan	1996	General		Constitution of the Islamic Republic of Pakistan
41	Qatar	2009	Art. 1 (conditionally)** Art. 5[a] (conditionally)*** Art. 2[a] Art. 9(2) Art. 15(1) (4) Art. 16(1)[a] [c] [f]		Islamic law; Existing legislation; Constitution; Qatari citizenship law; Family law and established practice
42	Saudi Arabia	2000	Any contradictory terms with Islamic law; Art. 9(2) and Art. 29.1		Islamic law

(continued)

Table 1 (continued)

No.	Country	Year ratified	Articles affected	Modification	Conflicting with
43	Senegal	1985	No reservations		
44	Sierra Leone	1988	No reservations		
45	Sudan	Not a signatory			
46	Somalia	Not a signatory			
47	Suriname	1993	No reservations		
48	Syria	2003	Art. 2 Art. 9(2) Art. 15(4) Art. 16. 1[c] [d] [f] [g] Art 16(2) and Art. 29.1		Islamic *Sharia*
49	Tajikistan	1993	No reservations		
50	Togo	1983	No reservations		
51	Tunisia	1985	General; Art. 9.2 Art. 15(4) Art. 16(1)[c] [d] [f] [g] [h] and Art. 29.1		Tunisian constitution; Tunisian Nationality Code; Code of Personal Status
52	Turkey	1985	Art. 15.2 Art. 15.4 Art. 16.1[c] [d] [f] [g] and Art. 29.1	All withdrawn by 2008	Turkish civil code
53	Turkmenistan	1997	No reservations		
54	Uganda	1985	No reservations		
55	United Arab Emirates	2004	Art. 2[f] Art. 9 Art. 15(2) Art. 16 and Art. 29.1		*Sharia*; Existing legislation
56	Uzbekistan	1995	No reservations		
57	Yemen	1984	Art. 29.1		

* Initial reports on state parties, Jordan, United Nations, CEDAW, CEDAW/C/JOR/1, 10 November 1997, available at http://www.un.org/womenwatch/daw/cedaw/cedaw22/jor1.pdf [accessed 16 July 2016].

** The Government of the State of Qatar accepts the text of article 1 of the Convention provided that, in accordance with the provisions of Islamic law and Qatari legislation, the phrase 'irrespective of their marital status' is not intended to encourage family relationships outside legitimate marriage. It reserves the right to implement the Convention in accordance with this understanding, available at http://www.bayefsky.com/html/qatar_t2_cedaw.php [accessed 10 October 2016].

*** The State of Qatar declares that the question of the modification of 'patterns' referred to in article 5[a] must not be understood as encouraging women to abandon their role as mothers and their role in child-rearing, thereby undermining the structure of the family, available at http://www.bayefsky.com/html/qatar_t2_cedaw.php [accessed 10 October 2016].

Source: Musawah (2011). *CEDAW and Muslim Family Laws in Search of Common Ground*, pp. 49–63.

with a visit to the holy shrine of Shah Jalal at Sylhet. Sheikh Hasina pledged not to enact any laws or formulate any regulations which goes against the *Quran* and the *Sunnah*.[25] The AL reintroduced secularism in Bangladesh and yet again promised in the tenth national parliamentary elections, 'No law contradicting the *Quran* and the *Sunnah* will be passed'

(Bangladesh Awami League, 2014). In the Gallup research study of 35 Muslim-majority nations between 2001 and 2007, John L. Esposito and Dalia Mogahed found that the majority of people in Muslim-majority countries want to see *Sharia* as a source of legislation (Esposito and Mogahed, 2008, p. 6). Furthermore, they found that the majority of people in Bangladesh want *Sharia* as the source of legislation (Esposito and Mogahed, 2008, p. 48). The majority of the population in Bangladesh does not want any legislation which is inconsistent with Islamic law. How can a secular approach like CEDAW be effective for women's liberation in a country like Bangladesh where Islam is so powerful? Mahmuda Islam (n.d.) undertook a research project to examine the possibilities of full ratification of CEDAW by the Bangladeshi government. She circulated 175 questionnaires and received 97 responses. The respondents were religious thinkers, university teachers, members of political parties, lawyers, journalists, students, representatives of NGOs and members of civil societies. Of the respondents, 21 per cent were from outside the capital of Dhaka and 29 per cent were women (Islam, n d., p. 112). She spoke of the difficulty in collecting the data (p. 119):

> very few respondents came forward voluntarily to fill in the questionnaire and most of them had to be persuaded to do so. Both the principal researcher and research assistant had to make follow up visits and telephone them several times. In some cases, the assistant had to fill up the questionnaire on the basis of the view expressed by the respondents. Despite our best endeavors, many did not cooperate mainly due to sheer apathy. This has led to the impression that people in general are either not aware of CEDAW or did not take due notice of it, or simply ignored information on the subject. There appears to be apathy towards women's development and a lack of commitment regarding rights of women. The situation cuts both ways. On the one hand, the government feels insecure about public reaction to ratification of provisions of the CEDAW which fall in the domain of *Sharia* laws. On the other hand, there is the prospect that if the government ratifies CEDAW in full, its action will go unnoticed and there will be little adverse reaction or active opposition.

The implementation of CEDAW depends on its acceptance. If people do not know about CEDAW, how will it be implemented? Is it possible to achieve gender equality without the support of the people? An-Na'im (2000) writes that without mass support the government cannot ratify human rights treaties and comply with the obligation to protect these rights. He argues that even if the elites who control the government want to respect some human rights, it is not possible for them to do so against the wishes of the masses. Only if people think that these rights are consistent with their religious beliefs can they accept such treaties (An-Na'im, 2000, p. 96). An-Na'im (2000, p. 95) also argues:

> The implementation of international human rights norms in any society requires thoughtful and well-informed engagement of religion (broadly defined) because of its strong influence on human belief systems and behaviour, regardless of the formal characterization of the relationship between religion and the state in any society. While it is true that the behaviour of believers is not always motivated by total fidelity to their faith, religious considerations are too important for the majority of people for human rights scholars and advocates to continue to dismiss them simply as irrelevant, insignificant, or problematic.

It would be very unethical for a democratic government not to inform the people and ratify CEDAW in full. Mahmuda Islam (n.d.) finds that the majority of her respondents suggested complete ratification of CEDAW without delay. She wrote, 'Since the majority represents a cross section of the population, the government may consider their views as reflective of effective public opinion and ratify CEDAW in full' (Islam, n.d., p. 123). How is it effective public opinion? She did not include people living in rural areas or lower-income groups in urban areas. This study, therefore, does not represent a good cross section of people. As the present AL government in Bangladesh promised before the election that they would not introduce any law contrary to the *Quran* and the *Sunnah*, how will the government withdraw the reservations on articles 2 and 16.1[c] of CEDAW? It has already ratified article 13[a], suggesting that state parties take all appropriate measures to ensure, on a basis of equality of men and women, the same rights, in particular, the right to family benefits, and article 16.1[d] which provides for the same rights and responsibilities as parents, also contrary to Islamic law. Can the government implement these articles of CEDAW which are contrary to the *Quran* and the *Sunnah*? Women's rights advocate Farida Akhter (2013) argues:

> it is evident that the CEDAW charter has not been accepted by scholars of other faiths as well and not just Islamic scholars in Bangladesh. The debate on the CEDAW is highly complicated and controversial. However, the mechanism of implementation of a charter of the UN in context of our cultural, social and religious norms should certainly be debated and dialogue and discussion in this regard is highly necessary.

Same responsibilities of men and women during marriage and its dissolution and same responsibilities as parents: how do these articles of CEDAW deprive women of financial rights accorded by Islamic law?

Article 16.1[c] of CEDAW demands that state parties ensure 'the same rights and responsibilities during marriage and its dissolution' and in article 16.1[d] there is an obligation to ensure 'the same rights and responsibilities as parents, irrespective of their marital status, in matters relating to their children; in all cases the interests of the children shall be paramount'. In this section I will deal with these two declarations. CEDAW assumes that without taking the same responsibilities a woman cannot enjoy the same rights as men and women do not deserve equal worth and equal dignity as men. Having the 'same responsibilities' means that a husband and a wife both should participate in paid and unpaid work. What would happen if the government of Bangladesh were to commit to ensuring that men and women had the same responsibilities during marriage and upon its dissolution and the same responsibilities as parents? Can a man share all types of unpaid work? Is women's paid work the only way of achieving equality between a husband and wife? Will women be deprived of financial rights accorded by Muslim personal law in Bangladesh? I will address these questions.

Can a man share all kinds of unpaid work?

In order to explore this question I need to explain what women do in their homes in Bangladesh. In Bangladesh there are differences between housework done by women who live in rural areas and that done by women who live in urban areas. In rural areas women cook for the family, collect firewood, dry and store rice straw for fuel and prepare cow dung cakes for fuel as well. Women clean ashes from the earthen stoves. They make bread and gut fish, prepare meat and vegetables and make curry with the ingredients. The spices used in cooking food are ground by women every day and the grinding takes a great deal of time and energy (Zaman, 1996, pp. 84–85). Women level earth around the house and use cow dung for washing the floors. They also make jute doors for their houses. Women repair household fences and plant grass and trees around the house. They fetch water and take care of their cows, goats, chicken and ducks. Women are also busy with washing and folding clothes, maintaining latrines and killing ants around the house. In addition, they do all the washing-up (Wallace et al., 1987, p. 74). Household tasks are mainly labour intensive. Cain et al. (1979) write, 'There is no electricity or running water in the village, collecting fuel and carrying water are both time-intensive activities. Food enters the household in forms that require much processing before being consumed' (p. 413). Another study (Wallace et al., 1987, p. 75) reports:

> Pre-harvest indirect economic contributions made by women are: sowing seed; spreading cow dung, weeding; harrowing the field; picking seedlings from seed beds; preparing seed beds; furrowing rows in the field; carrying seeds to the fields; and irrigating the field with a bucket and pond water. Women make indirect economic contributions to the household during harvest by helping in the harvesting of the crops and helping to carry the harvest to the house. Indirect post-harvest field activities are actually done by women around the house. Some of these activities are: drying, stirring, cleaning, threshing, parboiling, winnowing, and storing paddy; cleaning and preparing wheat, mustard, pulses for storing; cleaning and storing potatoes; preparing spices for storage; and drying and extracting fiber and seeds from jute.

Apart from these many tasks, women spend a great deal of time in making ***kantha*** (quilts), ***sikka*** (hanging rope), ***pankha*** (hand fans), ***pati*** (mats) and pillowcases for family use. In urban areas women also cook and clean but, unlike in rural areas, they do not use firewood or cow dung cakes for fuel. They have gas stoves or stoves that are run on ceresin oil. They make bread and gut fish, prepare meat and vegetables and make curry with the ingredients too. They supervise the construction of their own houses and decorate them. In urban areas, due to safety concerns, women take their children to school and collect them again afterwards. There are a lot of private tutors in Bangladesh and women in urban areas are very busy taking their children to private tutors after school. Women in both rural and urban areas of Bangladesh play social roles in maintaining relationships with relatives, neighbours and friends.

The committee's General Recommendation on Equality in Marriage and Family Relations recognizes women's unpaid work.[26] Can a husband and a wife share the above-mentioned unpaid work? The answer is: yes, they can. Now, the question is: can men be pregnant? Can men breastfeed? The answer is no to both. In that case, how can men and women take on the same responsibilities within marriage and its dissolution and the same responsibilities as parents? Pregnancy and breastfeeding – these differences between men and women cannot be ignored. Only women can perform these functions and the ability to do so is what differentiates women from men (Scales, 1981, p. 435). Although CEDAW emphasizes protecting maternity (articles 4(2), 5[b], 11(2) and 12 as well as CEDAW General Recommendation No. 24),[27] in its General Recommendation No. 21 (1994) the committee explains:

> The responsibilities that women have to bear and raise children affect their right of access to education, employment and other activities related to their personal development. They also impose inequitable burdens of work on women. The number and spacing of their children have a similar impact on women's lives and also affect their physical and mental health, as well as that of their children. For these reasons, women are entitled to decide on the number and spacing of their children.[28]

CEDAW assumes that if women decide on the number and spacing of their children, then they can perform these functions easily and at the same time get involved in the paid labour force and take the same responsibilities for their family and children as their husbands. In fact, every day, 830 women die from preventable complications during pregnancy and childbirth and 99 per cent of all maternal deaths take place in the developing world (World Health Organization, 2015a). In 2015, 303,000 women died during and following pregnancy and childbirth and almost all of these deaths took place in developing countries (World Health Organization, 2015a). The World Health Organization (2015a) reports:

> The majority of maternal deaths are due to haemorrhage, infection, unsafe abortion, and eclampsia (very high blood pressure leading to seizures), or from health complications worsened in pregnancy. In all these cases, unavailable, inaccessible, unaffordable, or poor quality care is fundamentally responsible. Maternal deaths are detrimental to social development and wellbeing, as some 1 million children are left motherless each year. These children are more likely to die within 1–2 years of their mothers' deaths.

Bangladesh records a high maternal mortality ratio of 176 deaths per 100,000 live births (World Health Organization, 2015b). Women in Bangladesh spend most of their time in childbearing and child rearing activities. Despite this situation, many rural women do not practise any form of birth control and some women deliberately do not practise birth control in order to try and have a son. This is observed in urban areas too. Most pregnancies of healthy mothers end with the birth of a live baby but, in many cases, childbirth is not the joyous event it should be. In some instances, it is a time of pain, fear, suffering and even death. A report says that many pregnancies are complicated by diseases which are aggravated by pregnancy, such as malaria, iron-deficiency anaemia, hepatitis, tuberculosis and heart disease (Ahmed et al., 1998, p. 1). Pregnancy-related complications are the main causes of maternal death in Bangladesh, these being: haemorrhage, eclampsia, unsafe abortion, sepsis and obstructed labour (Ahmed et al., 1998, p. 1). In addition to these complications, women in Bangladesh are at a greater risk due to the high fertility norm. The report further says, 'Although many women do not die, they suffer from various types of short and long term illness and disability, like obstetric fistulae, which may render them outcasts from their own family and society' (Ahmed et al., 1998, p. 3).

When women give birth to live babies, they devote much time to breastfeeding. Children are generally breastfed for two to two-and-a-half years. Infants in Bangladesh are generally fed on demand. Since infants sleep with their mothers, night feeds are the norm. Children who are fed on demand suckle more frequently to obtain more milk to meet their demands. In addition, breastfeeding is often used as a method of comforting the children (Huffman et al., 1980, p. 146). Children who are breastfed are closely attached to their mothers and always want to stay with them. When they are ill, they feel secure in their mothers' company. Breastfeeding ensures mother–infant interaction and closeness. Done on demand, breastfeeding guarantees that mother and child will be in close physical contact. Nursing mothers hold, rock and talk to their babies more. For this reason, sometimes it is not possible for fathers to take care of children who are or were on breast milk. These children prefer to stay with their mothers. Although CEDAW recommends that state parties ensure safe motherhood,[29] in reality childbearing and child rearing activities are not easy. Using data from the British Household Panel Survey, Gillian Paull (2008, pp. F25–F26) says:

> the continuing propensity for female workers to work substantially shorter weekly hours than male workers is closely related to the presence of children. Although a small gender gap in work hours exists prior to the arrival of any children, the most substantial movement towards part-time for women work occurs at the time of first birth, both through a shortening of hours from full-time to part-time and by the exit of a large fraction of full time workers from work altogether.

A Pew Research survey finds that in the United States working fathers attach more importance to a high-paying job, while working mothers prefer a flexible schedule (Parker and Wang, 2013).

Can paid work ensure equality between a husband and a wife?

Throughout the world, female labour force participation is 49.6 per cent and male labour force participation is 76.1 per cent (International Labour Organization, 2016, p. 6). In some regions female labour force participation is very low, for example, in South Asia it is 31.8 per cent, in the Middle East it is 18.7 per cent and in North Africa it is 24.4 per cent (International Labour Organization, 2012, p. 17). Globally, women work fewer hours in paid employment as they perform most of the unpaid household tasks and care work in both high- and lower-income countries in the world. When women are in the paid labour force, they still do the larger share of unpaid work in the household, including care work, and so they are unable to increase their hours in paid and formal work (International Labour Organization, 2016, p. xv). Women earn 77 per cent of what men earn in the world (International Labour Organization, 2016, p. xvi). Female labour force participation in Muslim-majority countries particularly is very low (Figure 1). The percentage of female labour force participation is very low in Syria, Afghanistan, Algeria, Iran, Iraq and Jordan (13–17 per cent). Gambia, Guinea and Senegal have the highest participation rate (66–72 per cent). The female labour force participation rate in Bangladesh is 58 per cent, while the male rate is 84 per cent (World Bank, 2014a; World Bank, 2014b). However, according to the *Labour Force Survey Bangladesh 2013*, female labour force participation is 33.5 per cent while that of males is 81.3 per cent (Bangladesh Bureau of Statistics, 2015, p. 46). Women still represent a distinct minority in high-status jobs (legal profession, senior officials or managerial jobs) throughout the world. The main factor behind women's low participation in the labour force is their family commitments. Career interruptions due to child rearing cause longer periods of unemployment for women, while men are easily able to move from one job to another. In addition, interruptions to labour market participation also result in skill obsolescence and reduced employability (International Labour Organization, 2012, p. 5).

CEDAW assumes that paid work is the key to women's liberation. But it ignores the fact that women's experience of work is closely affected by their class and parental and marital status (Fredman, 1997, p. 101). Bose (1985) finds that the status of housewife is higher than most working-class women's jobs (p. 56). A study (Karlekar, 1982) of sweeper women in Delhi finds that the husbands of two of the sweepers are clerks and they felt that it was demeaning for their husbands to have sweeper wives. One woman says:

> My husband mixes with big people at his place of work. He goes to interesting places. But at the end of the day he returns to this hovel and us. After all, what sort of job can he get me? I am illiterate and too old to learn anything now. But I hope my children will do better. At times I feel ashamed of my job.
>
> (Karlekar, 1982, p. 95)

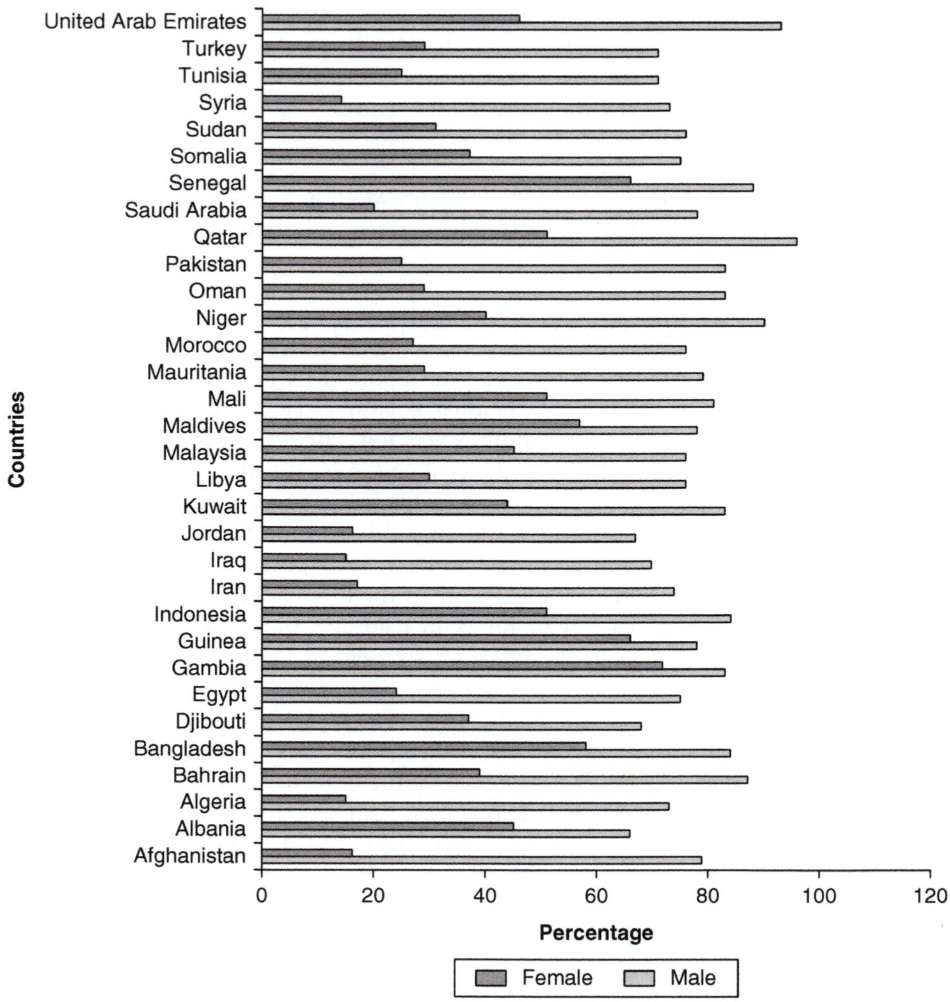

Figure 1 Male/female labour force participation rate in the Muslim countries (% of male/female population aged 15+)

Source: World Bank, 2014a; World Bank, 2014b.

Women take paid employment for many different reasons and, sometimes, increased employment is a sign of increased economic hardship or increased exploitation of women. In Bangladesh, 85 per cent of the total workforce in the garment industry are women. While many consider this as a positive step towards female empowerment, in fact, women are working in a highly exploitative situation. Most of the garment factories in Bangladesh are potential 'death chambers'. Shamim Ahsan (2005, cover story) writes:

> The factory buildings often do not have adequate ventilation facilities and are often too jam-packed with workers and machinery to allow any breathing space. Most of the

> garment factories do not impose the mandatory safety measures. Though fire incidents are rampant, most of the factories do not have fire-fighting equipment. Fire drills are not conducted in many factories. The exit staircase is a must, but they are a rare sight. When there is one it is often too narrow even for one person to comfortably get down.

On 24 April 2013 more than 1,130 people died and more than 2,500 people were rescued alive, but seriously injured, in the collapse of the Rana Plaza factory building, which was constructed illegally (Parveen, 2014). After the Rana Plaza collapse many of the survivors did not have any interest in going back to work in a garment factory again (Islam, 2013; Mahr, 2013). A report (Alam et al., 2011) on garment workers in Bangladesh finds that 60 per cent of the workers say that night shifts create problems in their family lives, especially for breastfeeding mothers. Low wages, long working days, excessive production targets, frequent night shifts and the lack of effective labour law enforcement severely affect the health and family life of women garment workers (p. 7). Female garment workers are recruited because they can be exploited as cheap labour. Female workers are harassed and abused in different ways. Garment workers suffer from many illnesses including eyesight problems and head- and ear-related complications. Due to overwork they always lose weight and look perpetually tired (Amin, 1998, p. 195). Garment workers are treated like disposable people. Many lose their jobs because they become unfit to work due to health reasons.

A majority of domestic workers in Bangladesh are young and female and they are much more prone to exploitation, sometimes even sexual harassment (Karim, 2009). Poverty forces poor parents to send their young girls to work at other peoples' houses, far away from their own homes. The poor parents know very well that there is every possibility that their girls will be 'treated badly, beaten up, not fed well, tortured, raped, or even killed' (Ahmed, 2009). Female domestic workers who work in Middle Eastern countries are having bitter experiences regarding low pay, long working hours, sexual exploitation, physical torture and lack of legal protection (Bhuyan, 2013). Although women in Bangladesh are going abroad as domestic workers because of straitened financial circumstances, they are considered a danger to the status of the family. One father of a female worker who is working in Malaysia said:

> We are very embarrassed that our daughter went to Malaysia even though we need the money she earns. We all know how the women behave there and that the environment is not good for them. Probably she will not find a husband after coming back.
>
> (Dannecker, 2005, p. 660)

In Bangladesh it is not possible for women to take any type of job at any time. Upper-class and upper-middle-class women seek high-status jobs. When they do not secure high-status jobs due to lack of adequate education and training, they prefer to be housewives. Lower-middle-class women can acquire clerical jobs, but if they marry men with high-status jobs, they must leave their jobs and live as housewives. Teaching at schools is regarded as appropriate for women of all classes. However, upper-class women do not work in Bengali middle schools because of the low salary but middle-class women do work in them. On the other hand, working as domestic servants is demeaning for lower-class women, although they are compelled to do so. A study finds that women working in the rice mills in a village are considered as 'spoiled women', because they are sexually exploited by their employers (Moin, 2002, p. 83).

For women, it is very difficult to take any kind of job without considering their class. Zarina Rahman Khan (1992) found that village women in Bangladesh were not interested in participating in earth cutting (p. 157). She points out, 'Women of higher social status, even if they were found to be just as poor, were hesitant to join such work' (Khan, 1992, p. 157). Women receive more prestige as housewives than in any kind of low-paid job. Epstein (1988) writes, 'For this reason, women often retreat to the home rather than face defeat in the workplace' (p. 213). Women whose husbands have money to maintain the family prefer to be housewives. For many women, paid work is an 'onerous necessity' with the added burden of domestic work. Women spend more time than men on unpaid domestic work. Working women with young children have difficulties in balancing dual demands and in many cases wives work part time or they do not join the paid labour force at all. Fifty-seven per cent of women are working on a part-time basis, while women constitute less than 40 per cent of total employment (International Labour Organization, 2016). Due to a lack of adequate education and training few women can get an upper-status job. Fredman (1997, pp. 128–129) argues:

> formal equality in marriage is undermined by the fact that in general, women have a lower earning capacity than men. Within an intact family unit, allocation of income between the partners is an important determinant of power relationships within the family. For example, in two-earner families, the man's income may be used for permanent ends, such as mortgage payments, whereas the woman's may pay for transient requirements, including weekly shopping or child care bills.

Can a husband and a wife take equal responsibilities within a family where the husband is a doctor and the wife is a clerk? Can a husband and a wife take equal responsibilities within a family where both are doctors, but the husband's income is higher than the wife's? How can formal equality be achieved when a husband and a wife cannot spend their income equally? In fact, when women are paid less than men in the marketplace, then women work longer hours at home than men. When the wage difference is significant, then women do all the housework (Chichilnisky, 2008, p. 829). Okin (1989, p. 154) writes:

> husbands with higher salaries and more prestigious jobs than their wives (the vast majority of two-job couples) are in a powerful position to resist their wives' appeal to them to do more at home, and it is husbands with the highest prestige who do the least housework of all.

Ericksen et al. (1979) also point out that high-income husbands do less housework then lower-income husbands (p. 310). Goode (1964, pp. 74–75) argues:

> Toward the lower strata, the husband is more likely to claim authority simply because he is male, but actually has to concede more authority to his wife. Toward the upper strata, men are less likely to assert the values of patriarchal authority, but in action manage to have more power anyway. On a common-sense basis, it can be seen that these men have resources by which to have their way. Their wives are less likely to work and even if they do work, they contribute a smaller percentage of the total family income than would be true in the lower social strata. Their husbands are less dependent on their wives' services, and can more easily purchase these services. Thus, the husband's position in the role bargaining is stronger.

For women, paid work sometimes imposes double or triple burdens (Olmsted, 2005, p. 115). According to a survey, men and women both spend a considerable time in the workplace in Bangladesh. Although men spend 6.9 hours while women spend 5.2 hours here, working women spend a significantly longer time doing housework. With regard to housework, women spend 3.6 hours doing this as compared to 1.4 hours by men (Khan, 2014). Gove and Tudor (1973) argue that when a married woman joins the paid labour force, she is in a less satisfactory position then married men (p. 815). Gove (1972, p. 35) writes:

> working wives would appear to be under a greater strain than their husbands. In addition to their jobs they apparently typically perform most of the household chores and this means that they are putting in considerably more hours of work per day than their husbands.

Do the provisions of same responsibilities deprive women of their financial rights granted by Islamic law?

I argue that if CEDAW is fully implemented, it will deprive Muslim women of their maintenance, dower rights and maintenance of children by their fathers. The law of maintenance derives from the injunctions of the *Quran*, the Prophet's tradition and consensus of the jurists. The *Quran* states:

> Men are protectors and maintainers of women, because *Allah* has given the one more (strength) than the other, and because they support them from their means. (4:34)

> The mothers shall give suck to their offspring for two whole years, if the father desires to complete the term. But he shall bear the cost of their food and clothing on equitable terms. (2:233)[30]

> Let the women live (in '*iddat*') in the same style as you live, according to your means. (65:6)

> Let the man of means spend according to His means; and the man whose resources are restricted, let him spend according to what Allah has given him. Allah puts no burden on any person beyond what He has given him. (65:7)

The Prophet said in his last speech:[31]

> O People! It is true that you have certain rights with regard to your women but they also have rights over you. Remember that you have taken them as your wives only under Allah's trust and with His permission. If they abide by your right then to them belongs the right to be fed and clothed in kindness. Do treat your women well and be kind to them for they are your partners and committed helpers.

Ali suggests developing women's rights by 'interpreting the basic texts of Islam from a woman's perspective' and categorizes the verses of the *Quran* related to women into four categories: protective, corrective, non-discriminatory and discriminatory (Ali, 2000, p. 5). She considers rights to dower and maintenance to be forms of protective rights (Ali, 2000, pp. 59–63). She writes about fathers' financial responsibility towards children (p. 63):

> This placing of the monetary responsibility for the welfare of the child and the nursing mother, although within the protective category of human rights, reinforces the stereotype roles of men as providers and women as passive consumers and men's liability.

Ali thinks that the provision of wives' maintenance cannot be used to achieve non-discriminatory status for women. However, although she assumes that if women achieve economic independence they would get the same status as men, she recommends further research on this issue (Ali, 2000, p. 65). Similar to Ali, a number of scholars argue that in Islamic law men are considered as the maintainers and protectors and this makes women dependent on them. Esposito and DeLong-Bas (2001) argue, 'Verses from the *Quran* have been used by different factions to both support a woman's subservience to a man and to defend her rights of equality' (p. 132). They divide the *Quranic* verses into two categories: the ethico-religious and the socio-economic. Men and women are equal at the ethico-religious level, but in the socio-economic sphere men achieve priority over women because of their financial responsibility towards women and women's dependency on men. Esposito and DeLong-Bas (p. 134) argue that the unequal status of men and women can be changed according to the social condition. They write:

> the social situation of women has increasingly and broadly changed in the twentieth century, so that many women are no longer completely dependent upon their husbands for maintenance and protection. Indeed, many women today are pursuing higher education and employment, making them contributors to the household's financial welfare. Consequently, the concept of the 'priority' of the husband over the wife in the socio-economic sphere is subject to change.

Fazlur Rahman (1982), who describes himself as a 'Muslim Modernist', writes that 'Islamic Modernism wants social reform through a new interpretation of Islamic sources' (p. 285). He argues that the *Quran* makes men superior to women, because men are responsible for household expenditure. He writes (p. 295):

> since these are basically socioeconomic functions and not inherent in the nature of sexes, there is nothing unchangeable about them. If they are changed, then, given necessary time, women will also acquire the same experiences and wisdom that men have accumulated over the ages.

Rahman thinks that women are dependent on men and are abused for their dependency, and can only be equal if they join the paid labour force (p. 295). Patriarchal ideology supports the notion that dower and maintenance grant husbands a type of ownership over their wives. This view ignores the statement of the *Quran* that 'husband and wife are each other's garments' (2:187). That means the relationship between a husband and wife is based on mutual support, mutual comfort and mutual protection. These laws are very useful for women, because many women in Islamic countries go to court for realizing dower and maintenance after divorce or separation to gain some relief from economic constraints. Some working women in Islamic countries even use these laws as a weapon to punish their husbands financially when their husbands divorce them without any valid reason. Werner Menski (2011, p. 126) argues:

> We can of course say that men and women 'shall' or should be the same because we are all human, or they 'shall' or should be treated equally because of human rights and all kinds of other concepts of equality, also before God in Islamic law. But we cannot make existing gender differences nonexistent by decrees of law and simple top-down declarations. The lived experience everywhere brings us back to the need to recognise many kinds of differences.

Azizah al-Hibri (1997) argues that one *ayah* of the *Quran* (4:34), highly controversial, is cited by some feminists to prove that Islam is 'structurally patriarchal' (p. 27). This *ayah* is translated by Abdullah Yusuf Ali in the following way:

> Men are the protectors and maintainers of women, because God has given the one more (strength) than the other, and because they support them from their means.

Azizah al-Hibri offers a different translation:

> Men are [advisors/providers of guidance] to women [because/in circumstances where/in that which] God made some of them different from some others and [because/in circumstances where/in that which] they spend of their own money.
>
> (al-Hibri, 1997, p. 29)

Azizah al-Hibri's (p. 30) analysis of this *ayah* is as follows:

> men are qawwamun[32] over women, is a general statement. But it is operative only when: (1) God has endowed a male (in a certain circumstance or at a certain time) with a feature, ability or characteristic which a particular woman lacks (and presumably needs in that circumstance or at that time) and (2) that male is maintaining that particular woman. Only under both of these conditions may the man presume to offer guidance or advice to the woman. The first element is important as to why the advisory role of the male is acceptable at all, the second element is important for limiting the advisory role to the man who is taking care of the woman as her provider (if the woman is indeed being provided for). Otherwise, she may be faced with droves of men who want to provide unsolicited advice (*fudhuliyun*).
>
> . . . the *Qur'an* was describing (and not recommending) in this ayah a situation akin to the traditional one existing at the time, where some women were financially dependent. In those circumstances, the ayah informs us, God gave the man supporting her responsibility (*taklif*, not privilege) of offering the woman guidance and advice in those areas in which he happens to be more qualified or experienced.

It seems that if a husband is unable to maintain his wife and the wife maintains herself, then the husband cannot be the advisor or provider of guidance to his wife; however, if a wife is financially dependent on her husband then only he can offer the woman guidance and advice.

Fadl (2001, pp. 210–211) also writes:

> the word *qawwamun* is ambiguous, and more importantly, the verse seems to hinge the status of being a maintainer, guardian or protector on objective capacities, such as the ability to provide financial support Arguably, if a woman is the one providing financial support, or stability, she becomes the one entrusted with the burden of guardianship. Furthermore, arguably, if financial responsibility is shared between the partners, then they become each other's guardians.

But I believe that this is not the intention of Allah, because in another *ayah* Allah says, 'The Believers, men and women, are protectors, one of another: they enjoin what is just, and forbid what is evil' (*Quran* 9:71) and al-Hibri (1997) also points out that this *ayah* is 'a suitable foundation for gender relations in today's Muslim societies' (p. 32).

In my view, Abdullah Yusuf Ali's translation shows the intended message of Allah. This *ayah* does not reveal or require a hierarchical patriarchal relationship in a Muslim family. It only states that the husband will take on the financial responsibility of the family because Allah gave him more strength. Here, strength means only physical strength, not mental strength. Allah did not ask women to maintain the family financially due to their child-bearing, breastfeeding and child rearing activities. Besides, sexual violence against women also adversely impacts women's employment in many countries. For these reasons, Allah did not make it mandatory for women to maintain themselves or their family. However, it does not necessarily follow that women are considered as inferior within Islam. The *Quran* considers women rational, because they have the same religious and moral duties and responsibilities as men.

Azizah al-Hibri argues that this *ayah* has been misused by the traditional jurists to confine women to the home and prevent them from participating in public life. It also perpetuates their financial dependence on men. Here, al-Hibri does not acknowledge that within marriage not only are women passively dependent on men, but men are also dependent on women. A wife's work includes satisfying her husband's sexual and emotional needs, giving birth to legitimate children, breastfeeding and raising children. Women undertake all of these duties and the fact that they do so enables men to work hard in paid employment. Although men earn money, they are dependent on women for their survival. Azizah al-Hibri ignores the fact that non-recognition of unpaid work done by women strengthens patriarchy. Constructing men as independent and women as dependent masks the dual dependency between men and women, whereby men (and children) are dependent on women's domestic and reproductive labour while women (and children) are dependent on men for the provision of income (Olmsted, 2005, p. 117).

Bhuiyan (2010) points out that women's position has changed in the modern twenty-first century and they are no longer dependent on their husbands for food and protection (p. 266). Is this the real picture of the world? In fact, female labour force participation is 49.6 per cent in the world (International Labour Organization, 2016, p. 6). How is it that women are not dependent on men for maintenance? Ali (2000, p. 65) and Islam (n.d.) argue that if women achieved financial autonomy, they would be accorded the same status as men. Does it not mean that women who do not have financial resources are inferior? In fact, Ali and Islam do not recognize the unpaid work of women. The *Quran* recognizes the unpaid work of women and so puts the responsibility of maintenance of wives and children on men, thus protecting women from a double or triple burden. It does not mean that women have no right to join the paid labour force. There is no decree in Islam that prevents women from seeking employment and there is no restriction on the use of women's exceptional talents in any area (Badawi, 1977, p. 141).

An-Na'im (1990b) interpreted verse 4:34 of the *Quran* and argues, 'The fact that men are generally physically stronger than most women is not relevant in modern times where the rule of law prevails over physical might' (p. 47). He ignores the fact that the rule of law is still absent in many parts of the world and women are victims of sexual violence. In Bangladesh, women are sexually harassed on the streets, in the marketplace, in every institution, even in the police station (Huda, 1999, p. 22). They are always insecure without men's company, although sometimes it is reported that women are sexually harassed, raped or killed in front of their own male family members. At university, female students are routinely sexually abused, harassed and raped by their male classmates, other students, political activists and even by some respected teachers. In Bangladesh, a woman is molested every 12 minutes and raped every 21 minutes (Imam, 2013). Furthermore, in 2014 in Bangladesh, 666 females were raped. Among these, 244 were women, 393 were children below the age of 18 and the age of 29 of them was unknown. Of the women, 31 were killed after being raped, 113 were victims of gang rape and 7 women committed suicide after being raped. Seventy-one women and children were victims of attempted rape (Odhikar, 2014, pp. 90–91). Although professional women are also facing harassment, the forms this takes are different from the experiences of working-class women. Young garment workers and domestic servants are vulnerable and powerless, and experience harassment at every stage of their daily lives (Huda, 2003, pp. 53–54). In her study on garment workers Majumder (2000, pp. 15–16) observes:

> In the existing social context of Bangladesh, living alone is not safe and secure for the young women. . . . The female garment workers living in rented accommodation always remain occupied with the fear of attack by the local touts, people traffickers, drug addicts and above all by the landlords and their sons.

One 18-year-old garment worker (an SSC graduate, who was harassed by her supervisor and left her job after one week) expresses her feelings:

> I'm willing to work for just one taka, but with my honour intact . . . It feels terrible when someone screams and abuses you this way. I can't put it out of my mind. I replay the incident over and over in my mind until my head begins to throb. It makes it difficult to concentrate on what I'm doing. My whole history comes back to me then. My life flashes before my eyes. I have to ask myself why on earth I even entered this line of work. Why am I working? I feel like crying. I get so depressed.
>
> (Siddiqi, 2003, p. 46)

In the post-divorce situation, paid work does not ensure equality between ex-husbands and ex-wives. The idea of formal equality in reforming family law neither addresses nor ameliorates the actual differences between men and women with regard to employment, earning capacity or the problems of balancing child care with a full-time job, especially for women who have custody of children (Mossman, 1994, p. 24). Fineman (1991, p. 35; 2009, p. 445) points out that 'sameness of treatment' perpetuates inequality, especially in the context of family law. She argues for the separate treatment of spouses after divorce:

> The idealized feminist solution of shared, equal responsibility for domestic chores is hard to implement when the unit is broken. The Chores still have to be done, children must be cared for, and a home must be established and maintained, but there are no longer two adults to divide the burdens. If women assume these responsibilities after divorce, as they do in the overwhelming majority of cases, they may need more assets or financial resources than their ex-spouses to have effective access to market opportunities. This need is further complicated by the fact that a woman is statistically likely to earn far less than her ex-spouse after divorce even if she is working.
>
> (Fineman, 1983, p. 823)

Lenore J. Weitzman (1981) found that in California men had a 42 per cent improvement and women had a 73 per cent loss in their standard of living after divorce (p. 1251). In her view, equality cannot be achieved by legislation where men and women are differently situated (Weitzman, 1985, p. 365). Weitzman (1981) writes about divorced mothers having very little time for work, retraining, child care, household chores or a new social life due to the extreme pressure to earn money (p. 1261). Treating men and women equally at divorce ignores the economic inequalities between them. In her study (Weitzman, 1985) she found that divorcing couples had very little property and so an equal distribution of marital property meant the forced sale of the family home (p. 362). She writes:

> If the divorce rules do not give her a share of his enhanced earning capacity (through alimony and child support awards), and if divorce rules expect her to enter the labour market as she is, with few skills, outdated experience, no seniority, and no time for retraining, and if she continues to have the major burden of caring for young children after divorce, it is easy to understand why the divorced woman is likely to be much worse off than her former husband. Faced with expectations that she will be 'equally' responsible for the financial support of their children and herself, she has been unequally disadvantaged by marriage and has fewer resources to meet these expectations. The result is often hardship, impoverishment, and disillusionment for divorced women (and their children).
>
> (Weitzman, 1985, p. xii)

Formal equality conceals real discrimination. As Becker (1987, p. 216) has also written:

> treating women and men as though they are equal when, in fact, they are not has worsened the post-divorce economic position of women and children, especially those women (and their children) who are most in need because they are least like men.

In addition, CEDAW promotes the equal responsibilities of parents. Most mothers always want to keep their children after divorce or separation. How can mothers take care of their children and at the same time join the paid labour force? CEDAW ignores the fact that in most of the developing countries day care facilities for children are simply not there. Even in Canada I had to wait two years to obtain subsidized day care. The provision of same responsibilities also makes children vulnerable. In recognizing women's vulnerability, especially because of the absence of the rule of law, Islam did not put the responsibility of earning on women. CEDAW ignores the vulnerable position of women, especially in developing countries and, in the name of formal equality, it places the same responsibilities as men on women in the family. It encourages women to join the paid labour force at any cost, and if CEDAW is implemented fully, it will deprive Muslim women of their maintenance and dower rights and maintenance of children by their fathers in the name of having the same responsibilities.

CEDAW assumes that the formal equality approach in family relationships will work well for achieving gender equality. But for whom and in what contexts? It will work best for upper-class or upper-middle-class women in Bangladesh whose lives closely approximate the male norm, but for women who are unwilling or unable to integrate, this model will not offer anything for them. Becker (1987, p. 214) writes about formal equality in America:

> Formal equality has actually hurt many women. Formal equality is likely to help most, and hurt least, professional women who either have no children or who hire other women to care for their children and are able to compete with men on men's terms. These women have tended to control the women's movement. And it is likely to hurt most mothers and wives who are not well-paid professionals.

Conclusion

Islam is so powerful in a country like Bangladesh that a secular approach like CEDAW cannot be effective for women's liberation. The effectiveness of family law reform in Bangladesh depends on its acceptance by the people of Bangladesh. In my view, if reform is done within an Islamic framework, then people will accept it. Some provisions of CEDAW are clearly inconsistent with Islamic law. The concept of equality between men and women in Islamic law is different from CEDAW's concept of equality. Both CEDAW and Islamic law incorporate formal and substantive notions of equality. However, in family law CEDAW mostly adopts a formal equality approach and Islamic law mostly adopts a substantive equality approach. Articles 16.1[c] and [d] of CEDAW, which deal with family law, are not consistent with Islamic law. Article 16.1[c] imposes an obligation on state parties to ensure that men and women have the same responsibilities during marriage and its dissolution, and article 16.1[d] obligates state parties to ensure that they have the same responsibilities as parents. In these articles, CEDAW adopts a gender-neutral formal equality approach and Islamic law adopts the substantive equality approach. I argue that if CEDAW is implemented fully, it will deprive Muslim women of their maintenance, dower rights and maintenance of children by their fathers. The idea of formal equality in the family does not consider the actual differences between men and women with regard to employment, earning capacity or the problems of balancing child care with a full-time job, especially for women who have custody of children (Fineman, 1991, p. 35; 2009, p. 445). Moreover, in recognizing women's vulnerability, especially due to childbearing and child rearing activities and the absence of the rule of law, Islam does not put the responsibility of earning on women. CEDAW ignores the vulnerable position of women, especially in developing countries, and in the name of formal equality it places the same responsibilities as men on women. I argue that working women are taking *more* than equal responsibilities.

Women's organizations in Bangladesh are demanding complete ratification of CEDAW. Feminists in Bangladesh do not think that women will lose the right to maintenance, dower and maintenance of children by their fathers as granted by Muslim personal law in Bangladesh if CEDAW is fully implemented. It will not be a problem for the elite-class women who control the women's movement in Bangladesh as they are self-sufficient, but it will hurt the majority of women in Bangladesh who are not in the paid labour force and who are working under insecure and exploitative working conditions. In the name of men and women having the same responsibilities during marriage and its dissolution and the same responsibilities as parents, it will encourage women to join the paid labour force at any cost. It is not possible to achieve gender equality at home even if gender equality is achieved in all areas outside of the home in Bangladesh. In most cases there will be inequality between husbands and wives in terms of education, training and income. Although the women's movement in Bangladesh has many positive achievements, it is dominated by the urban educated upper and middle class. The women's movement in Bangladesh has been strengthened by the money and ideas of donor agencies (Jahan, 1995, p. 107). Akhter (2006) writes:

> The overwhelming presence of NGOs and dictation of International agencies through their counterparts has often marginalized the voices of Bangladeshi women. Bangladesh had only a few middle- and upper-class women seeking jobs at the national and international organizations and therefore they became the 'implementers' of the suggestions made by foreign 'gender consultants'.

The elite women who lead the feminist movement in Bangladesh make demands for a change they consider desirable by imposing its cost on other women. One of the reasons for women's subordination is that others have defined and dictated what the women of Bangladesh want, instead of actually listening to their thoughts and feelings. Ali (2000, p. 285) correctly recognizes that the equality movement in the Muslim countries will be successful if it comes from within those societies and women's active participation is essential in that struggle. It is not possible for a government to ignore 'the politically articulated wishes or positions of powerful groups or segments of its population who might want to maintain religious and customary laws' (An-Na'im, 1994, p. 169). The purpose of CEDAW should not be to force women into lifestyles with which they do not agree (Venkatraman, 1995, p. 2011).

Notes

1 CEDAW was adopted by the United Nations General Assembly by 130 votes to none. Ten countries abstained from voting (Bangladesh, Brazil, Comoros, Haiti, Mali, Mauritania, Mexico, Morocco, Saudi Arabia and Senegal) and twelve countries did not vote (Albania, Djibouti, Dominica, Equatorial Guinea, Iran, Malawi, Papua New Guinea, Saint Lucia, Seychelles, Solomon Islands, South Africa and the United Republic of Cameroon) (Chinkin and Freeman, 2012, p. 7).

2 UN Women, Declarations, Reservations and Objections to CEDAW, http://www.un.org/womenwatch/daw/cedaw/reservations-country.htm [accessed 9 October 2016].

3 Article 2. State parties condemn discrimination against women in all its forms, agree to pursue by all appropriate means and without delay a policy of eliminating discrimination against women and, to this end, undertake:

[a] To embody the principle of the equality of men and women in their national constitutions or other appropriate legislation if not yet incorporated therein and to ensure, through law and other appropriate means, the practical realization of this principle;
[b] To adopt appropriate legislative and other measures, including sanctions where appropriate, prohibiting all discrimination against women;
[c] To establish legal protection of the rights of women on an equal basis with men and to ensure through competent national tribunals and other public institutions the effective protection of women against any act of discrimination;
[d] To refrain from engaging in any act or practice of discrimination against women and to ensure that public authorities and institutions shall act in conformity with this obligation;
[e] To take all appropriate measures to eliminate discrimination against women by any person, organization or enterprise;
[f] To take all appropriate measures, including legislation, to modify or abolish existing laws, regulations, customs and practices which constitute discrimination against women;
[g] To repeal all national penal provisions which constitute discrimination against women.

16.1[c] The same rights and responsibilities during marriage and at its dissolution.

4 'Rights Activists Call for Full Implementation of CEDAW', *New Age*, 4 September 2014.

5 Comm. On the Elimination of Discrimination Against Women [CEDAW] *General Recommendation No. 25 on Article 4, Paragraph 1 of the Convention on the Elimination of All Forms of Discrimination Against Women, on Temporary Special Measures*, available at www.un.org/womenwatch/daw/cedaw/recommendations/General%20recommendation%2025%20%28English%29.pdf [accessed 25 July 2016].

6 Comm. On the Elimination of Discrimination Against Women [CEDAW] *General Recommendation No. 25 on Article 4, Paragraph 1 of the Convention on the Elimination of All Forms of Discrimination Against Women, on Temporary Special Measures*, available at www.un.org/womenwatch/daw/cedaw/recommendations/General%20recommendation%2025%20%28English%29.pdf [accessed 25 July 2016].

7 Article 1, CEDAW.

8 CEDAW, *General Recommendation No. 12 (eighth session, 1989)*; *General Recommendation No. 19 (eleventh session, 1992)*, available at www.un.org/womenwatch/daw/cedaw/recommendations/recomm.htm#recom12 [accessed 25 July 2016].

9 Comm. On the Elimination of Discrimination Against Women [CEDAW] *General Recommendation No. 21 of the Convention on the Elimination of All Forms of Discrimination Against Women, on Equality in Marriage and Family Relations*, available at www.un.org/womenwatch/daw/cedaw/recommendations/recomm.htm#recom2 [accessed 25 July 2016].
10 *General Recommendation No. 17 (tenth session, 1991)*; *General Recommendation No. 21 (thirteenth session, 1994)*; *General Recommendation No. 24 (twentieth session, 1999)*, available at www.un.org/womenwatch/daw/cedaw/recommendations/recomm.htm#recom2 [accessed 25 July 2016].
11 CEDAW, *General Recommendation No. 21 (thirteenth session, 1994)*, *Equality in Marriage and Family Relations*, available at www.un.org/womenwatch/daw/cedaw/recommendations/recomm.htm#recom21 [accessed 25 July 2016].
12 Article 10[c], CEDAW.
13 Article 5[a], CEDAW.
14 UN Women, Declarations, Reservations and Objections to CEDAW, http://www.un.org/womenwatch/daw/cedaw/reservations-country.htm [accessed 9 October 2016].
15 UN Women, Declarations, Reservations and Objections to CEDAW, http://www.un.org/womenwatch/daw/cedaw/reservations-country.htm [accessed 9 October 2016].
16 UN Women, Declarations, Reservations and Objections to CEDAW, http://www.un.org/womenwatch/daw/cedaw/reservations-country.htm [accessed 9 October 2016].
17 UN Women, Declarations, Reservations and Objections to CEDAW, http://www.un.org/womenwatch/daw/cedaw/reservations-country.htm [accessed 9 October 2016].
18 UN Women, Convention on the Elimination of All Forms of Discrimination against Women, http://www.un.org/womenwatch/daw/cedaw/cedaw.htm [accessed 9 October 2016].
19 Article 15[2], CEDAW.
20 UN Women, Declarations, Reservations and Objections to CEDAW http://www.un.org/womenwatch/daw/cedaw/reservations-country.htm [accessed 9 October 2016].
21 UN Women, Declarations, Reservations and Objections to CEDAW, http://www.un.org/womenwatch/daw/cedaw/reservations-country.htm [accessed 9 October 2016].
22 UN Women, Declarations, Reservations and Objections to CEDAW, http://www.un.org/womenwatch/daw/cedaw/reservations-country.htm [accessed 9 October 2016].
23 UN Women, Declarations, Reservations and Objections to CEDAW, http://www.un.org/womenwatch/daw/cedaw/reservations-country.htm [accessed 9 October 2016].
24 UN Women, Declarations, Reservations and Objections to CEDAW, http://www.un.org/womenwatch/daw/cedaw/reservations-country.htm [accessed 9 October 2016].
25 *New Age*, 16 December 2008.
26 Comm. On the Elimination of Discrimination Against Women [CEDAW] *General Recommendation No. 21 of the Convention on the Elimination of All Forms of Discrimination Against Women, on Equality in Marriage and Family Relations*, available at www.un.org/womenwatch/daw/cedaw/recommendations/recomm.htm#recom2 [accessed 25 July 2016].
27 CEDAW, *General Recommendation No. 24 (twentieth session, 1999)*.
28 CEDAW, *General Recommendation No. 21 (1994)*, available at www.un.org/womenwatch/daw/cedaw/recommendations/recomm.htm#recom21 [accessed 25 July 2016].
29 *General Recommendation No. 24 (twentieth session, 1999)*, available at www.un.org/womenwatch/daw/cedaw/recommendations/recomm.htm#recom24 [accessed 25 July 2016].
30 It refers to maintenance when the wife is divorced.
31 The Last Sermon of Prophet Muhammad (PBUH). This speech was delivered on the Ninth Day of Dhul-Hijjah, 10 A.H. (632 CE) in the Uranah valley of Mount Arafat in Makkah at the pilgrimage. It is also known as the Farewell Pilgrimage, available at *www.cyberistan.org/islamic/sermon.htm>l* [accessed 20 July 2016].
32 According to Azizah, 'qawwamun' means advisors/providers of guidance.

5 Dowry, women and law in Bangladesh

Dowry has now become more significant than dower in Bangladesh. The distinction between dowry and dower is often misunderstood. Dower is religiously sanctioned but dowry is not supported by state law and personal laws. Marriage is a civil contract that legalizes sexual relationships between a man and a woman in Islamic law and dower is an essential part of Muslim marriage. Islamic law does not specify any maximum amount of dower, but makes it obligatory for a husband to pay whatever amount has been fixed and whatever amount is assessed if not fixed (Monsoor, 2008, p. 24). The dower is paid by the husband to his wife as an honour and to show respect, and to indicate that he seriously desires to marry her with a sense of responsibility and obligation (Monsoor, 2003). On the other hand, dowry refers to 'the transmission of large sums of money, jewellery, cash and other goods from the bride's family to the groom's family' (Monsoor, 2003). The dowry system increases the vulnerability of girls and women in Bangladesh, turning them into liabilities for their family.

After Bangladesh became independent on 16 December 1971 the problem of dowry became so widespread that women activists and some enlightened men demanded legislation to eradicate this practice. Daulatunnessa Khatun introduced a 'Dowry Prohibition Bill in parliament, and under pressure, the government passed it as the Dowry Prohibition Act of 1980' (Begum, 2006, pp. 225–229). The act makes the giving and taking of dowry, or demanding dowry a punishable offence. According to the act, dowry means 'any property or valuable security given or agreed to be given either directly or indirectly', as follows:

(a) by one party to a marriage to the other party to the marriage; or
(b) by the parents of either party to a marriage or by any other person to either party to the marriage or to any other person.

The Dowry Prohibition (Amendment) Ordinance 1984 extended the definition of dowry to 'any property or valuable security given at the time of marriage or at any time' which substituted the earlier words 'at, before or after the marriage'. It states:

> [at the time of marriage or at any time] before or after the marriage as consideration for the marriage of the said parties, but does not include dower or mehr in the case of persons to whom the Muslim Personal Law (*Shariat*) applies.

Section 3 of the act provides the punishment for giving or taking dowry:

> If any person, after the commencement of this Act, gives or takes or abets the giving or taking of dowry, he shall be punishable with imprisonment which may extend to [five years and shall not be less than one year, or with fine, or with both].

Section 4 of the act sets out the punishment for demanding dowry:

> If any person, after the commencement of this Act, demands, directly or indirectly, from the parents or guardian of a bride or bridegroom, as the case may be, any dowry, he shall be punishable with imprisonment which may extend to [five years and shall not be less than one year, or with fine, or with both].

Despite this legislation, dowry-related violence has been increasing in Bangladesh. Odhikar noted in 2014 that 237 females had experienced dowry-related violence. Of the 237 women, 4 were under-age brides. Additionally, among the 233 women, 120 were allegedly killed, 103 were physically abused and 10 resorted to suicide because of dowry-related demands and dowry-related violence. Among the four under-age brides, one had committed suicide and three were killed. Children are often also victimized alongside their mothers in these situations. Odhikar reported that during the same time period one female child was killed while a male child was injured. Furthermore, Odhikar found that ten relatives of victims were also physically abused due to dowry-related domestic abuse (Odhikar, 2014, p. 87).

How does the dowry system work in South Asia? How did the dowry system emerge in Bangladesh? How does the dowry system work in Bangladesh? What are men's expectations from their wives or wives' families? What are the limitations of the anti-dowry law in Bangladesh? I will address these questions in this chapter. I argue that dowry increased with the expansion of capitalist relations, which help men in Bangladesh to accumulate capital. It has been turned into 'demand, extortion, material gain, and profit maximization' (Samuel, 2002, p. 205). The most common motives behind the dowry system are the grooms' and their families' greed, growing consumerism, excessive materialism, status seeking and rising expectations of a better and luxurious life.

The dowry system in South Asia

The practice of dowry is becoming more widespread in India despite there being anti-dowry law, modernization and women's increasing participation in the market economy (Srinivasan and Lee, 2004, p. 1108). The Dowry Prohibition Act 1961 was passed for combating dowry-related violence and dowry murders in India. The act was amended in 1983, 1984, 1985 and 1986 (Menski, 1998, p. 122). Menski (1998) writes, 'These various amendments, in their combined strength, have given the Indian legal system and particularly the judiciary enormously powerful weapons to punish any violations of the Dowry Prohibition law' (p. 122). Despite having anti-dowry law, women are in a disadvantaged position on the marriage market and must pay for it in India (Edlund, 2006, p. 542). Dowry turned into a 'coercive transaction' in which the amount of dowry determines women's value and marrying a daughter is impossible without a large dowry (Srinivasan, 2005, p. 600). Dowry is conserved as 'a means of female competition for desirable (that is wealthy) husbands' (Gaulin and Boster, 1990, p. 997). Upadhya (1990, p. 42) writes:

> Dowry is essential in that a woman cannot get married without it, and a large dowry is necessary to attract a good husband. The main goal of the bride's father is to marry her into a 'good family' – one with plenty of land and respectable ancestry – or to marry her to an educated, employed, urban migrant boy. Moreover, to offer or receive a large dowry is in itself status-enhancing.

Tambiah (1973) argues that dowry is female property or female right to property which is transferred during marriage as a kind of pre-mortem inheritance. A bride receives a marriage portion which is known as *stridhan* (women's wealth). *Stridhan* is the exclusive property of a woman and is considered as a substitute for the right of inheritance (Tambiah, 1973, pp. 70–71). In addition, dowry also consisted of a portion known as *dakshina* destined for the bridegroom and his family. *Dakshina* includes gifts that are given on special occasions after the marriage (Rudd, 2001, p. 516). Rudd (2001, p. 516) writes:

> In India, when a gift or *dakshina* is given to a Brahmin priest, it is given without reciprocation, which blesses the giver and renders the gift sacred. The same principle applied to dowry. A father received no material gain when he properly dowered his daughter, but he did achieve status and family honor, along with blessings. Religious values then, were extremely important in perpetuating the Indian marriage and dowry system.

Dowry was a gift that came with the gift of the virgin (*kanya dana*) and it was aligned with the status game of hypergamy, where a family of lower status, although not necessarily inferior in wealth, wants to raise its status through a superior marriage for its daughters and sisters (Tambiah, 1973, p. 64). Social status or caste was determined by birth. Women can change their caste status, but men cannot change theirs. When a lower-caste woman marries a man from a higher caste, she and her children are inducted into the man's caste. When a woman from a higher caste marries a man from a lower caste, she and her children become members of the lower caste. Society does not allow a woman from a higher caste to marry a lower-caste man, although a lower-caste woman is encouraged to marry an upper-caste man (Self and Grabowski, 2009, p. 70). Billig (1991, p. 349) writes:

> Hypergamy arose as a way to preserve the male advantage in the competition for spouses, at least for those males whose social dominance is at stake. Since higher status men are scarce relative to the number of women who are 'competing' for them, the parents of girls are pressed to marry off their daughters at young ages and offer large amounts of groomprice for the privilege of marrying their daughters into prestigious households.

Dowry was closely connected with high status (Goody, 1973, p. 19). The ancient scripts of Manu (a holy text) restricted dowry to the Brahmin caste (Tambiah, 1973, p. 69). Rastogi and Therly (2006, p. 68) write:

> In prehistoric times women were regarded as chattel and so it was the bride's father, and not the bridegroom, who was regarded as justified in demanding a payment at the time of marriage. The father lost control over the labour of his daughter after her marriage and was paid in kind to compensate for it. There is contradictory evidence in Hindu scriptures to suggest that women who are economically privileged used to bring large amounts of gifts to the husband's family after marriage. However, these presents were not called dowries for they were voluntarily made after the marriage, and out of pure affection.

Kandiyoti writes that in classic patriarchy, the dowry is directly given to the grooms' kin and brides do not have any control over it (Kandiyoti, 1988, p. 279). Samuel also finds that brides have no real control over their dowry gifts (Samuel, 2002, p. 221). Artefact gifts do not benefit the brides and neither does money given for wedding expenses, such as the feast, decorations and other accompaniments (Kumari, 1989, p. 50). When brides become older they are involved actively with the dowry system as givers (mothers of brides) and as receivers and redistributors (mothers of bridegrooms) (Sharma, 1993, p. 342). Kishwar (1986, pp. 6–7) writes:

> In actuality, a woman is seldom allowed to have control even over things that are supposedly for her personal use. Gold and other jewellery are traditionally supposed to be a woman's personal security, but, in practice, the gold usually stays in the custody of her mother-in-law or husband. It is up to them to give her what they wish for her personal use and daily wear . . . It is fairly common for certain items of her jewellery to be incorporated into her husband's sister's dowry.

When parents arrange the marriage of a son, they always expect to receive dowry at the wedding and that is why they always look at whether the bride's family has the ability to give dowry (Sharma, 1993, p. 343). Parents start to collect items for their daughters' dowries well in advance of their weddings. Sometimes, the girls themselves prepare some of the items, for example embroidered bed covers, cushions, etc. and at the present time daughters who are in paid employment buy some items from their income. Most parents, whatever their financial status, receive some help from other relatives (Sharma, 1993, p. 344). A family wants to show that it is capable and important by giving huge dowries (Srinivasan, 2005, p. 603). Great expenditure is incurred on weddings to show the status of the bride's family (Srinivas, 1984, p. 27). Srinivas (1984, p. 27) argues:

> Care is taken to invite as many important acquaintances as one can, and these become indicators of one's status just like the number of cars parked outside the wedding hall. It must be made clear that both the kin groups coming together in the wedding are sensitive to considerations of family status or honour, though the bride's kin are usually a little more eager to impress everyone, especially the groom's kin.

At present in India among the high and educated castes, bridegrooms demand all the wedding costs including the cost of their travel to the bride's city or town and they also demand a 'grand' wedding (Srinivas, 1984, p. 28). Dowry harassment is one of the techniques by which a husband and his family humiliate a wife to 'accept a subordinate position within the family and feel grateful for being allowed to survive at all in the marital home' (Kishwar, 1986, p. 4). Dowry practice indicates the gender inequality in Indian society. Srinivas (1984, p. 11) writes:

> The groom's family expects that it is the responsibility of the bride's family to make them happy and satisfied, often making unexpected and sudden demands and looking for faults within wedding arrangements and gifts. The bride's family has to tolerate all the demands and complaints from the groom's side as they believe that they are inferior.

Similarly, Jhutti's (1998, p. 189) research on the Sikhs in Britain has found:

> demanding a dowry is a way for the groom and his family to improve their wealth and social position. Most importantly, however, it is a way to demonstrate to the wife and her family who is boss, and to keep them in their place. Where a dowry is demanded or

> expected, the groom's family has power, while the bride's family are vulnerable because they never know whether what they have given is enough.

The growth of the cash-based economy and commercialized dowry further lowers the position of women. The cash-based economy redefined the social hierarchy. Formerly, social status was determined by caste, but now class determines everything. As Jane Rudd (2001, p. 516) writes:

> Education and an expanding economy, as well as government employment, have created an urban middle class. The centuries-old tradition of dowry becomes one way for an upwardly mobile family to demonstrate its wealth and make ties among higher social groups.

She points out, 'dowry is part of the class system and the "maintenance" of the superiority of higher groups over lower' (Rudd, 2001, p. 517). Billig (1991) argues that a new form of hypergamy has emerged. Parents wants to marry their daughters to educated men who have urban jobs because they have higher and certain incomes and their wives do not need to do the hard work of rural life. Generally, they do not live with their parents-in-law (Billig, 1991, pp. 355–356).

The age structure of the population became younger as a result of the infant and child mortality level. Thus, there was a surplus of younger women of marriageable age. Moreover, the number of widowers decreased drastically (Bhat and Halli, 1999, p. 144). Caldwell et al. (1983) argue, 'In a seller's market, created by relative scarcity, there was no alternative but to offer a dowry with one's daughter' (p. 347). Now, parents do not want to marry off their daughters to men of a higher caste who do not have sufficient education and bright employment prospects (Billig, 1991, p. 356). Young men who were in salaried jobs were attractive as bridegrooms in the marriage market. They were 'scarce commodities', and their scarcity was increased due to the rule of '*jati* endogamy' and the necessity of marrying off girls at an early age (Srinivas, 1984, p. 11). Educated bridegrooms can demand larger dowries because parents of girls want to marry them off to salaried men. They prefer bridegrooms who have government or professional jobs and live in cities (Srinivas, 1984, p. 21). Oldenburg (2002) also finds that the parents are looking for educated, employed and attractive men of good character, and eligible bridegrooms demand big dowries because the supply of their kind is small (p. 31). Billig (1991, p. 356) argues:

> In the newly monetized economy, where much of the wealth has become concentrated in urban centres, ritual rank no longer ensures the kind of good life and overall status that it did only a generation ago. Within one's own *jati*, marrying a doctor or engineer or business executive has become more desirable than marrying an undercredentialed scion of a family with caste prestige.

Population growth created a surplus of women in the marriage market and caused the rise of dowries in India (Rao, 1993, p. 676). Epstein (1973) considers the interaction between four variables in the changeover from bridewealth to dowry in South India (p. 199). First, the peasants enjoy the increased wealth which allows them limitless spending on weddings in order to gain social recognition. Second, women from wealthy peasant families do not work on the land and while it gives them prestige, it makes a peasant wife a liability. Epstein (1973) argues that, 'the groom's family now want to be paid for taking over the responsibility of keeping her where previously they had been prepared to compensate her father for the loss of the productive contribution.' Third, the parents of young educated males feel justified in demanding dowry as compensation from the brides' families. They invest in a son's education and expect to be rewarded when he gets married. Finally, the peasants imitate the lifestyle of Brahmin – the high caste – and following this they practise the dowry system. In the words of one peasant, 'What is good enough for Brahmins is good enough for me!' Srinivas (1984, p. 20) also points out:

> since independence there has been a sharp increase in the emulation of the higher caste by the lower. Such emulation was facilitated by the latter's increased access to education, and jobs in the organized sector, and in the growing erosion of the moral authority of the dominant castes to prevent the dependant caste from emulating their betters.

Samuel (2002) explores the dowry system in India using the theory of modified capitalist patriarchy. She argues that, along with capitalism and patriarchy, the caste system and religious beliefs are responsible for the existence of the dowry system in India. She points out, 'there is a caste within every class and a class within every caste'. Class/caste interaction patterns are influenced by the process of Westernization and Sanskritization. Samuel (2002, p. 194) argues:

> The process of Westernization consists of the integration of customs and beliefs based on the misrepresentation of a capitalist system in the colonial and neo-colonial period. Most upper castes adopted the 'western' lifestyle and the social custom of dowry during the period of colonialism, with the practice assuming consumeristic overtones during the neo-colonial period. Sanskritization, a process whereby the lower castes assimilated the norms and values of the upper castes, facilitated the lower castes imbibing the custom of dowry from the upper castes.

With the expansion of capitalist relations, the practice of dowry increased. It helped men accumulate capital using violence against women. Dowry is used for material gain and profit maximization and it is acquired by men and their families through demand, extortion or violence. Capitalism in fact promotes greed, materialism and consumerism and the dowry practice is an easy way for many men to move up the social ladder. Samuel (2002) also finds that women were harassed for dowry regardless of their educational and occupational background. Dowry harassment exists in all three religious communities (Hindu, Christian and Muslim) and almost all caste/class groups. The middle-class/caste urban population is more affected by the dowry system, because they 'aspired to emulate the lifestyle of the upper caste/class'.

From the 1990s the process of economic modernization began in India and it increased cash flows and availability of consumer goods and led to rising aspirations for a better and luxurious life (Srinivasan, 2005, p. 605). Modern dowry is closely related to a new consumerism, status seeking and rising expectations of a lifestyle that men cannot achieve with their own income (Stone and James, 1995, p. 127). Srinivasan (2005, p. 605) points out:

> well-off families could have easily shifted to giving the latest consumption goods as part of their daughter's dowries because they could afford it. The problem of course is that this behavior is not a function merely of financial affordability, that is, it is not limited to only those who can afford or have the means. An even greater impact of market liberalization is the increasing importance of material status and opulent life styles as a desired state to be pursued. Under the pressure of maintaining 'face' and social imitation, the not so well-off and the poor pay a huge price, as economic reforms have not benefitted all and/or to the same extent, which brings us to some of the indirect ways in which these reforms have a bearing on the practice of dowry.

Colonialism, Western consumerism and mothers-in-law are responsible for the dowry practice (Greenberg, 2003, p. 835). In India, the higher castes practised dowry marriage and the other castes practised bride price in which the groom used to give gifts to the bride and her family. The British colonial government reinforced the marriage system of high caste on the presumption that other forms of marriage system were not valid (Greenberg, 2003, p. 830). Today, Indian men consider dowry as a way of upgrading their economic position. In the post-independence period middle-class families became the target of consumerism and Western-style advertising and it created an 'insatiable greed' in the grooms' families (Kumari, 1989, p. 38; Greenberg, 2003, p. 830). Ram (1991) found that in a fishing community in southern India dowry was used in capital equipment purchase (p. 197). Grooms and their families improve their wealth and social position by demanding dowry (Jhutti, 1998, p. 189).

Mies (1986) argues that there is a relationship between dowry demands and capital accumulation. In India, the dowry money is used in many cases to start a business – a lawyer's office, a private practitioner's clinic, an engineering office, etc. (p. 162). Mies (1986, p. 162) points out that the institution of dowry can be considered as 'a source of wealth which is accumulated not by means of the man's own work or by investing his own capital, but by *extraction, blackmail and direct violence*':

> The command over dowry gives all men the chance to get hold of money which they have not earned and to have access to modern consumer items which they might otherwise not be able to buy. The dowry creates a market for such goods, even among people who have to take up consumption loans in order to secure their survival. It paves the way for the spread of market-values and market-commodities, even among the poor.

A report (1974) on the status of India found that educated girls require more dowry because they expect better qualified husbands. The report says:

> where the girl is allowed to earn and is capable of earning her own dowry, education may be an advantage, but it does not lessen the dowry. Only where a girl has taken up a career or has a permanent job will the boy's people be satisfied with a modest dowry.
> (Government of India, 1974, p. 75)

Klaas van der Veen (1971) studied the Anavil Brahmans of South Gujarat and found that girls who had undertaken higher education brought smaller dowries than girls with less education (p. 40). Murickan (1975) found that for the women of Kerala, 'neither education nor employment of the bride reduces the incidence of dowry' (p. 83).

Despite religious and cultural differences, the practice of dowry in Pakistan exists and the causes are similar to those in India. However, research on the dowry system in Pakistan is very limited compared to India. In Pakistan, the traditional custom of dowry is considered the pre-mortem inheritance of a daughter and it is still practised in rural areas, despite the fact that she receives less than what she is entitled to according to the law. In urban areas, however, the dowry practice turned into a groom price payment (Anderson, 2000, p. 38). The relevant legislation in Pakistan is the Dowry and Bridal Gifts (Restriction) Act 1976 and rules made under that act, and the Dowry and Bridal Gifts (Restriction) (Amendment) Ordinance 1980. Pakistan also passed the Marriages (Prohibition of Wasteful Expenses) Act 1997 to take steps to control increased expenditure at weddings (Menski, 1998, pp. 107–108). Menski (1998, p. 108) writes:

> Interestingly, the Act appears to have effectively stopped the huge wasteful dinner parties in often lavish five star surroundings. An instant repercussion, I was told, which definitely remains to be researched, has been that the groom's side may now expect the actual savings from the prohibited lavish dinners to be transformed into higher dowry payments!

Makino (2014) argues that higher dowry increases women's decision making power in the household and it helps women stay protected from domestic violence in the rural areas in Pakistan (p. 15). Many parents are always worried about providing large dowries and the dowry practice causes the neglect of daughters in Pakistan. The quote 'God should give daughters to rich families only' indicates the financial cause for son preference in Pakistani society because daughters require a dowry to get married and they will not look after their parents (Winkvist and Akhtar, 2000, p. 80). The financial cause for son preference is strong in rural areas of Punjabi society and in urban areas parents are more concerned about the fate of their daughters in their marital families (Winkvist and Akhtar, 2000, p. 80). For many families, dowry becomes a burden; many parents have to take loans to provide the dowry and sometimes daughters in poor families remain unmarried because of their inability to meet the demands from grooms' families (Ali et al., 2013, p. 86). Sometimes, dowry is demanded after the wedding and the inability to meet the demands causes physical, psychological and verbal abuse (Ali et al., 2013, p. 88). In a study on dowry in Pakistan one respondent related the story of her sister:

> After marriage, the in-laws started teasing and beating my sister. When she got conceived, they charged her by saying that she was not a virgin at the time of marriage and denied to own the child. All this was done just to snatch some money from my family.
>
> (Perveen et al., 2011, p. 33)

Tazeen Saeed Ali et al. (2013, p. 88) write:

> If a wife doesn't bring dowry, sometimes the in-laws will not accept her into the family. She will sometimes be treated like a servant, expected to do all house chores and sexually satisfy her husband to gain her respectable place within the family.

Seventy to 90 per cent of women in Pakistan are the victims of domestic violence. Homicide or 'stove burns', and suicides give husbands an opportunity to pursue another marriage and receive more dowry (Niaz, 2004, p. 60). Perveen et al. (2011, p. 15) note:

> the extreme form it takes includes driving a woman to suicide or engineering an accident through the infamous 'stove-burning' – usually when the husband, often in collaboration with his side of the family, feels (or is made to believe) that the dowry or other gifts he had expected from his in-laws were not forthcoming or/and he wanted to marry again or he expected an inheritance from the death of his wife.

Dowry is an unacknowledged form of violence and is considered to be a part of social customs and norms in Pakistani society (Perveen, 2014). Dowry increases because of media attention and consumerism. The media promotes consumerism and the custom of dowry through dramas, movies and advertisements portraying luxurious wedding parties, costly bridal dresses and jewellery, etc. Influenced by the media, parents take out loans to provide the dowry and then spend their whole lives paying back the loans (Perveen et al., 2011, p. 32). Perveen et al. (2011, p. 31) find:

> dowry normally includes a TV, a refrigerator, a deep-freezer, clothes, gold, furniture, bed sheets, quilts, utensils, carpets, curtains, cosmetics, and other accessories of daily use. Average expenditure on dowry in a middle class family is above 0.3 to 0.4 million rupees.

The brides' families continue giving gifts on other occasions after the marriage. Parents are compelled to give gifts to maintain their prestige and to ensure their daughters' security. Not long after the wedding, brides' in-laws, grooms and their relatives and friends are invited to a lavish lunch or dinner hosted by the brides' families at which they receive yet more gifts. Furthermore, on different social and religious occasions the brides' families are expected to send gifts to the grooms' families. If brides' families are unable to send gifts, brides face psychological or physical harm (Perveen et al., 2011, p. 33). Dowry is used to attract a more suitable match (Perveen et al., 2011, p. 14). It is also used to attract more suitable grooms for brides' younger sisters. Two respondents said in a study on dowry in Pakistan, 'My parents gave me a large amount in dowry and that resulted in finding good matches for my younger sisters' (Perveen et al., 2011, p. 31). Dowry may increase the worth of brides, but it does not always ensure security in their married lives. Many times, women face violence, separation and divorce on grounds of dowry demands (Perveen et al., 2011, p. 32). In Pakistan, dowry demands are always made informally, mostly by grooms' mothers or sisters. If girls are less beautiful or over-aged for marriage according to society, then the dowry covers up the gap. Fathers' high status and financial solvency also help to cover up such a gap (Perveen et al., 2011, p. 32). At present, forms of dowry have changed as more women are joining the paid labour force in Pakistan. Their income is considered as an alternative to dowry and can be given throughout their lives (Perveen et al., 2011, p. 32). Perveen et al. (2011, p. 32) argue:

> Nowadays, girls having some source of earning/job are preferred for marriage because she becomes a source of income. Where Islam considers a woman's earnings her own, declaring it a man's obligation to support the family, the current expectation is that she will bring her earning capacity as well as dowry into the marriage, and her income cannot be spent at her own discretion.

The emergence of dowry in Bangladesh

Amin and Cain (1997) argue that the emergence of the dowry system in Bangladesh was caused by a surplus of women relative to men of marriageable age which began in 1960 (p. 290). They note that (p. 298):

> in 1950 there was an excess of girls of only 10 per cent, rising to 22 per cent in 1965 and 43 per cent in 1975, then falling to 26 per cent in 1985 and further to 15 per cent in 1995.

They point out that bride price existed until 1964 and after that the dowry system emerged (pp. 290–291):

> The value of brideprice was relatively invariant and typically consisted of several pieces of jewelry for the bride and some cash. The cash component of brideprice was intended to

> defray some of the costs of entertainment related to the marriage ceremony, which are typically incurred by the bride's father. When dowry first appeared, the most common form of payment was jewelry for the bride. In recent years cash dowries have become more common, and the groom will occasionally ask for radios, watches, gold rings, and items of clothing.

Rozario (1998) also argues that recent practice regarding dowry is related to a new surplus of unmarried women in Bangladesh (p. 269). She writes: 'the shift from bridewealth to dowry in the Bangladeshi context is a consequence of women's devalorization, which is justified through the ideology of purity' (Rozario, 1998, p. 269). She points out that village men started to postpone marriage until they were between 25 to 30 years of age because of increased urbanization and education. Men value female purity and, therefore, do not want to marry women of their own age. They consider such women to be sexually suspect. Men can remain unmarried until the age of 30 or even 40. On the other hand, a woman of 20 years of age is considered unmarriageable (Rozario, 1998, p. 272). Rozario observes that the number of never-married women is increasing, that parents are worried about the marriage prospects of their daughters and that this compels them to make dowry payments (Rozario, 1998, p. 272). Although the number of never-married women is increasing, Rozario's observation about purity and marriage is disputable. Village men in Bangladesh want to marry very young girls, because young girls are thought to have greater sexual and procreative power than older girls (Chowdhury, 2004, p. 247). Rozario fails to understand the attitude of rural men in Bangladesh.

Lindenbaum (1981) observed that there had been a change in the direction of the flow of wealth at marriage in Bangladesh between the 1950s and 1970s (p. 396). The burden of marriage expenses had shifted from the groom's family to the bride's family. Lindenbaum did her field work in Shaitnal, an area in Comilla District, in 1964. The general perception of the people of that area was that the then current marriage transaction emerged as a result of the surplus of young unmarried women in the 1960s, but Lindenbaum believed that this was not the case (Lindenbaum, 1981, p. 394). In the earlier system, if the status of the bride's family was considered as superior or equal to that of the groom's family, the groom's family used to provide gold ornaments and a sum of money (*khailoti*) to the brides' fathers. Nothing was provided if the bride's family was considered to be inferior. Until 1950 the maximum value of the *khailoti* was 600–700 taka. After that the system was abolished. Lindenbaum found that, currently, the bride's father or guardian paid for the cost of the wedding and most of the daughter's jewellery. He also paid some money to the groom (Lindenbaum, 1981, pp. 394–395).

The new marriage custom started in urban areas and among wealthy families in the 1950s. It spread to the rural areas in the 1960s and among poorer families in the early 1970s (Lindenbaum, 1981, p. 395). Lindenbaum (1981) argued, 'In the past, the focus of marriage was on a desirable bride, and the groom's kin bore the economic costs. Now, greater attention is directed toward a desirable groom, one with a monthly salary' (p. 396). She observed that new groom payments were called a 'demand'. Lindenbaum (1981) noted that from the 1950s to the 1960s grooms started to demand objects which were not of Bengali origin or manufacture. Rural grooms started to demand fountain pens, watches and sometimes transistor radios. The city grooms demanded tape recorders, record players and television sets that were manufactured in Japan or the United States. Some demanded bicycles that were made in the United Kingdom and Germany and suits of clothing mostly from the United Kingdom. The dowry demands reveal the emergence of Bangladesh as a consumer of goods from industrialized countries and this was one of the ways in which it entered into a relationship with the capitalist world (Lindenbaum, 1981, p. 396). In the 1950s and 1960s a small but significant number of Muslim middle-class small traders, shopkeepers and professionals emerged, who depended in part on foreign aid from capitalist countries. In the 1950s, the sons of Muslim farmers started to seek waged employment. Lindenbaum (1981) noted that, '[t]he prestige system begins its shift from one based on land and aristocratic values to one based on the accumulation of money, allowing for the translation of occupational and commercial success into a new kind of social position' (p. 396). The dowry system emerged initially among the relatively wealthy families who were the first to become involved in urban employment and commerce.

Ahmed and Naher (1987, pp. 187–188) found that after independence a nouveau riche class emerged in Bangladesh who accumulated immense wealth within a very short period of time. They wrote:

> The *nouveau riche* class had to spend their wealth somewhere and marriages became the occasion for splurging money in order to show off wealth. Huge sums of money were involved and each wedding had to be bigger, better and costlier. This is how the newly affluent classes of Bangladesh, who had earlier been poor step cousins to the British and Pakistani bourgeoisie, spent their wealth and felt proud of doing so.

At the same time, the new affluent class looked for grooms who were wealthy or who had occupations that created wealth so that their daughters could lead lives of leisure and comfort. For this reason, many parents 'willingly' gifted things to the grooms (Ahmed and Naher, 1987, p. 188). The authors argued (pp. 188–189):

> Matches were also made in cases where the girl's side was urban and wealthy and the prospective groom from a rural background who had become a doctor or engineer after great difficulties due to financial hardships. When the girl's parents showed interest or eagerness to make the match, the groom would agree subject to being given cash, land or other wealth since he himself had no asset or wealth except for his profession. Many such weddings took place in posh city hotels and ill-dressed rural relatives of the groom could be observed wandering about feeling ill-at-ease among all the glitter and gold. Thus, the birth of Bangladesh opened up many avenues, occupations, employment and opportunities for striking rich overnight. And it was primarily men who were the beneficiaries and who took advantage of such opportunities.

These trends in marriage transactions were emulated by the poor classes, and grooms started demanding something at the wedding (Ahmed and Naher, 1987, p. 189). As the age range during which women are marriageable is much shorter than for men, prospective grooms for marriageable women are always few (Ahmed and Naher, 1987, pp. 190–191). Ahmed and Naher (1987) used the word 'demand' instead of dowry. The demand system existed in Bangladesh during both the British and Pakistan periods, but to a more limited extent (Ahmed and Naher, 1987, p. 197). In the urban areas during the 1930s, 1940s and 1950s, some parents married off their daughters to grooms who had strong job prospects, but did not have sufficient money to continue their studies, on condition that the father-in-law would bear all the expenses until the groom completed his education and found a job. In the Pakistan period, CSP (Civil Service of Pakistan) officers were highly desirable grooms. Some wealthy families married off their half-educated daughters to those CSP officers who had status, but were yet to become rich. The authors argue, 'From these origins, the demand system has reached a stage where it is not a question of nabbing a "highly desirable" groom any more but of getting a more or less "ordinary" groom for one's daughter at quite a cost' (Ahmed and Naher, 1987, p. 197). In India and Bangladesh too, dowry increased with the expansion of capitalist relations and thus men were helped to accumulate capital. Dowry has been turned into 'demand, extortion, material gain, and profit maximization' (Samuel, 2002, p. 205). The most common motives behind the dowry system are the grooms' and their families' greed, growing consumerism, excessive materialism, status seeking and rising expectations of a better and luxurious life.

Men's expectations from their wives or wives' families during marriage

The dowry system indicates the superiority of the man and is a way to establish patriarchal norms (Huda, 2006, p. 258). Demanding dowry or agreeing to pay dowry displays the fact that women's position is lower compared to men, which leaves space for violence (Naved and Persson, 2010, p. 851). Huda reports a village woman commenting, 'Boys and their guardians think they are special and that the girl does not amount to much' (Huda, 2006, p. 258). The amount of dowry is an indication of the groom's worth. Women must have property in order to attract husbands of equal or higher rank. Dowry is the price parents pay to buy their daughter's security, happiness and a good, timely marriage. Educated people can mask the dowry system in the name of social obligation. Geirbo and Imam (2006) cite a comment of a highly educated male: 'The problem of demand is very acute among the lower and lower middle-income group of people. They bargain the price of the bride openly. But among us it is not a claim, it is a social obligation' (p. 13). Suran et al. (2004, p. 7) explain about the practice of dowry payments in Bangladesh:

> The family of the bride will often disclose to their friends, neighbors, and marriage brokers the amount of dowry they are willing to pay for a suitable groom, particularly if the proposed amount of dowry is relatively high. Both parties to the marriage contract often haggle about the price, and a marriage broker will mediate between them, often going back and forth several times with offers and counter offers. It is not uncommon for a negotiation to 'fall through' if an agreement regarding the dowry cannot be reached. A portion of the dowry may be given before the marriage ceremony takes place to help defray expenses the groom will incur at the marriage. The remaining transaction usually occurs at the marriage ceremony. Among poorer families and for marriages taking place during non-harvest periods, the parties may agree in advance that a portion of the dowry will be paid later (after the harvest, for example).

The strongest motivation behind paying the dowry is the daughter's security. Women are considered vulnerable to physical and social risks and marriage is the ultimate security for them. An abusive marriage is often preferred, because being unmarried poses great physical and social risks. Geirbo and Imam (2006, p. 28) point out:

> A common notion is that fathers give demand to ensure a happy married life for the daughter. If a daughter brings a large demand, her parents hope that she will be well treated in her in-laws' house. They hope she will get her needs provided for, be loved and respected. The demand is expected to have this effect only if it is paid in full. If it is not paid in accordance with the schedule negotiated, the daughter is in danger of being abused.

In Bangladesh, dowry is an element in the competition for an eligible groom. One village woman said, 'If I do not pay dowry for my daughters, someone else will pay and get an eligible husband for their daughter' (Huda, 2006, p. 257). The size of dowry depends on factors such as the 'quality' of brides and bridegrooms, age, beauty, education and fathers' status. Geirbo and Imam (2006, p. 14) explain:

> the quality of the bride can also be a significant factor. If she is perceived as being of high quality compared to the groom, he might be willing to reduce his *demand* to marry her. If she is perceived as being of low quality compared to him, he might be willing to marry her in exchange for a higher *demand*. A female college teacher told that in her family they usually pay two or three lakh[1] in demand. However, for one of her relatives, they had paid ten lakh because she is dark skinned and the groom has a good government job.

If a girl is not attractive, the parents need to add something to attract the bridegroom. However, unemployment and the shortage of prospective grooms mean that parents now need to pay even if their daughter is considered beautiful (Ahmed and Nahar, 1987, p. 175). Education is deemed an important indicator of earning ability, especially for sons, so dowry gives grooms' families an easy way of obtaining reimbursement for money spent educating their sons (Rozario, 1992, p. 146; Huda, 2006, p. 254). In the villages, a man who can provide good living conditions for his wife and children is considered a high-quality groom. A good lineage or family background is considered a desirable quality for both brides and grooms. A good family background embraces such things as having a good reputation, no history of engaging in conflicts, no serious diseases, no extramarital affairs in the family and no family history of criminality (Geirbo and Imam, 2006, p. 8). An ideal bride must have a good lineage and a good family background and, in addition, she must be obedient and skilled and have the ability to adapt to the new environment in her husband's family (Geirbo and Imam, 2006, p. 8). Child marriages occur because the dowry is usually smaller when the bride is very young. The demand is much higher when the girl is not beautiful. Less attractive girls tend to face discrimination in their parents' family, and even educated girls who are less attractive have difficulty finding grooms (Chowdhury, 2009, p. 619). In the villages, girls with a fair complexion and attractive appearance are regarded as beautiful, but slim girls are not considered beautiful, as in the villages most of the girls are slim because of malnutrition. It is thought that girls who are not big and healthy will become ill after the birth of their children. In Bangladesh, most women who become ill after giving birth do so because of malnutrition and hard work. Girls with smooth skin are considered beautiful, but the villagers do not regard height as an important criterion of beauty (Chowdhury, 2004, p. 251). However, this is slowly changing due to globalization. In the urban areas a girl is considered beautiful if she is tall, fair complexioned and slim.[2] These standards have been shaped by advertisements, films, beauty contests and pornography where women are used as sexual objects to accumulate capital. Hossain (2008) writes:

> Girls are starting to become sexual objects from a very early age, and being 'sexy' has become something very important, empowering, and a precondition of women's success. . . . In Bangladesh, women today are more conscious about how they look, what they wear, what they eat, and how much they weigh, than they were even ten years back. Women have been fed this message very, very clearly over the past decade that, however successful or educated one might be, one's looks and sex appeal comes [sic] first. No woman in today's world is allowed to carry body fat and appear unattractive, she has to be pretty and sexy in order to win the race.

In the villages, literacy is considered desirable in a bride, but it is better to have education only as far as class five. Villagers think that, in an ideal marriage, the groom should have a higher educational qualification than the bride (Geirbo and Imam, 2006, p. 8). In the cities, the qualification should be the same or higher. An unemployed groom with a good education is not valued in the marriage market (Geirbo and Imam, 2006, p. 9). Now, highly educated and professional grooms not only look for highly educated brides, but also prefer brides with an educational background in business administration, engineering or medical science, because education in these subjects brings money. It is very difficult to marry off well-educated girls because educated grooms are very expensive and demands are higher. Geirbo and Imam (2006, p. 15) report one mother as saying:

> If I give more education to my daughter, I have to give more demand at her marriage, as in that case I have to find a groom with a salaried job (*Chakri*). An educated girl would never agree to marry a van driver or a day labourer. He has to be businessman or have a salaried job. But to get a groom like this one must pay a very high demand.

Arends-Kuenning and Amin (2001) argue that 'families emphasize the value of education as a desirable attribute in the marriage market, or, in other words, as a form of marriage capital' (p. 130). Educated grooms demand higher dowry and Arends-Kuenning and Amin (2001) find that '[s]ome parents intend to limit their daughters' education before they complete secondary school because they are concerned that they will not be able to pay dowry for an educated groom' (p. 131). Both the bride and the groom need to be strategic in finding a spouse; however, brides are not able to be assertive as marriage proposals are generally initiated by the groom's family according to social customs (Amin and Huq, 2008, p. 9).

Although *Bhodra* (educated and cultured) families do not directly demand that brides' parents make provision in cash or kind, I found from the 'Looking for Brides or Grooms' advertisements in the newspapers that a highly educated female (beautiful, tall, slim, fair skinned and settled in Dhaka) lecturer in a private university was looking for a highly educated groom. The advertisement stated that the bride's siblings are doctors, engineers and PhD holders (to show the bridegroom parties that her family is well established and wealthy) and that, if necessary, the bride's family would arrange a scholarship for the groom to pursue higher studies in Japan.[3] Another advertisement says that a tall, beautiful, religious medical student is looking for a groom who is a doctor. The bride is an only daughter and her parents are established in Dhaka.[4] This means that the bride's parents are wealthy and have their own house in Dhaka. By saying she is the 'only daughter' the parents are indicating that their daughter would get the whole share of their property. Another advertisement says that the bride has an MBA and is working in a private bank. She is the only daughter and has a house and car in Dhaka.[5] These advertisements reveal that it is expensive to attract a highly educated groom. Brides whose parents own houses or apartments, especially in Dhaka, are considered desirable. The grooms' families will think that even if they do not get the property at the wedding, they will have a share of it after the death of the brides' parents. Many brides' families request their friends, relatives or acquaintances to look for a suitable groom and at the same time inform them that the brides have their own houses or apartments. Sometimes, they publish advertisements stating: 'Looking for a groom. The bride has her own apartment.'[6]

Upper-class people always want the marriage to be within that class. A matchmaking organization, Mehedi, advertises that it is 'only for respectable upper class aristocratic family members'.[7] Another advertisement states: 'Only for the residents of Baridhara, Gulshan,

Dhanmondi, Banani who are from respectable upper class aristocratic families.'[8,9] Upper-class families do not demand dowry. They know that they will benefit economically and socially from connections between their families. In these marriages, the families of grooms and brides spend large sums on wedding parties. Grooms' families buy wedding dresses for brides and brides' families buy wedding outfits for grooms. Both exchange gifts for their family members. But it is also assumed that women are inferior, and brides' families therefore feel they need to give expensive gifts to keep favour with the grooms' families. In this way, they also hope that their wealth and power will prevent their daughters being neglected in the in-laws' home. In these marriages, the brides' families provide expensive household items for the couple and after the marriage they give expensive gifts to the grooms' families.

However, if a girl from an upper-class family is less desirable in terms of physical beauty or a poor education, the parents will attempt to marry her to a highly educated, professional groom with a middle- or lower-middle-class background. Highly placed officials, rich businessmen and powerful politicians are considered desirable in-laws for grooms from a middle- or lower-middle-class background. Many people in Bangladesh say that to have a poor father is bad luck, but to have poor in-laws is stupidity. Some men who have a poor family background are highly educated professional people. They want to marry the daughters of wealthy and powerful parents. In these cases they are sometimes prepared to marry less beautiful girls or girls who are less well educated. In this way a man becomes connected with wealthy and powerful families and the less desirable daughter marries a highly educated, professional groom. Sometimes, these grooms do not demand dowry directly, but they know that the relationships will bring them power and resources and enhance their status. In every class, grooms want to have living in-laws so they can enjoy care, attention and gifts from the brides' families. I have seen a groom's family choose a beautiful, highly educated girl for their son only to reject her when they heard that the girl's father was dead. It is also more difficult to attract grooms for women who are over 35. It is believed that women in their thirties experience a decline in fertility and are more likely to suffer complications during pregnancy. Higher levels of education and delayed marriages lead to a higher dowry. Grooms' families also demand large wedding parties. They determine the number of guests, and the brides' families must agree to feed them. The number of people depends on the class. The grooms also determine the items of the marriage feast. One newspaper reported:[10]

> There were many items in a marriage feast. There were pulao (rice cooked with ghee), beef, goat meat, chicken, shrimp, vegetables and salad. Only there was no egg. For this reason the bride takers became angry. The bride's father wanted to make them understand that he did not get 700 eggs together in the market for the marriage feast. But the bride takers strongly insisted that it was agreed by the bride's family that there would be eggs in the marriage feast. So, they need eggs. Finally with the help of the some senior men the egg problem was solved. The bride takers took the bride to the groom's house. After arriving at home the groom's family started humiliating and swearing at the bride. The groom was extremely mad. At one point, he cracked 19 eggs on the bride's head and she got hospitalized.

For some grooms, especially ones who are educated but unemployed, the most desirable Bangladeshi brides are those living in Western countries. Sometimes, meritorious students who want to pursue higher education in Western countries look for immigrant brides in the United Kingdom, Canada, the United States, Australia or New Zealand. One advertisement says: 'Looking for a beautiful widow bride (age 23–27) who is settled abroad. All help is needed for the groom to settle abroad with financial support.'[11] Another advertisement says that the groom obtained an honours degree at the University of Dhaka and is currently doing his MA. He is looking for a bride who is a citizen abroad and able to bring the groom to her country; a divorcee woman is acceptable (Barman, 2009). Another advertisement says that the groom, who did his master's in commerce and is employed in a high position in an established company, is looking for a bride who is an American citizen. It also mentions that the groom has a house in Dhaka (Barman, 2009). This indicates that the groom is rich, but still wants to go to the United States. Some men use the dowry money to increase their business profits. One published an advertisement saying that he was a smart, honest, hard worker whose business was suffering because of the world economic recession. He needed Tk. 3,000,000–4,000,000, which he would pay back. He was asking the parents of potential brides to contact him directly if they were able to help him.[12]

Khundker (2006) did research in 31 villages of Manikganj District in Bangladesh and found that in 51 per cent of the cases, the dowry money is spent on the costs of the wedding. Dowry is also used as a means of acquiring resources, such as land or an investment in business (p. 10). Khundker (2006) also finds that in most of the cases the parents of the groom had control over the dowry money (p. 11). She observes: 'Interestingly, dowry transactions were less common in "love marriages", i.e. where the parents had little or no control over the marriage negotiations' (Khundker, 2006, p. 11). If the parents accept the union, dowry is given to 'strengthen the marriage and to increase the status of the bride in the in-law's house' (Geirbo and Imam, 2006, p. 10). A husband may later demand money, goods or privileges from his wife or her family, even in dowry-free love marriages (Naved et al., 2001, p. 100).

Parents of daughters work hard to save money for the dowry. People in Bangladesh sell livestock, agricultural products and land to do this. Sometimes they borrow money and sometimes they use microcredit to cover the wedding costs and dowry (Faraizi et al., 2011, p. 89; Uddin, 2015, p. 83). There are instances where half the money is used for business and half for dowry. Occasionally, parents will take out a loan to cover the wedding costs. Rozario (2002, p. 69) argues:

> While microcredit has not benefited the poorest of the poor and many other poor in rural communities, it has increased the consumption capacities of many poor and lower middle to middle class families, for example through improved housing and the ability to make higher dowry payments.

Geirbo and Imam (2006) write, 'If the microcredit officer comes to check how the loan was used, a neighbor's cow or rickshaw van is sometimes shown' (p. 21). If very poor women do not have sufficient money, they start begging for dowry (Geirbo and Imam, 2006, p. 21) Karim argues that microcredit acts as a form of dowry and she observed that NGO officers encouraged poor people to take loans instead of begging to provide their daughters' dowries (Karim, 2011, p. 83). According to the Grameen Bank rules, members are not allowed to take or receive dowry, but Karim (2011) observed that both employees and borrowers are not following the rules. She writes about her experience in a Grameen loan meeting:

> I said to the manager who was sitting there, collecting and counting money, that his members did not follow the rules of Grameen. In response he said. 'You can never teach these people anything.' To show me that he did his duty, he then asked the women, 'Why do you take dowry?' The women in turn questioned him, 'Did you not

> take dowry when you got married?' The manager then replied in the negative. Then one woman laughed and said, 'Sir, you are wearing a large gold ring. Who gave you that?' When he did not reply she went on to add, 'That's a lot of gold. You educated people take dowries as well. What are you going to teach us?'
>
> (Karim, 2011, p. 84)

In rural areas, money, land, gold and silver jewellery, furniture, bicycles, televisions, video cassette players, etc. are used in dowry transactions. Sometimes trees, livestock, sewing machines or tin for houses are given as dowry. Dowry money is also used to enable grooms to acquire salaried jobs or to cover the cost of temporary migration abroad for employment (Khundker, 2006, p. 10). To get a job as a primary schoolteacher, one has to pay a bribe of between Tk. 80,000–100,000 (Geirbo and Imam, 2006, p. 23). In Bangladesh, dowry is increasingly used as a source of capital for the groom as men use dowry to gain access to modern goods, salaried jobs and new business opportunities or expansions of existing ones (Gibson et al., 2004, p. 16; Rozario, 2009, p. 48; Nasrin, 2011, p. 35). Dowry demands also include securing jobs in Dhaka or the Middle East and the promise of a business (Ahmed and Naher, 1987, p. 160; White, 2013, p. 13). The dowry system provides men with an additional opportunity to 'accumulate capital and appropriate wealth' (Arens, 2014, p. 72). Rao (2012) writes:

> parents seek overseas migrants as potential grooms for their daughters and willingly finance their migration. Dowry takes new forms, like provision of visa papers, travel documents and imported consumer goods that help build a new social identity, rather than clothes, sweets and local goods, or capital to finance a small enterprise.

Instead of demanding the abolition of the dowry practice in India, Madhu Kishwar (1988) argues for an effective equal inheritance right for women (p. 13). She writes, 'If women's inheritance rights were to become real, dowry in its present form would almost certainly disappear' (Kishwar, 1988, p. 13). Following Madhu Kishwar, Rozario (2004) suggests that women's inheritance rights should be transferred during their marriages, which would be 'a natural complement to a campaign against dowry' (p. 48). She argues that women's inheritance rights would be an alternative to dowry and would help the newly married couple financially, which would then protect women's interests in their in-laws' families (Rozario, 2004, p. 49). However, Rozario's (2004) argument is debatable as many families in Bangladesh do not own land or properties and therefore would not be able to pass anything on to their daughters. If this were to be enforced, potential grooms and their families would only look for wealthy brides whose parents have the ability to pass on large pieces of land, or properties. How would the daughters of financially disadvantaged parents get married and what would their positions be in society? Why do women have to bring something into their in-laws' families? In reality, Rozario's (2004) argument would reinforce the structure of the dowry system, because a woman's worth would be determined by what she brought into her new family and women would be completely transformed into objects.

Dowry and law in Bangladesh

The Dowry Prohibition Act 1980 has been ineffective in preventing the practice of dowry in Bangladesh. The act leaves much discretion to the court with regard to reducing the sentence, and punishment may be imprisonment, which could extend to five years and would not be less than one year, or a fine, or both. Again, a fine is not fixed (Begum, 2004). Begum (2004, pp. 256–257) recommends:

> Given the alarming increase of dowry incidents, the discretionary power of the judge should be removed. Rather, provisions may be made that the specified penalty can be increased when the taking of dowry exceeds the financial ability of the socially under-privileged father of the bride.

The act provides the same punishment for dowry givers. It does not recognize the social reality of women in Bangladesh. Parents of brides feel compelled to give dowries to arrange their daughter's marriage. Kotalova (1996) wrote, 'Universally in Bangladesh, it is felt that "a woman must be given (*bie dawa*) in marriage at least once"; and more, she should be married "in time"' (p. 190). A study (Aziz and Maloney, 1985, pp. 55–56) reveals that both parents and their unmarried mature daughters have a sense of guilt if the daughter remains unmarried. Parents consider them as burdens and as 'the spine of a fish stuck in the throat' (*galay atkano kata*). The act should recognize this and be amended so that only dowry takers or abettors are criminalized (Begum, 2004, p. 258). Section 4 of the 1980 act made 'direct or indirect' demands an offence. Begum (2004, p. 259) writes:

> the Act does not define the term 'indirect demand', while the burden of proof is entrusted with the bride under the adversarial trial system in Bangladesh. There are no guidelines developed by the judiciary in the country to this direction. In the absence of such clarification, many undue expectations of the in-laws and their fulfillment might remain beyond the scope of 'indirect demand'.

The Dowry Prohibition (Amendment) Ordinance 1982 allows a person to proceed with a dowry complaint without the prior sanction of a government officer (Monsoor, 1999, p. 230). The Dowry Prohibition (Amendment) Ordinance 1986 made the dowry offence non-cognizable, non-bailable and compoundable.[13] Monsoor (1999, p. 232) writes:

> The reported cases concerning the issue of dowry have primarily struggled with the definition of dowry, whether what is claimed as dowry constitutes dowry under the Dowry Prohibition Act of 1980 or whether such demands were made as a consideration for the marriage to fulfill the condition of the Act. This shows that the cases were more concerned with technicalities in the application of the Act rather than the protection of women.

In *Poddar* v. *Saha* (1985), the High Court held that the demand for dowry was not a consideration for the marriage and so it did not recognize it as a dowry. However, in *Rezaul Karim* v. *Mst. Taslima Begum* (1988, p. 362), the court took a different view and gave 'marriage' an extended meaning. Marriage, the court elucidates, means and includes:

> not only the ceremony of marriage but also the newly created legal status for both the husband and wife, to be continued, asserted and recognized to be available always in everyday life, till death separates one from the other or till the marriage subsists. Marriage, thus, is not only a ceremony but the creator of a status without which status it cannot exist. A husband or a wife has a right to claim and assert that status with all its corresponding rights and duties during the continuation of their marriage and can

> demand it as of right and it calls for no consideration in terms of money or valuable security except those that are embodied in the contract of marriage or kabinnama.

The court reasoned (pp. 362–363):

> demanding money or other valuable security from the wife, or her relations by the husband after she is married for giving her the status of a wife namely maintaining her as a wife and giving her a shelter would amount to demanding money in consideration for the marriage. The expression 'In consideration for the marriage' as it appears in section 2 of the Dowry Prohibition Act, need, out of necessity, be given that extended meaning, otherwise the scheme of the whole Act which prohibits demand of Dowry by the husband, terming it to be an illegal act, to be visited with the vengeance of the law, would be frustrated and become redundant. Otherwise a crafty husband without demanding money at the time of marriage or immediately before or after the marriage would wait for an opportune moment to demand that money from the wife or father or guardian, refusing otherwise to take her home or refusing to give her the status of a wife, with impunity and when confronted will reply saying that he is only demanding money and not dowry in consideration for the marriage because the marriage is already over and he is already married and he never demanded the money before and afterwards, thus, asking to allow him to do something after the marriage which he is prohibited from doing before the marriage or at the marriage. This cannot be the intention of the legislature.

In *Abul Basher Howlader* v. *The State and another* (1994, p. 173), the Appellate Division of the Supreme Court gave an extended meaning to dowry observing:

> if a fresh demand for dowry is made after solemnization of marriage about which there was no prior agreement and which demand does not fall strictly within the definition of dowry in section 2, then the word 'dowry' in section 4 is repugnant in the subject or context to the definition itself. 'Dowry' in section 4 has therefore to be understood in its ordinary meaning, namely, property brought by [a] woman to her husband at marriage or vice versa. It must be held therefore that in the Bangladesh Act the legislature has taken care to see that not only the taking or giving of dowry or abetment thereof before or at the time of marriage is made an offence but also the demand thereof after the marriage.

In *Mollick* v. *State* (1996), the High Court said, 'It has now been settled that if dowry is demanded after the marriage then also the offence under section 4 will be attracted' (p. 330). As regards penalties, the Women and Children Repression Prevention Act 2000 (which replaced the Oppression of Women and Children (Special Enactment) Act 1995) provides, in section 11, that:

> If the husband of a woman or husband's father, mother, guardian, relatives or any other person of the husband's side causes death or attempts to cause death to that woman for dowry [or causes grievous hurt or simple hurt to that woman][14] that husband, husband's father, mother, guardian, relatives or persons:
>
> (a) shall be sentenced to death for causing death or shall be sentenced to imprisonment for life for attempting to cause death and in both cases shall also be liable to [a] fine;

(b) shall be punishable with lifelong rigorous imprisonment or maximum twelve years or minimum five years rigorous imprisonment and shall also be liable to [a] fine for causing grievous hurt;
(c) shall be punishable with maximum three years, but minimum one year rigorous imprisonment and shall also be liable to [a] fine for causing simple hurt.[15]

The act does not, however, make provision for psychological abuse. Despite the existence of anti-dowry laws, dowry victims are denied justice because the legal process is expensive and lengthy, there is a lack of witnesses or direct evidence and because the police are dishonest (Taher and Jamaluddin, 2015, pp. 86–88). Begum (2004, pp. 256–257) observes:

> The Dowry Prohibition (Amendment) Act 1986 allows police to arrest the accused of dowry violence without a warrant. However, police seldom enforce arrests in proportion to the total numbers of incidents and are very reluctant to recognize dowry as a crime. In numerous instances, police refused to arrest the criminals and even denied registering the case brought by women, believing that victims provoked the violent incidents. Likewise, the manipulation of the investigating process by the police has been one of the serious barriers to getting a favourable remedy in dowry cases. There is ample evidence in Bangladesh that dowry deaths are frequently labeled as accidental or suicidal. On some occasions, no action is taken, even after years, 'until evidence disappears'. The failure of the police to investigate and to take proper action helps many offenders to go legally unchallenged, while the state places arrest at the discretion of the police. Without any legal compulsion to arrest, police are often improperly occupied with their self-interest in arresting abusers, especially those who are influential in terms of economic and political power. Such an approach ignores not only the 'vulnerable position' of a female victim in an unequal abusive relationship but also presents serious flaws in the criminal laws of the country.

Conclusion

The dowry system indicates the superiority of the man and it is a way to establish patriarchal norms of superiority. Parents of brides feel compelled to give dowries to arrange their daughter's marriage because marriage is universal in Bangladesh. The new dowry system started first in urban areas and among the wealthy families in the 1950s. It spread to the rural areas in the 1960s and among the poorer families in the early 1970s. After independence a nouveau riche class emerged which accumulated immense wealth within a very short period of time. The new affluent class looked for grooms who were wealthy or had occupations that made them wealthy so that their daughters could lead lives of leisure and comfort. For this reason, many parents 'willingly' gifted things to grooms. The birth of Bangladesh opened up many opportunities for becoming rich overnight and it was primarily men who were the beneficiaries. These trends in marriage transactions were emulated by the poor classes and grooms started demanding something at the wedding. Women's age range for marriage is much shorter than that of men, so prospective grooms for marriageable women are always few. Dowry increased with the expansion of capitalist relations. Dowry has been turned into 'demand, extortion, material gain, and profit maximization' (Samuel, 2002, p. 205). The most common motives behind the dowry system are the grooms' and their families' greed, growing consumerism, excessive materialism, status seeking and rising expectations for a better and luxurious life. Despite the existence of anti-dowry laws, dowry victims do not receive justice because of the difficulties and expense of the legal process.

Notes

1 One lakh is a hundred thousand taka.
2 This observation is made from consulting the 'Looking for Brides or Grooms' advertisements in the Bangladeshi daily newspapers.
3 *Daily Ittefaq*, 2 January 2009.
4 *Daily Ittefaq*, 17 July 2009.
5 *Daily Ittefaq*, 24 April 2009.
6 *Daily Ittefaq*, 20 February 2009.
7 *Daily Ittefaq*, 20 June 2009.
8 Baridhara, Gulshan, Dhanmondi and Banani are the rich residential areas in Dhaka.
9 *Daily Ittefaq*, 1 May 2009.
10 *Prothom Alo*, 22 February 2009.
11 *Daily Ittefaq*, 30 January 2009.
12 *Daily Ittefaq*, 19 June 2009.
13 In section 8 the words 'bailable and non-compoundable' have been substituted for the words 'non-bailable and compoundable' (Monsoor, 1999, p. 306).
14 The words [or causes grievous hurt or simple hurt to that woman] and brackets were substituted for the words and quotation marks 'cause injury or attempt to injure' by section 6 of The Women and Children Repression Prevention (Amendment) Act 2003.
15 Sub-sections [b] and [c] were substituted for the earlier sub-section [b] by section 6 of The Women and Children Repression Prevention (Amendment) Act 2003.

6 Women, income and dowry in Bangladesh

In recent times there has been a significant change in the attitude towards women taking up paid employment in Bangladesh. With the erosion of the extended family system and increasing poverty, large numbers of women from landless and middle-class families are in need of economic support. Women from such families seek out any available employment. As a result, they shed age-old inhibitions and prejudices. Changing male attitudes towards employed women, the expansion of educational and employment opportunities and rising expectations of consumption have also helped bring about changes in female participation in paid employment. Both urban and rural women are no longer hesitant to join the paid labour force when opportunities arise (Khan, 1993, p. 3).

This chapter deals with women's income and dowry in Bangladesh and will address the question, 'How has the dowry system shifted as a result of women's increasing paid labour force activity?' I argue that the dowry system has shifted as a result of women's increasing paid labour force activity. The general perception in Bangladesh is that women's power increases when they earn money. In reality, however, many Bangladeshi women cannot control their income. In most cases, husbands or in-laws control and appropriate women's income (Rashid, 2006, p. 156; Chowdhury, 2010, pp. 1–10). Husbands consider their wives' income to be a source for their own wealth accumulation. This must be acknowledged as reality and the Dowry Prohibition Act amended. Here, I also argue that wives' income, appropriated or controlled, should be considered as dowry and, therefore, the practices of appropriating or controlling it are criminal offences.

Women and employment

A significant number of women are joining the paid labour force because of globalization and trade liberalization in Bangladesh (Kabeer and Mahmud, 2004, p. 93). The Bangladeshi government followed privatization programmes and public sector reforms due to pressure from the World Bank and the IMF (Uddin and Hopper, 2003, p. 740). The rate of female participation in the labour force in Bangladesh increased continuously between 1991–2010, while during the same period the rate of male participation dropped from 87.4 per cent to 82.5 per cent. The rate of female participation in the labour force was only 14 per cent between 1990–1991, while the male rate was 86.2 per cent. Between 2006–2010, the rate of female participation in the labour force increased by ten percentage points, from 26.1 per cent to 36.0 per cent (Rahman and Islam, 2013, p. 18). However, the rate of female participation in the labour force in Bangladesh decreased in 2013. In this year, the rate of female participation in the labour force was 33.5 per cent, while the male rate was 81.3 per cent (Bangladesh Bureau of Statistics, 2015, p. 46). With regard to women, 44.5 per cent are in skilled agricultural work, 23.6 per cent are in craft and related trade work and 12.1 per cent are in elementary occupations. Women make up 20.3 per cent of those employed in the industrial sector and in the service sector 10.7 per cent of women are administrative and commercial managers (Labour Force Survey Bangladesh, 2013, p. 130).

Employment opportunities for women are not being created, and insecurity in the workplace and a lack of women-friendly work environments contribute to decreasing women's participation in the workforce. Women are still not safe in the workplace or outside of it either, because of sexual harassment and violence. In addition, women are not able to spend the same amount of time or put in as much effort at work as their male counterparts because of their dual roles as working women and housewives (Alamgir, 2016). Moreover, most banks in Bangladesh are not interested in giving low-cost credit to ordinary women. A lack of marketing opportunities and a bad law and order situation in Bangladesh also deny women the possibility of becoming businesswomen.[1]

Among the women who face sexual violence in the workplace, most of them do not file complaints against the perpetrators mainly because of the fear of losing their jobs.[2] Working mothers are forced to quit their jobs in order to nurse their newborns, because of a huge shortage of day care facilities in Bangladesh. The number of day care centres run by the Bangladeshi government and NGOs is completely insufficient to meet the rising demand of working mothers in the country. There are only 56 government-run day care centres in Bangladesh and only 3,820 places are available for children aged six months to six years old. Bangladesh Bank, BRAC, BRAC Bank, Grameen Phone, Robi, Banglalink and a few other NGOs and privately run organizations offer day care facilities for working mothers. Among the banks, Bangladesh Bank was the first to introduce day care facilities for children of working mothers (Das, 2016).

The garment sector is a major source of formal employment for women. In Bangladesh, 85 per cent of the total workforce in the garment industry are women and more than 90 per cent are migrants from rural parts of the country (Afsar, 2003). While many consider this as a positive step towards female empowerment, women actually work in a highly exploitative situation. Bangladesh is the second largest exporter of ready-made garments in the world, after China. Garments make up almost 80 per cent of Bangladesh's export earnings and contribute to more than 10 per cent of the GDP (Human Rights Watch, 2015). Most garment factories in Bangladesh are potential 'death chambers'. The Rana Plaza factory collapse in Bangladesh is considered the world's worst garment factory disaster. On 24 April 2013, more than 1,134 people died and about 2,500 people were injured in the Rana Plaza collapse.[3] Many survivors do not have any interest in going back to work in the garment industry again (Islam, 2013; Mahr, 2013). Five months before the Rana Plaza tragedy, the Tazreen Fashions factory was the site of Bangladesh's deadliest factory fire, which killed at least 112 people.[4] In Bangladesh, more than 1,000 workers have been killed and over 3,000 injured in around 275 factory accidents between 1990 and 2012 (Venkatesan, 2013). Female garment workers often experience suffocating conditions both at home and in the workplace: malnutrition, disease and ill-health caused by overwork, low food intake or starvation, and abuse, sexual harassment, rape and even death (Muhammad, 2011). International companies are clearly aware of the many accidents and lack of safety measures in Bangladeshi factories, which is why they avoid dealing directly with many of them. Companies are aware that accidents are common; however, as an inevitable result of capitalism, instead of pushing for worker safety they push for lower prices. In order to cut costs, buildings in which factories are located are either not built for industrial use or are built with substandard materials and violate building codes and safety regulations (Venkatesan, 2013). Rock-bottom prices, constantly cutting costs, lack of worker representation, extremely low wages, failure of industry initiatives, negligence of factory owners and lack of action from the government all contribute to dangerous working conditions for workers in Bangladesh (Venkatesan, 2013). Trade unions are legal in Bangladesh; however, workers seeking to form unions often experience violent retaliation, termination of employment, harassment, arbitrary barriers to registration, and retaliation once a union is established. Workers involved in creating trade unions find themselves victims of extreme violence from managers or local criminals, who work on behalf of factory managers. Additionally, workers involved in setting up unions experience threats, intimidation and increased workloads. In some cases, the factory management even threatened to rape workers for engaging in trade unions (Human Rights Watch, 2015). Most garment factory owners prefer to hire unmarried girls for fear of pregnancy-related problems and many female workers do not want to disclose their marital status in order to get the job (Preetha, 2012). Mushrefa Mishu, general secretary of the Democratic Revolutionary Party and president of the Garment Workers Unity Forum says:

> According to the compliance law 2006, expecting women, working in the garments factories, are to be given a four-month maternity leave with pay. But in reality, that is not happening, despite the fact that the compliance law is being strictly implemented. I have been working in this industry for the last 15 years and I have witnessed plenty of problems caused due to expecting female workers not getting their pay and/or their leaves accordingly. Only a handful of these industries and factories actually abide by the compliance law. Similar problems are seen with female employees in the NGO sector as well, where the number of women workers is increasing every day.
>
> (Karim, 2010)

Middle-class rural women started working as government and semi-government employees in the mid 1970s because of the rapid expansion of the Integrated Rural Development Programme (IRDP), the family planning programme and rural women's cooperatives. The introduction of rice mills increased the number of poor women who joined the paid labour force in rural areas in the late 1970s The Food for Work programme was introduced and poor women in rural areas engaged themselves in road repairing, brick breaking and construction work; however, lower-middle-class women were interested in government work (Feldman, 2001, p. 1107). Currently, the NGO sector in Bangladesh employs many young urban and rural women as field workers and organizers and is recruiting many poor rural women into credit, training and educational schemes (Feldman, 2001, p. 1107). However, most women work in the informal sector and in traditional domains. These include handicrafts, food and snack preparation, sewing and domestic work. Some women are involved in petty trading (Asian Development Bank, 2010, p. 14).

Women are also employed in construction work, domestic service, electronics, pharmaceuticals, shrimp processing, the jute industry, textiles, rice mills, restaurants and medical clinics (Khatun, 2009). Women labourers in Bangladesh are being exploited because of their gender. Female construction workers earn less than men and they have never heard of maternity leave. Every woman who is a construction worker has been denied maternity or sick leave (Hussain, 2006).

Income from employment favours men as the average wages for rural women are only 60 per cent of men's (Asian Development Bank, 2010, p. 2). A newspaper report finds that female labourers in rural areas continue to face serious wage discrimination compared to their male counterparts. These female labourers are engaged in work in crop fields, brickfields, hotels and restaurants, in houses as domestic servants, in small industrial units, bidi factories and on construction sites, to name just a few places, and they receive as little as one-third of the wages received by men for the same work. Middlemen take advantage of women's poverty and hire them for very low wages to work in crop fields and other places. Several female labourers working on road construction in a village reported that they were hired for a daily wage of Tk. 80–100 each, while a male labourer earned Tk. 250–300 a day for the same work (Roy, 2014).

Domestic workers are considered to be informal labourers in Bangladesh. The number of domestic workers in Bangladesh is 2 million. Among them, 83 per cent are female (Khan, 2016). Domestic workers do not have any legal rights in Bangladesh. They are excluded from the Labour Act 2006 and do not have a fixed wage rate or fixed working hours (Karim, 2009). The Domestic Workers Protection and Welfare Policy 2015, which was approved by the Cabinet to protect the rights of domestic workers, has not been implemented either. There are no formal rules or regulations for domestic workers and a majority of them are young females who are much more prone to exploitation, sometimes even sexual harassment (Karim, 2009). Poverty forces poor and financially disadvantaged parents to send their young girls to work at other people's houses, far away from their own. The parents know very well that there is every possibility that their daughters will be 'treated badly, beaten up, not fed well, tortured, raped, or even killed' (Ahmed, 2009). The following story proves that Bangladeshi society does not even recognize abuse against domestic workers:

> When Samia arrived at the lawyer's office with her friend she was hoping to get advice on how to file for a divorce. The lawyer asked her some obvious questions about what was wrong with the relationship and whether she had children, etc. When she told the lawyer that her husband had molested two teenage maids in the house, Samia expected the lawyer to be in full solidarity with her decision. The lawyer did not display much emotion, what she said in response shocked Samia instead. 'This is quite normal for men of our country', she said. Instead of pointing out to Samia that her husband had committed a punishable crime which she was an eye-witness to, the lawyer was showing her commiseration and in a meandering way saying that this was not serious enough for the dissolution of a marriage.
>
> (Ahmed, 2009)

A survey on domestic workers in Dhaka finds that 50 per cent of them are between the ages of 5 and 15 years and 76.67 per cent are female. Among these, 46.6 per cent ended up in this kind of job due to poverty, lack of education and lack of skills required for other jobs. Although domestic workers are very low paid, they are forced to work longer hours. Only 60 per cent of workers receive their wages on a regular basis. In many cases, they do not even have a separate room to sleep in. Forty per cent of domestic workers sleep in living rooms or on bedroom floors, 33.33 per cent in the kitchen, 16.67 per cent on a balcony and 3.33 per cent in storerooms. Only 6.67 per cent sleep in separate rooms. Domestic workers do not have any days off during the week and they do not enjoy any regular holidays (Siddiqua, 2010).

Out of 236,194 Bangladeshi women who took jobs abroad from 1991 to April 2013, 98 per cent found employment in Middle Eastern countries as domestic aides and about 2 per cent were skilled workers. The monthly salaries of domestic aides range between US$150–200. Domestic workers have bitter experiences regarding low pay, long working hours, sexual exploitation, physical torture and a lack of legal protection (Bhuyan, 2013). One woman

Table 2 Percentage of females in different levels of education in Bangladesh

Level	*Female*	*Total*	*% Women*
Junior Secondary	217,990	367,510	59.32
Secondary School	4,272,188	8,046,366	53.09
Higher Secondary	179,979	349,078	52
University	179,354	597,153	30.03

Source: Ministry of Education (2014). *Education Statistics*, available at http://www.moedu.gov.bd/index.php?option=com_content&task=view&id=300&Itemid=301 [accessed 25 July 2016].

who returned from Lebanon said that she would never go to work in the Middle East again (Biplob, 2013). A report said that 18 female workers returned from Jordan empty handed when they refused to be further sexually abused.[5] Access to education for girls has improved in Bangladesh, but learning outcomes are poor (Asian Development Bank, 2010). Gender disparity between boys and girls is significant in university education (Table 2). The percentage of female students in university is only 30.03 per cent (Ministry of Education, 2014). With regard to jobs that require higher education, women's participation is very low.

Traditionally, engineering, physics, the judiciary, law enforcement and health service administration are considered 'male' jobs, while teaching, library work and care giving are considered 'female' jobs. At present, an increasing number of Bangladeshi women are working as lawyers, judges, journalists, pilots, defence officials, architects, engineers, bankers, IT professionals, scientists, construction inspectors and even professional drivers. Women have traditionally been encouraged to participate in medical science, but most female practitioners have focused on areas such as gynaecology and ophthalmology, and neurology and cardiology are considered difficult for women. Many women hold high positions in the police force but, in most cases, female police officers are assigned desk work in different branches or provide security to VIPs. Only a few women engage in the kinds of challenging jobs that male police officers do, such as criminal investigations (Al-Mahmud et al., 2010).

During the last decade, women have been doing important work as journalists in Bangladesh, but their numbers are fewer than men in both print and electronic media. Women journalists identified 'stereotyped attitudes, unfair treatment, harassment by male colleagues and job insecurity' as the causes for giving up the profession (Babul, 2010). Despite the increasing number of women journalists in last few years, only 4 per cent of women have been able to continue working in mainstream journalism (Babul, 2010). They are paid less compared to male colleagues and they work under 'immense social pressure and mobility problems' (Babul, 2010). In 2005, all newspaper correspondents were male, while in 2010 and still in 2015 only 8 per cent of correspondents were female. With regard to the television in 2005, 78 per cent of presenters were female and 29 per cent of reporters, which reduced to 66 per cent and 19 per cent respectively in 2015. In 2005, 100 per cent of presenters and reporters on the radio were female, which fell to 67 per cent and 33 per cent respectively in 2015.[6] Women's position in the Bangladeshi Civil Service is also low. Only 3.9 per cent of females had attained the rank of Secretary (administrative head of the ministry) while 5.2 per cent had attained the rank of Additional Secretary. Furthermore, the percentage of females holding the rank of Joint Secretary was 9.8 per cent, that of Deputy Secretary 11.9 per cent, that of Senior Assistant Secretary 20.2 per cent and that of Assistant Secretary 25.9 per cent (The Women in Public Service Project, 2014, p. 8). The number of women in higher positions is extremely low. The main problems with regard to the low numbers of women working in the Bangladeshi Civil Service are the absence of day care centres, inadequate transport facilities and residential accommodation, no hostels to accommodate career women, non-cooperation of male colleagues and a lack of security (Jahan, 2007, pp. 57–60). Teaching is considered to be a prestigious job for women. However, the number of female teachers at the junior secondary level was only 27.39 per cent, at secondary level 24.14 per cent and at higher secondary level 23 per cent, while in universities the percentage of female teachers was 22.84 per cent in 2014 (Ministry of Education, 2014).

The percentage of female staff in banks decreased significantly in 2014 from the previous year. In 2013, the percentage of entry-level female staff was 16.88 per cent, which decreased to 13.70 per cent in 2014. At mid level, the percentage of female staff was 16.66 per cent in 2013, which decreased to 14.18 per cent in 2014. Female participation at senior management level also declined to 7.46 per cent from 10.91 per cent. The percentage of female staff aged 30–50 was 15.64 per cent in 2013, decreasing to 12.98 per cent in 2014, and female staff who were aged over 50 years reduced from 9.61 per cent in 2013 to 6.91 per cent in 2014. Female members on the board of directors also decreased from 13.73 per cent in 2013 to 11.27 per cent in 2014 (Uddin, 2015). The main reason behind these reductions is that banks are reluctant to give promotions. A number of banks usually reject female job applicants from the viva board although they successfully pass the written test. Banks' viva boards generally want to know whether female applicants are newly married, because of the fear of having to grant maternity leave in the near future (Uddin, 2015). Currently, 51 banks grant six-month maternity leaves. Bank management does not show normally much interest in recruiting females due to the provision of the six-month maternity leave. Female bankers face discrimination regarding promotions as the months taken during maternity leave are counted as negative in the Annual Confidential Report (ACR) (Sultana, 2016). In many banks, women are compelled to work beyond regular office hours, although the Bangladesh Bank several times issued a circular instructing that they were not to be kept at work after 6 p.m. (Sultana, 2016). A former female employee in a globally established bank said that her male bosses often left the office early when they had emergencies with their children, but she observed that when her female colleagues wanted to leave early for the same reasons they were penalized. She was forced to leave her job when she found out that she would not get a promotion. She said, 'I had to take care of my father who became extremely ill, but I put in more than my fair share of hours at work, often staying until 11 p.m.' Once, she wanted to leave the office early to take care of her father and her colleague asked her, 'Don't you have a brother who can take care of this?' (Ghosh, 2016). Although the government passed the Parents Maintenance Act 2013, under which every child, both male and female, is responsible for ensuring the maintenance of his or her parents, the attitude that women are not responsible for taking care of their own parents still persists in Bangladesh (Government of the People's Republic of Bangladesh, 2013).

Only 25 banks have a policy for dealing with complaints about harassment, despite many females alleging that they are facing different forms of harassment in the workplace, including sexual harassment. However, they have not filed any complaints with the regulatory authority. The female bankers 'either dealt with the situation internally with the help of other colleagues or left the bank to avoid [an] unwanted situation' (Sultana, 2016). Over 81 per cent of women in Bangladesh reported being sexually harassed at some point in their lives. For girls aged 10–18 the percentage is 87 per cent and it is 82.5 per cent for women aged 18–30 (Islam, 2010). The sexual abuse that Bangladeshi women face in the public sphere is tremendous. Women are sexually harassed on the streets, in bazaars and shops and surprisingly even in police stations where they turn to for protection. Living alone without a male is very difficult for Bangladeshi women, however in many instances even male company cannot protect them from sexual harassment and abuse, rape or killings. In universities, it has become much more common for female students to be sexually harassed and abused or even raped by male students and student political activists. In addition, recently reports of sexual abuse by male professors have been rising, even without taking into account the many cases that remain unreported. Although professional women face harassment, the forms of this are different from what working-class women experience. Young garment workers and domestic servants are vulnerable and powerless, and experience harassment at every stage of their daily lives (Huda, 2003, pp. 53–54). Dilara Choudhury (2005, pp. 80–81) argues:

> sexual harassment of women at [the] workplace does exist in Bangladesh. However, its range and intensity varied from sector to sector depending upon the organizational structure, male–female power relations within the organization, awareness, and socio-economic background of the women and whether or not there exists [a] sexual harassment policy and sexual grievance procedure within the organization.

Fear of sexual harassment prevents many women from participating in the paid labour force. Many girls do not pursue higher education due to colleges and universities being some distance away. Despite having an interest in pursuing higher education, many girls in Bangladesh cannot get college or university degrees due to a lack of security. This in turn further reinforces the difficulty of getting highly paid jobs and strengthens patriarchy. Many women in Bangladesh, even after obtaining college or university degrees, have to worry about which jobs will provide them with the most security. For this reason, women in Bangladesh cannot apply for any type of job like men do and thus the employment rate of women is lower than that of men.

Women's income and dowry in Bangladesh

Ability to earn is sometimes considered a good quality for a bride, but it does not change traditional expectations: fair skin, beauty, submissiveness, youth and chastity (Huda, 2006, p. 254). Samuel (2002) writes about India, 'both unemployed and employed women are vulnerable to dowry and dowry harassment. In fact, in some families, fathers, who are poor or have too many daughters, expect their "earning" daughters to save for their own dowries' (p. 199). Kishwar (1986, p. 12) writes that instead of giving dowry, parents should provide their daughters with the means of acquiring an independent income, and White (1992) also believes that 'this is a much more satisfactory approach' (p. 103). However, in my view this is not a practical solution. In a study of Indian students, Rao and Rao (1980) found that one-third of male students expected dowry even if their wives were equally educated. Despite women's education and status, society still considers them inferior to men and their parents need to compensate the grooms' families for saving their daughters' lives through marrying them. I undertook interviews with 50 middle-class working women in Rajshahi, one of the divisional cities in Bangladesh, to determine the extent to which married women are able to control their own income.

I found that most husbands, and in some cases mothers-in-law, control wives' income directly or indirectly (Chowdhury, 2007; Chowdhury, 2010). Sometimes, working women in Bangladesh have to hear things such as, 'There are many rich people's daughters in Bangladesh. We could have brought them. If we brought them we would have got *lakh lakh* (hundreds of thousands of taka), cars, houses from their in-laws and husbands.' Even a class one officer in the Bangladeshi government said that her husband talked about his friends receiving money, cars and houses as dowries. A female college teacher's parents gave her bedroom furniture, but her husband and in-laws expected more from her family. They always say to her, 'Your parents gave you birth, but they don't know what to give their daughter. You are a beggar's child.' A woman working as a deputy director in an autonomous institution, whose husband is a teacher at a government college, said that her mother-in-law told her, 'My son has a government job. I could get more dowry, *lakh lakh* (hundreds of thousands of taka).' The wife replied, 'Is it not sufficient that you are getting a lot of money monthly?' A university teacher said that her husband demanded a large marriage feast. Her financially disadvantaged parents had to borrow a large sum of money to arrange this. When she asked her husband why he had demanded it, he replied, 'If your family didn't arrange a large marriage feast, how did you expect me to marry you?' Currently, men in Bangladesh are interested in marrying women whose fathers are rich, so that daughters can inherit property and their husbands can gain control over their wealth. Men also want working wives so that they can appropriate their wives' income. A woman who has inherited property as well as having her own income is considered the most desirable type of bride to grooms' families. If a woman is unable to join the paid labour force, but owns property from her parental family, she is taunted. Hearing phrases like, 'you are doing nothing, only eating and sleeping' is not uncommon for many married women. On the other hand, when a woman is in the paid labour force but does not own parental property, she is constantly compared to those who own parental property and is psychologically abused by her in-laws or husband.

Ahmed and Naher (1987) found that after independence a nouveau riche class emerged in Bangladesh who accumulated immense wealth within a very short period of time (p. 187). Despite the introduction of socialism,[7] the gap between rich and poor widened after independence and it continued to increase after the introduction of free market economic policies in the mid 1970s. Competition started among the people of Bangladesh with regard to accumulating capital and wealth and corruption became common. Zafarullah (2001, p. 483) points out:

> Bribery, nepotism, and favoritism, misuse of power, neglect of official duties, fraud, misappropriation of funds, false and inflated invoices are some common forms of corruption in the public sector. Other types of corruption like terrorism, extortion, defaulting of bank loans, black marketing, trafficking of children and women, adulteration of food and medicine and even contract killings are now common in Bangladesh society.

Income inequality is consistently increasing in Bangladesh. As prices of essential commodities increase, the middle class struggle to pay for rent, education, medical bills and taxes. Consequently, those in the lowest economic bracket are continually fighting for basic survival. In this context, men increasingly started controlling their wives' income and accumulating wealth to enhance their own standards of living. In Bangladesh, middle-class educated people know that demanding dowry is a criminal offence and that they cannot demand dowry publicly. When women started participating in paid employment, middle-class men adopted various strategies to accumulate wealth from their wives. Their attitude is: 'We do not want dowry. We want working women.' Women's income is considered as 'sufficient compensation for waiving dowry demands' (Kabeer, 1997, p. 299). On the surface, it seems as if men want women's emancipation, but their main intention is to control their wives' income and accumulate wealth to enhance their own standards of living. The general perception in Bangladesh is that women's power increases when they earn money. In reality, however, many Bangladeshi women cannot control their own income. Salma Ali, Executive

Director of the Bangladesh National Women Lawyers' Association, said:

> most of the women do not enjoy economic freedom. In many cases, women earn, but cannot spend the money according to their will. Women work but remain unpaid. Many home-based women workers do not get money in their hands, as the work of marketing is done by their husbands.
>
> (Fatima, 2016)

Paul-Majumder (1997) showed that only 35 per cent of female garment workers in Bangladesh spent their income according to their own discretion, 43 per cent spent their own earnings according to a joint decision with others and 23 per cent reported that they had no control over their earnings (pp. 138–139). In another study, 24 per cent of women who took out credit/a loan from NGOs spent their money by themselves and 50 per cent spent it along with their husbands. In the remaining percentage, the women's loan money went directly to their husbands (Haider and Akhtar, 1999, p. 61). Salehin (2016, pp. 153–154) writes:

> it is not just about control over credit; rather that credit imposes a burden upon women. This burden is two-dimensional: the woman's husband pressures her to obtain credit from the NGO and on the other hand the NGO pressures her to repay the loan every week. Although the woman has no control over the credit, she is the one who has to face all the hurdles in repaying the loan.

Another study found that some female members of parliament in Bangladesh have little control over their own earnings (Chowdhury, 2013b, p. 85). One female MP said:

> After I obtained the position of Member of Parliament, my husband asked me to maintain our family financially. In maintaining our family financially I had to go deeply into debt. In three years I had to spend all of my income. Now I do not spend all the money for family maintenance. I saved some amount of money. But I am scared that anytime my husband will take my money. I cannot imagine what I will do after completing five years' tenure in this parliament. I think it is better to take a job even in a garment factory. After being elected as a Member of Parliament my husband did not give me any saris even as an Eid gift. He questioned me, 'Now you earn money, why do you need a gift?'

Salway et al. (2005) write that when slum women in Bangladesh make a greater economic contribution to the home, many men become less responsible for managing the family and withdraw financial support (p. 343). Kibria (1995, p. 299) describes a garment worker who wanted to save money and kept 20 per cent of her income, but when her husband discovered this she had to stop:

> After that time I stopped keeping money for myself; every time I get paid I come home and give all the money to my husband. I see some of the marriages of women in the garment factory be ruined over money; they don't give all the money when he asks for it, the husband leaves her, and then she and her children will be struggling to find rice to eat. After all, women have only one dream in life, to remain with their husband forever.

Kibria (1995) also reports that lower-middle-class women gained control over their wages, whereas working-class women surrendered control over their wages to men (p. 306). However, I have found that most of the income of middle-class married women in Bangladesh is controlled by husbands and in some cases by mothers-in-law. Out of the 50 middle-class working women that I interviewed, only 8 spent their income independently. Among these, one was divorced for trying to spend her income independently. Ten women spent their money through joint decisions with their husbands and the incomes of 28 were controlled by their husbands. In these cases, the husbands' families always encouraged the husbands to do this. A highly educated woman who works in an NGO told me, 'Whenever my husband and I visit my in-laws's house they say, "How much did you save? Both of you are working. You should not waste your money."' Thus, they pressure her husband to control her money. One woman resisted having her income controlled, and finally she divorced her husband. The income of four women was controlled by their mothers-in-law. Among the 32 respondents who could not control their income, 5 had to give dowries to their husbands. These five women were paying twice – through direct dowry and by allowing their husbands to control their income. Sometimes, fathers-in-law also control women's income. Sabina reports that a father-in-law in an urban slum in Dhaka wanted his garment worker daughter-in-law's income because his son did not get dowry from her family. The father-in-law did not even let her keep the child when she got pregnant because he wanted her to continue working to give him money (Rashid, 2006, p. 156). The daughter-in-law explains:

> A couple of months after my marriage I began to feel weak and tired all the time. The doctor did a check-up and informed me that I was pregnant. When we were leaving the clinic, my husband said, 'Let's not keep the child, you are not well at all. You look so sick.' My grandmother-in-law brought medicine [abortion medicine] from the local healer . . . [voice shaking] my father-in-law wants me to work and bring money for the household. If I fall pregnant I cannot work, can I?. . . She brought the [indigenous] medicines the very next day, but when nothing happened, my father-in-law spoke to the health workers about a possible MR. I overheard them discussing the costs of the MR . . . I thought to myself what is the point of me saying anything. My father-in-law has no intention of letting me keep the baby. If I don't listen to him, I will have to suffer and hear words. Then who will feed the baby if no one wants the baby in the household? I felt very sad initially. It was our first child . . . when I got married and I came to this home my father-in-law said to me 'you have to work for two years and give me all your earnings' . . . Well, if he had got his son married he could have got taka 50,000 for him in dowry money so I have to make up for it.

In South India, Mencher (1988) showed that 'a very high percentage of the income earned by females goes to household maintenance, whereas a lower percentage of male income is comparably spent' (p. 119). In a lower-income Cairo neighbourhood, Hoodfar (1988) found that financial issues were notable sources of family conflict. She reported that money was a 'constant source of fights and bitterness' (p. 138). The power of married women may be reduced when they earn money because while their husbands use more of the money that comes into the household for their own personal expenditure, women pay for collective family expenditure (Jephcott et al., 1962; Phal, 1980, p. 322). Whitehead (1981) writes about industrial Britain, 'a wife's wage enters the household and she loses control of it' (p. 107). I have found that in Bangladesh husbands of middle-class women adopt a number of strategies to control their wives' income in order to accumulate wealth. I characterize this appropriation of wives' income as a new form of dowry.

The strategies that husbands employ to control wives' income

Husbands withdraw their financial support

Out of the 50 middle-class working women interviewed, 4 indicated that their husbands withdrew financial support to their families. Jori is a highly educated woman who received her education from a European university and is a class one officer in the Bangladeshi government. She married a college teacher, and after their marriage Jori and her husband lived in Jori's government quarters so her husband did not need to pay any rent. Moreover, she found that her husband did not spend any money on their day-to-day expenses either. She even bought all the furniture for their home herself. Jori's mother-in-law also started living with them. When Jori asked for money for family expenditures, her husband replied, 'I will not give you a lot of money. Before marriage, my day-to-day expenses were much lower. Why do I need to give you more money?' Jori's husband did not want to understand that maintaining a family requires spending a lot more money. When Jori got pregnant he did not take care of her or use any money for expenses related to childbirth. Jori had a C-section to deliver the baby and she alone had to pay for all the medical expenses and the doctors' bills. When she asked for money, her husband started quarrelling with her, which led to him beating her up at least three times. Finally, Jori divorced him. Jori said, 'When I realized that he married me only because of my money, I divorced him.' Like Jori's husband, many husbands do not want to pay the medical expenses related to childbirth.

Polly works in an NGO as an officer and earns Tk. 11,000 per month. When she was pregnant the doctor said that she might need a C-section to deliver the baby and Polly's husband asked her to deposit her full salary into his bank account in order to save up money to deliver the baby. Polly did not give her full salary to her husband. Before the date of her delivery, her husband and mother-in-law brought her some medicine and asked her to take it in order to avoid the C-section and its associated costs. They also asked her not to disclose this to the doctor. Polly did not take the medicine they gave her because she did not believe them and thought that they might have wanted to kill the baby, already knowing that it was a baby girl. When Polly's mother-in-law heard that the baby was to be a girl, she said angrily to her son, 'Now you have to save Tk. 500,000 for your daughter's dowry.' After the C-section, Polly's husband and mother-in-law started quarrelling with her. She then gave her husband a cheque to pay for the operation, handing it over at a time when her husband's friend was present. When the friend left the hospital her husband angrily asked her why she had handed him the cheque in front of his friend. In this particular situation, Polly's husband wanted all her money, but at the same time he did not want to disclose this to other people in order to maintain his status, because cultural norms in Bangladesh oblige the husband to bear all the expenses of his wife and children. Moreover, he did not want to publicly recognize the contributions of his wife, wanting to make her subordinate.

Sometimes, husbands in Bangladesh do not even want to pay for the education of their children. Shipi has three children who are studying at college. She has to take them to private tutors, which is very expensive, in order that they can obtain better results in school. However, Shipi's husband knows that if he does not pay these educational expenses, then his wife will be compelled to pay them. Whenever Shipi needs to pay the private tutors' fees her husband says that he does not have any money. Many husbands use their wives as money-making machines and many men specifically marry working women so that they can withdraw their financial support and thus accumulate wealth and enhance their own standard of living.

Sabera is a schoolteacher. Her first husband died after one year of marriage and she remarried. Her current husband does not have enough income and thought that Sabera had valuable assets from her first husband. He married Sabera only for the purpose of appropriating these. Unfortunately, Sabera's first husband's brother took everything that she had inherited from her husband and her second husband was very disappointed about this. They had one son and her husband started studying medical science. Sabera said:

> He did not spend money for family expenditure and rather took money from me for his educational expenses. I paid all his expenses, but he always wanted more money. He asked me to take another job with a higher salary all the time. I did not want to leave school teaching, because while the salary may be low it is still a prestigious job. When he did not get enough money from me, he married another woman to get more dowry. He visits me every three or four months and did not divorce me out of greed for my pension money.

Husbands want money from their wives for day-to-day expenses to save their own money and accumulate assets

Nine women reported that their husbands took their income for day-to-day expenses. Nipu is a banker and her husband wanted her full salary, but she did not agree to give him all her money, because she has to send money to her mother and younger brother. Every month she gives Tk. 5,000 to her husband, which he uses to pay for the house rent and all the bills as well as their three children's educational expenses. Her husband was able to save money from his own income, but he was still very unhappy that he had to pay for some of the other expenses. Sahara is a lawyer and her husband has a well-paid job in an autonomous institution, but her husband takes all her income. He says things like: 'We need to buy a television, give me your money'; 'We need to buy a dinner set, give me your money'; and 'I don't have any money today and the bank is closed. I have to do the grocery shopping so give me your money.' This is how he controls Sahara's income. Rasheda is a clerk in an autonomous institution. She said:

> I give my full salary to my husband. My husband wants my salary. I have no other alternative except handing over my entire salary to him. It's my second marriage and I have a daughter from my first marriage. My older sister is raising her. I send a very little amount of money from my salary to my daughter. If I want to give her more, I have to give it secretly.

Mala is a doctor who inherited two flats and some land from her father. Her husband controls all her income and is now building a house with it. She said:

> I don't even know how much he is getting from my flats and land. He also spends my salary. He bought a car and I had to pay for half of the cost of the car. I don't know how much he saves. If I asked then there would have been a conflict or I know he would have lied and given me wrong information. He doesn't want to say, because he thinks that then I will not let him control my income. I didn't want any conflicts in my family. I feel that I am exploited, but I don't protest to avoid my family breaking down.

Rupa is a university teacher and her husband gives her a little amount of money to manage the family, but wants her to manage everything with her own salary:

> He gives a little amount of money and asks me to manage the family. I can't save my money managing the family. I have to spend almost all my money. He bought a piece of land and he borrowed some money from me. He still didn't buy it in my name. Later, he bought another piece of land and I gave 50 per cent of the cost and he included my name. He bought a car and took 50 per cent of the cost from me. Actually, he takes all my money and sometimes I find that even if I want to buy a sari, I have to ask for it.

Husbands threaten their wives with not allowing them to continue working

The husbands of three women threatened them with not giving them permission to continue working in their jobs if they did not hand over their earnings to them. Dora is an officer in an independent institution. She did her bachelor's degree after her marriage, but her mother paid for all her educational expenses. She said:

> After ten years of marriage I got the job in 1978. First, my husband did not let me work, but my mother-in-law inspired him by saying that if I work then I could bring in money for the family. My husband always takes all my income. Sometimes I even find that I don't have money to buy snacks for guests. I gave all my income to my husband, otherwise he would not allow me to do the job. I inherited some land from my father and I receive a good amount of money from paddy cultivation. But I also have to give him this income. My husband thinks that I will waste my money, but I think that if I could control my income I would have saved more. I spent all my income building a house on his land. I built this house, but he is the owner. I did not even buy one sari more than I needed.

Monu is a clerk in a bank. She said:

> If I did not contribute financially, my husband would not have allowed me to continue my job. At the beginning, I gave him all my income. Now I keep money for my transportation expenses and give him the rest of my money. Every day I don't want to ask him for my transportation expenses. I contributed a lot to build his house, but he does not want to buy even a sari for me. I contribute a lot to my family, but I have to request him to buy me a sari when I need one.

Abeda has an administrative job which she got in 1987. First, she joined as a clerk and until 1998 she used to give her husband her full salary. He was very happy with this arrangement, but Abeda did not want to give her full salary to him. Unfortunately, she did not have the courage to resist or say anything to him. She explains her situation:

> My husband thought that I earned a much higher salary, but I concealed it and gave some of my salary to my parents. That is why he always argued with me and was always suspicious about the amount of my salary. In 1998 I decided not to give him any of my salary. He said all right, if you don't give me your salary, I won't even spend one taka on day-to-day family expenses. He then started asking me to leave my job. He said, 'You are doing the job with my permission, so you have to give me all of your salary.' He also

> called me a disobedient woman, saying that I would rather leave him than leave my job. When I tell him that it is his responsibility to maintain our family financially, he responds by arguing that he will take full responsibility when I quit my job. But before, when I didn't have a job, he didn't provide enough money for me and my daughter and we had to live in my parents' house.

Husbands repay their own loans

Rebeka is a class one officer working for the Bangladeshi government and her husband is an engineer in an NGO. Her husband bought two plots of land for building houses and in order to buy these plots of land he took out loans. He obviously has to repay the loans; however, hiding behind the repayments, he does not hand over any money for family expenditures. Rebeka told me:

> When he bought the two plots of land, I asked him to buy them in my name. He did not agree. I pay the rent, bills, everything. I save some money in a provident fund, but that's all. I have to buy clothes, cosmetics and everything for myself. He doesn't buy anything for me.

It should be noted that some husbands even provide false information about having loans. They claim that they took out the loans before their marriage. Nahid got a clerical job just after her marriage which her husband helped her to get. Her husband told her that he needed money to repay a loan and said, 'I arranged the job for you, so you have to give me your money. I allowed you to do this job, so you can't keep your salary. I deserve your salary.' Nora earns Tk. 10,000 per month and after her marriage her husband wanted her to deposit all her salary in his bank account. He told Nora that he would only give her Tk. 10 per day. He did not even want her to buy a sari. He indicated that he had taken out some loans before marriage and now he had to repay them. He severed all relations with Nora's parental family so that they could not give her any advice on financial matters. Moreover, he wanted to keep Nora isolated from her family so that she would feel helpless and thus give him all her money. He wanted Nora to wash his clothes and cook every day. He was always rude to her, but Nora had to passively do everything to satisfy her husband's wishes. Nora had substantially more education than her husband, but was told by him all the time that she knew nothing. When they visited friends Nora had to be quiet, otherwise her husband would tell her that she 'talked too much'. She could not argue with her husband, but one day when she did, he slapped her.

Husbands invest in businesses

Two women said that their husbands take their money to invest in personal businesses. Tuli is an officer in an autonomous institution. She said:

> My husband wants all my money. I don't want to give it to him. I have to spend for family expenditures and he only spends on groceries. He always observes how much I spend. If I spend less, he says that this month you didn't spend much. He asks, where is your money? When I save Tk. 30,000–40,000, I have to give it to him. He takes my money to invest in his business and I have to give it to him. But when he leaves the house for business purposes, he does not want to tell me where he is going.

Saleha is a clerk in an NGO. She said:

> I have to spend all my money for family expenditures. After spending all my money, I cannot buy anything for myself. My husband does not care about that. I don't have any savings. If he has problems with capital in his business, I have to give him money. My in-laws told him you have a working wife, tell her, she will solve the problem. My husband takes my money and he doesn't return the money to me. I can't ask him, how much do you have in your bank account? This question will make him mad and angry at me.

Husbands maintain their large parental families

Four women reported that their husbands take all their income to maintain their large parental families. Seema said that she had nine brothers- and sisters-in-law. To look after them, her husband had to take her income. She said that if she had had a family that large, nobody would have married her. Liza is a college teacher. She said:

> My husband used to take all of my income. Now I spend all my money, but it is my responsibility to maintain the family. I spend for family expenditures and he looks after all of his brothers and sisters. He has 11 brothers and sisters. He also saved his money and built a four-storey building with loans. He is now repaying the loans. I don't have any savings or any resources. He and his family disconnected my relationship with my parental family. They think that if I maintain a relationship, maybe I will give them money. One of my sisters died. She left behind two little kids and they thought that I would bring the kids and look after them. So he and his family quarrelled with my relatives, so that they couldn't come to my house. I can't buy anything for myself. I always have to buy for my sisters-in-law and he always pressures me into giving all my income to him.

Jahanara had a clerical job, but got a promotion and is now working as an officer in an NGO. She said:

> First I did not want to do the job, but my husband compelled me to do it. My husband has a big family, he has eight brothers and sisters. He is the oldest among all. I had to hand over my entire salary. I wanted to give gifts to my parents and sisters, but I couldn't. I always want to buy things for my two children, but I can't afford it. I have to maintain his big family. I don't buy anything that is more than necessary for myself.

Sathi is a schoolteacher and she started her job in 1970. She got married in 1982. Her husband did not demand dowry from her family, because he thought she herself was an asset. She and her husband earn the same salary: Tk. 8,000 per month. Sathi said:

> After my marriage I spent all my salary for family expenditures. My brother-in-law has two sons and he was unable to pay for their educational expenses. My husband asked me to spend for their educational expenses and I paid for all of their educational expenses. If I had to contribute financially to my parental family, I would not be able to do it after marriage. This is the social norm. I also don't want my daughters-in-law to look after their parents or other relatives.

Mothers-in-law control women's income

Kandiyoti argues that in classic patriarchy (Bangladesh is an example of classic patriarchy), women are under control of all men and at the same time they are also subordinate and controlled by senior women, especially by their mothers-in-law in the in-laws' home (Kandiyoti, 1988, p. 279). Sangari also points out that the role of the mother-in-law produces tensions in the family (Sangari, 2002, p. 377). In my study, out of 50 working women, 17 stated that they were living with their mothers-in-law. Three indicated that they used to live with their mothers-in-law. Among them, one woman's mother-in-law died and two had to convince their husbands to live separately. Out of 17 women, 6 said that they did not have any problems with their mothers-in-law. Moreover, their mothers-in-law were helping to raise their children. Eleven respondents said that they had problems with their mothers-in-law. The women said that their mothers-in-law and other members of the in-laws' family took the attitude that they were not contributing to the family. Sometimes, their mothers-in-law did not look after their children when they went out to work.

In my study, in general, it is observed that mothers-in-law also want to control women's income. Reba is a college teacher who faced difficulties with her mother-in-law. She had to do all household tasks by herself and had to take care of her mother-in-law, who could not move independently because of health complications due to old age. Her mother-in-law could not tolerate her good relationship with her husband and when her husband returned from work, her mother-in-law would always tell her husband bad and untrue things about her. She had to be very tactful with her mother-in-law. She had to pay her entire salary to her husband, because her mother-in-law instructed her to do so. Reba said:

> I cannot give any gifts to my parents because of my mother-in law. Even if I buy a sari, I always buy one for my mother-in-law. Still, she is not happy. If my husband buys anything for me, he has to give it to me secretly. I cannot maintain a relationship with my parental family, my mother-in-law does not want me to maintain a relationship. I have to tolerate all this oppression, because I am childless. And I love my husband very much, I don't want him to think about a second marriage to have children.

Rakhi's mother-in law takes all her salary in the name of repaying their loans. Sometimes, she does not want to contribute all her salary and she observes that her husband beats her for silly matters. She gives all her salary to avoid beatings. Afroza works in an NGO. She said:

> My mother-in-law took Tk. 50,000 as dowry from my father. I have to stay with my in-laws' family. My husband's office is in Nowgoan, he comes every week. I receive Tk. 4,000 per month and I give Tk. 1,000 to my mother-in-law for my food. Besides that, I have to buy all the necessary things for the family. If I go to a birthday party or wedding with my mother-in law, I have to buy the gifts. One day my mother-in-law asked me to take my grandfather-in-law to the dentist. I had to take him and I had to pay all the dental expenses for him. It was a big amount. My mother-in-law wants to control my money.

Ruhi lives with her mother-in-law. Her mother-in-law manages the whole family. After her marriage, she is always saying to Ruhi, 'My son is giving only Tk. 2,000 for food, I can't manage the whole family.' It means, indirectly, that she wants money from Ruhi. In addition, her mother-in law always wants her to do all the housework after work. One day Ruhi only gave the paltry sum of Tk. 1 to their maid, who is eight years old, to buy chocolate. Her husband and mother-in-law shouted at her and warned her not to do it again. Ruhi has gold jewellery and needs to pay *zakat*.[8] They asked her to give her *zakat* money to her husband's relatives. However, according to Islam, it should be Ruhi's decision as to who she wants to give her *zakat* money to. When Rahela received her first salary, she gave it to her husband. But her husband asked her to give the salary to his mother. After getting her salary, her mother-in law was very happy and now Rahela also wants the same kind of obedience from her daughter-in-law. She said:

> Now when my daughter-in-law took the job, we were angry because she did not take our permission. But my son has more of an interest in her job. My son made us understand that our daughter-in-law will get Tk. 15,000 and from her salary my son can save Tk. 10,000 to buy a flat. The rest of the money can be spent for family expenditures.

In Saleha's case (see above, 'Husbands invest in businesses'), it can also be noted that her mother-in-law instructed her husband to take money from her to invest in his business.

Women give their income to their husbands to make them happy and husbands do not need to use any strategies

Sometimes, husbands and in-laws' families do not need to use any particular strategies, because women happily hand over their income to their husbands or take all financial responsibility for the family. They do it only to make their husbands happy and thus they protect their family lives. Women who do not have children are particularly helpless, and it is observed that highly educated women without children hand over all of their income so that their husbands or in-laws' families would not think about a second marriage. Farida works for an NGO and started her job after her marriage. She deposits her income into her husband's bank account and thinks that it is divine law that she should give all her income to her husband. Moreover, she is childless. Earlier on in their marriage, Farida and her husband did not have any medical tests, but after 25 years Farida came to know that the problem was her husband's. Uptil then she had believed it was her own fault she could not have children. She raised one of her husband's nephews and spent all her money on him. To make her husband happy, she had to give money to her husband's family members, but she could not give any money to her own parental family. Milu also does not have a child. She said:

> Actually, I thought that if I don't give him my money he would think that I gave my money to my parents. Besides, he didn't demand any dowry. I think that if a wife wants to save her money, then there will be conflict. I deposit all my money to his account. If he gets this money, then everything is all right.

Although Shamoli has two sons, she always wants to make her husband happy and hands over her monthly salary to her him. She said:

> I didn't ask my husband to spend for our day-to-day expenses. If I asked him for money, then there would have been conflict. He bought land in his name. I don't think about myself, because I think that my children will inherit his assets. I always have to serve him and his relatives. This is the norm of our society that wives should talk less, should be obedient to their husbands, wash their clothes. When husbands come home at midnight after hanging out with their friends, their wives should serve them dinner and sit in front of him. I want to make him happy and avoid a family breakdown.

Lindenbaum (1981) argued that rural women might participate in the paid labour force to provide their own dowries (p. 398). Citing Abdullah and Zeidenstein (1980) she wrote, 'educated rural women work for rural cooperatives, gain status, and use their income to support a parent, or to provide education for siblings and nieces. Cooperative workers are often seen as highly desirable brides' (Lindenbaum, 1981, pp. 398–399). It was observed that a bride with skilled employment could marry with a lower demand. In one particular study a respondent commented, 'A service-holder bride is herself considered as a demand. She is a source of income for the whole life' (Geirbo and Imam, 2006, p. 15). Khundker (2006) also finds that '[t]he increase in employment opportunities for women have thus not sufficiently empowered them to do away with the dowry system. In fact, many girls from rural areas are sent out to urban factories to earn their own dowry' (p. 14). Dannecker (2002) finds that most of the married female garment workers regularly sent part of their income to their in-laws' families and thus a new marriage arrangement developed. Traditionally, the bride's family had to make a one-off payment of a certain amount of money to the bridegroom's family, but now these female workers take this responsibility by contributing their salary (p. 163). A female garment worker said:

> I am married now, therefore I do not give any money to my parents. I have to give the money to my husband who transfers part of it to his parents, otherwise he would be disappointed and his family would think that I am not a good daughter-in-law. See I come from a poor family but his parents did not mind, they said that they do not want any dowry but that I should go on working, sending money from time to time. If I need some money for myself I try to get something from my parents.
>
> (Dannecker, 2002, p. 162)

Rozario (1998, p. 266) considered garment workers' income as a form of dowry. She wrote:

> Often, when the parents have given up trying to arrange a marriage for their daughters, the girls find partners for themselves in urban centres. Their income in the garment factories, for instance, is attractive to poor and semi-employed men such as rickshaw-pullers, day labourers, etc. . . . these men marry the factory girls because they have an income, and in this sense their income can be seen as a form of dowry.

Conclusion

The legislators of Bangladesh still do not acknowledge that the dowry system has shifted as a result of women's increasing paid labour force activities. Women in Bangladesh join the paid labour force to contribute financially to their families. This raises a number of questions. Can men marry working women in order to withdraw financial support to their families and thereby accumulate wealth and enhance their own living standards? Should husbands expect financial contributions from their wives for day-to-day expenses, thus saving their own money to increase their assets? Is it right for husbands to threaten their wives with not allowing them to continue their jobs if they do not pay the day-to-day expenses? Should women have to maintain their husbands' families and sever all relationships with their own parental families? Is it fair that women cannot financially assist their own parental families? Why can women not give to charity according to how they choose? Why is it that they cannot even buy a sari with their own income without the permission of their husbands? Do women not even deserve Eid gifts from their husbands because of their earning capacity?

Islamic law prohibits the appropriation or control of a wife's income by her husband or in-laws. Dower is an essential part of Muslim marriage and maintenance is the lawful right of the wife to be provided at the husband's expense and encompassing food, clothing, accommodation and other necessities of life in Bangladesh. This law derives from the injunctions of the holy *Quran*, the Prophet's traditions and the consensus of jurists. In Bangladesh, a wife is entitled to maintenance whether she is economically solvent or not. In *Mst. Amena Khatun* v. *Sherajuddin* (1965) the lower court took the view that the husband was absolved from his duty to maintain his wife, because she was a woman of means. C. J. Murshed held that, legally, such a proposition is not tenable. The competence of the wife does not absolve the husband from his duty to maintain her (*Mst. Amena Khatun* v. *Sherajuddin*, 1965, p. 690). According to Islam, women have every right to spend their income independently and to control their money. A wife is not required to spend her resources or income on the household. Badawi (n.d., p. 16) writes:

> No married woman is required to spend any amount at all from her property and income on the household. In special circumstances, however, such as when her husband is ill, disabled or jobless, she may find it necessary to spend from her earnings or savings to provide the necessities for her family. While this is not a legal obligation, it is consistent with the mutuality of care, love and cooperation among family members.

According to maintenance law, a husband cannot force his wife to use her own earnings for family expenditures. What is the point of joining the paid labour force and taking a double burden if wives cannot control their income and their income is appropriated or controlled by their husbands or in-laws? Is it not a new form of dowry? To prevent appropriation of wives' income, Bangladeshi law should recognize it as a new form of dowry and criminalize the practice. The operation of the dowry system has shifted as a result of women's increasing paid labour force activities and the Dowry Prohibition Act 1980 must be amended.

Notes

1 *New Age*, 13 March 2016. 'Decline in Women's Share in Workforce Worrisome'.
2 *New Age*, 7 March 2016a. 'Women Facing Sexual Violence at Workplaces Don't Complain Fearing Job Loss: Dialogue'.
3 *The Guardian*, 24 October 2013. 'Primark Offers Long-Term Compensation to Rana Plaza Factory Collapse Victims: Clothing Retailer Calls on Other Brands to Help Injured Workers and Families of Those Killed in Bangladesh Disaster', available at www.theguardian.com/world/2013/oct/24/primark-compensation-rana-plaza-factory-collapse-bangladesh [accessed 25 July 2016].
4 *Daily Star*, 25 November 2012.
5 *Financial Express*, 5 April 2013.
6 *New Age*, 7 March 2016b. 'Women's Presence, Participation in Media Comes Down in 10 Years'.
7 After independence on 16 December 1972, Bangladesh instituted a fully fledged constitution and socialism was declared as one of the four guiding principles of that constitution. However, the ruling party – the AL – never spelled out what it meant by a socialist economy. It seemed that by socialism it meant a policy of nationalization. Despite having socialism as one of the state principles, the AL continued to depend on the surplus of farmers in the villages who were its old power base. In the urban areas it depended on lawyers, businessmen and educated professionals (Jahan, 1980, p. 101).
8 It is an obligation for Muslims to pay 2.5 per cent of their wealth to specified categories in society when their annual wealth exceeds a minimum level. *Zakat* is one of the five pillars of Islam.

7 Conclusion

With the erosion of the extended family system and increasing poverty in Bangladesh, large numbers of women from landless and middle-class families sought any available employment and shed age-old inhibitions and prejudices. Changing male attitudes towards employed women and the expansion of educational and employment opportunities also helped bring about changes in female participation in paid employment. Both urban and rural women are no longer hesitant to join the paid labour force when opportunities arise (Khan, 1993, p. 3). The ability to earn is sometimes considered a good quality for a bride, but it does not change traditional expectations: fair skin, beauty, submissiveness, youth and chastity (Huda, 2006, p. 254).

Despite women's education and status, society still considers them inferior to men and their parents need to compensate the grooms' families for saving their daughters' lives through marrying them. Sometimes, working women in Bangladesh have to hear things from their in-laws and husbands such as, 'There are many rich people's daughters in Bangladesh. We could have brought them. If we brought them we would have got *lakh lakh* (hundreds of thousands of taka), cars, houses.'

After independence, a nouveau riche class emerged in Bangladesh which accumulated immense wealth within a very short period of time (Ahmed and Nahar, 1987, p. 187). Despite the introduction of socialism, the gap between rich and poor widened after independence and it continued to increase after the introduction of free market economic policies in the mid 1970s. Competition began among the people of Bangladesh with regard to accumulating capital and wealth and Bangladeshis became more corrupt as a result. In this context, men increasingly started to use the dowry system in order to control their wives' income and accumulate wealth to enhance their own standards of living.

The dowry system indicates the superiority of the man and it is a way to maintain patriarchal norms of superiority. Parents of brides feel compelled to give dowries to arrange their daughters' marriages as marriage is universal in Bangladesh. The new dowry system first started in urban areas among wealthy families in the 1950s. It spread to rural areas in the 1960s and among poorer families in the early 1970s. After independence, a nouveau riche class looked for grooms who were wealthy or who had occupations that would make them wealthy, so that their daughters could lead lives of leisure and comfort. For this reason, many parents 'willingly' gifted things to grooms. The birth of Bangladesh opened up many opportunities for becoming rich overnight and it was primarily men who were the beneficiaries. These trends in marriage transactions were emulated by the poor classes and grooms started making demands at weddings. As women's age range for marriage is much shorter than that of men, prospective grooms for marriageable women are always few. This is why the demands of grooms and their families at the time of a wedding are higher and these demands are almost always met passively by brides and their families.

Dowry increased with the expansion of capitalist relations and dowry has been transformed into 'demand, extortion, material gain, and profit maximization' (Samuel, 2002, p. 205). The most common motives behind the dowry system are the grooms' and their families' greed, growing consumerism, excessive materialism, status seeking and rising expectations for a better and more luxurious life. Despite the existence of anti-dowry laws, dowry victims do not receive justice because of the difficulties and expense of the legal process.

The increase in employment opportunities for women did not empower them to escape the dowry system. In fact, many young girls from rural areas are sent to work in urban industries to earn their own dowries. Men who marry garment workers do not demand dowry, as the women's income is considered as 'sufficient compensation for waiving dowry demands' (Kabeer, 1997, p. 299). In Bangladesh, middle-class educated people know that demanding dowry is a criminal offence and they cannot demand dowry publicly. When women started participating in paid employment, middle-class men adopted various strategies to accumulate wealth from their wives. Their attitude is: 'We do not want dowry. We want working women.' On the surface, it seems that they want women's emancipation, but their main intention is to control their wives' income and accumulate wealth to enhance their own standard of living. The general perception in Bangladesh is that women's power increases when they earn money. In reality, however, many Bangladeshi women cannot control their own income. Many garment workers in Bangladesh have no control over their income (Kibria, 1995, p. 299; Paul-Majumder, 1997, pp. 138–139). Many women cannot spend their credit/loan from NGOs independently as the money from their loans goes directly to their husbands (Haider and Akhtar, 1999, p. 61). When women living in slums in Bangladesh make a greater economic contribution to the home, many men become less responsible for managing their families and withdraw their financial support (Salway et al., 2005, p. 343). Even some women MPs in Bangladesh have little control over their own earnings (Chowdhury, 2013, p. 85).

My study finds that most of the income of middle-class married women in Bangladesh is controlled by husbands and in some cases by mothers-in-law (Chowdhury, 2007; Chowdhury, 2010). Sometimes, fathers-in-law also control women's income (Rashid, 2006, p. 156). My study suggests that, in Bangladesh, husbands adopt a number of strategies to control their wives' income in order to accumulate wealth. The strategies are: withdrawal of their financial support; directly taking all their wives' income; saving their own money while expecting their wives to meet family expenditures; threatening their wives by saying that they will not allow them to continue their jobs unless they hand over all their income, buying land or property in their own names by taking loans which they then repay with their own income, thus compelling their wives to meet family expenditures; giving false information about their loans to their wives and attempting to take all their wives' income to 'repay' these; attempting to use their wives' income to invest in businesses; and appropriating their wives' income to maintain their parental families. Furthermore, husbands do not look after their wives' families. In some cases, mothers-in-law control the money that women earn and in all cases the in-laws' families encourage and support husbands in controlling their wives' income. My study also finds that women could not even pay *zakat* according to their own choice. They were sometimes victims of physical assault for not handing over their incomes and many respondents reported that they could not even buy a sari when they needed to. Moreover, in most of the cases their husbands stopped giving them gifts, even for Eid. One woman asked her husband to give her some gifts for Eid and her husband replied, 'You earn money. Why do you need gifts from me?'

Islam plays a very important role in society and politics in Bangladesh and the people of Bangladesh have strong attachments to Islam, so much so that no one would risk retribution by criticizing Islamic customs, practices and beliefs. The ruling AL promised that laws contrary to the *Quran* and the *Sunnah* would not be enacted. After assuming power with an absolute majority, the AL reintroduced secularism. Although it claims itself to be a secular party, it is still using religion in politics to get mass public support. The question now is: does Islam allow appropriation of wives' income? What are wives' rights in Muslim family law in Bangladesh? Does Muslim family law in Bangladesh allow appropriation of wives' income?

The relationship and roles of men and women in Islamic law are based on the notion of both formal and substantive equality. Some verses of the *Quran* reveal that men and women are equal (*Quran* 3:195; 4:124; 9:71; 33:35). Islam follows a formal equality approach in the context of full possession and control over women's wealth. It guaranteed women complete control over what they earn and possess. Certain provisions in family law afforded women complete equality. For example, women have the right to marry of their own free will (Ali, 2000, p. 38). The substantive approach of equality recognizes differences (Wentholt, 1999, p. 55). Similarly, Islamic law recognizes physical and biological differences between men and women and it gives importance to the 'complementary but equally important roles of men and women' in the family (Venkatraman, 1995, p. 2004). Considering physical and biological differences, Islamic law gives financial responsibility for wives and children to men. The right to maintenance and dower was introduced to ensure women's economic security within a marriage. Furthermore, sexual violence against women also sometimes prevents them from taking up certain forms of employment in many countries of the world. For these reasons, Allah did not make it mandatory for women to maintain themselves or their families. However, it does not follow that women are considered inferior within Islam. The *Quran* considers women rational, because they have the same religious and moral duties and responsibilities. In fact, Islamic law acknowledges unpaid work that is done by women, especially childbearing, child rearing and breastfeeding activities. Islamic law does not put double or triple burdens on women, but this does not mean that women do not have any rights to join the paid labour force. There is no decree in Islam that prevents women from seeking employment and there are no restrictions with regard to using women's exceptional talents in any area (Badawi, 1977, p. 141). Working wives also have the right to maintenance and dower.

I draw on both formal and substantive models of equality within Islam. Using formal equality, I argue that Muslim women have the right to control what they earn and possess. Using substantive equality, I argue that a wife's ability to earn does not absolve her husband from his duty to maintain her. Dower and maintenance, to be provided at the husband's expense, encompassing food, clothing, accommodation and other necessities of life, are the lawful rights of a wife. A husband cannot force his wife to use money for family expenditures. I think that the ability to control their resources, whatever they may have, is important for the empowerment of women, and Bangladeshi women can achieve this through Islamic law.

Islamic law prohibits the appropriation or control of a wife's income by her husband or in-laws. Dower is an essential part of Muslim marriage and maintenance is the lawful right of the wife to be provided at the husband's expense with food, clothing, accommodation and other necessities of life. This law derives from the injunctions of the holy *Quran*, the Prophet's traditions and the consensus of jurists. In Bangladesh, a wife is entitled to maintenance whether she is economically solvent or not. In *Mst. Amena Khatun* v. *Sherajuddin*, the lower court took the view that the husband was absolved from his duty to maintain his wife because she was a woman of means. However, C. J. Murshed held that, legally, such a proposition is not tenable. The competence of the wife does not absolve the husband from his duty to maintain her (*Mst. Amena Khatun* v. *Sherajuddin*, 1965). According to Islam, women have every right to spend their income independently and to control their money. Badawi (n.d.) writes:

> No married woman is required to spend any amount at all from her property and income on the household. In special circumstances, however, such as when her husband is ill, disabled or jobless, she may find it necessary to spend from her earnings or savings to provide the necessities for her family. While this is not a legal obligation, it is consistent with the mutuality of care, love and cooperation among family members.

I argue that Bangladeshi society misinterprets Islam in order to make women inferior. It is believed that women are transferred to their husbands' families through marriage. Husbands consider their wives as their property and Bangladeshi patriarchal culture teaches girls that it is their religious duty to make only their husbands and husbands' families happy. In Islam, women not only have responsibilities towards their parents, but they also have the same religious and moral duties and responsibilities as men. In the interests of men, Bangladeshi patriarchal society does not convey to women these messages of their broader responsibilities. Bangladeshi society only spreads the message that women have responsibilities exclusively towards their husbands, children and members of their in-laws' families.

Women in Bangladesh are not educated with regard to what Islam says and are unaware of their rights and responsibilities in Islam. They are not encouraged to acquire knowledge and apply reasoning in understanding the *Quran*. Although Bangladeshi men claim that they are devout Muslims, when the question of women arises they misinterpret Islam and oppress women. Women do not know that in Islam, 'the sole basis for superiority of any person over another is piety and righteousness not gender, color, or nationality' (Badawi, n.d.).

It is Bangladeshi society that considers women to be passively dependent on men. Bangladeshi people ignore the fact that men are also dependent on women. A wife satisfies her husband's sexual and emotional needs, gives birth to legitimate children, breastfeeds and raises children, etc. and these in turn help a man to work in paid employment. Although men earn money, they depend on women for their survival. Islam recognizes the unpaid work done by women, but Bangladeshi patriarchal society fails to acknowledge it.

According to social norms in Bangladesh, women must take care of their in-laws, but they cannot look after their own parents in the same way. In addition, husbands do not take care of their wives' parents in the same way that their wives take care of their in-laws. Married women who are in the paid labour force also experience this situation. When the *Quran* instructs as to responsibilities towards parents, it does not only instruct men. However, Bangladeshi patriarchal society does not teach girls about this instruction in the interests of husbands and husbands' families. For this reason, girls are considered as liabilities in their natal families. Women also have responsibilities to kinfolk, orphans, those in need, neighbours and friends, but in Bangladesh they are taught not to think beyond their husbands, children and husbands' families. When Bangladeshi women are aware of their rights and responsibilities in Islam, only then will they resist the oppression and exploitation against them. Women must have proper Islamic knowledge in order to protest and also to protect them from the oppression of men in the name of Islam.

The effectiveness of family law reform in Bangladesh depends on its acceptance by the people of Bangladesh. Many Bangladeshis do not perform mandatory religious practices, but most display their devotion to Islam in public. In my view, if reform is done within an Islamic framework, Bangladeshis will accept it. At present, CEDAW is perceived as the 'magic remedy' for women's liberation by women's organizations in Bangladesh. Bangladesh ratified CEDAW with reservations on articles 2, 13[a] and 16.1[c] and [f] as they conflict with '*Sharia* law based on the Holy Quran and *Sunnah*'.[1] Bangladesh later withdrew its reservations from articles 13[a] and 16.1[f]. It still has reservations on articles 2 and 16.1[c] (Islam, n.d.).[2] Women's organizations, however, are demanding complete ratification of CEDAW.

Women and men are the same: this is the assumption of CEDAW's definition of discrimination, despite the fact that it goes beyond equality of opportunity and deals with the concept of equality of result, and provides affirmative action programmes and protection against indirect discrimination. The term 'discrimination against women' is defined as:

> any distinction, exclusion or restriction made on the basis of sex which has the effect or purpose of impairing or nullifying the recognition, enjoyment or exercise by women, irrespective of their marital status, on a basis of equality of men and women, of human rights and fundamental freedoms in the political, economic, social, cultural, civil or any other field.[3]

In CEDAW, equality is defined as being like a man, except in special circumstances, such as pregnancy (Charlesworth, 1991, p. 632). The provision of affirmative action programmes in article 4 of CEDAW assumes that these measures will be used temporally to let women perform exactly like men. Equality is presented in CEDAW as women being treated in the same way as men, or women having the same opportunity to be treated like men; it did not consider whether male standards are appropriate for women. Western notions of formal equality on human rights ignore the socio-economic realities of many women around the world (Wright, 1988, p. 262).

I argue that in the name of equal responsibilities, working women are taking *more* than equal responsibilities. CEDAW assumes that paid work is the key to women's liberation, but paid work cannot ensure equality between a husband and a wife at home. CEDAW ignores the presence of conflicting human rights principles, such as equality between men and women on the one hand and the right to freedom of religion, culture and custom on the other. If CEDAW is fully implemented, it will deprive Muslim women of their maintenance and dower rights and the maintenance of children by their fathers. CEDAW ignores the vulnerable position of women, especially in developing countries, and in the name of formal equality it puts the same responsibilities that men have on women in the family too. It encourages women to join the paid labour force at any cost, which perpetuates inequality. Introducing the same responsibilities for both husbands and wives will hurt the majority of women in Bangladesh who are not in the paid labour force or who are working under insecure and exploitative working conditions. It is not possible to achieve gender equality at home even if gender equality is achieved in all other areas in Bangladesh. In most cases, there will be inequality between husbands and wives in terms of education, training and income.

Legislators of Bangladesh still do not acknowledge that the dowry system has shifted as a result of women's increasing paid labour force activities. Women in Bangladesh join the paid labour force to contribute financially to family expenditure. This raises a number of questions. Can men marry working women to then withdraw their financial support so that they can accumulate wealth and enhance their own living standards? Should husbands expect financial contributions from their wives for day-to-day expenses and then save their own money to increase their assets? Is it right for husbands to threaten their wives with not allowing them to continue their jobs if they do not pay day-to-day expenses? Should women have to maintain their husbands' families and sever all relationships with their own parental families? Is it fair that women cannot contribute to their own parental families? Can women not give to charity according to their own choice? Can they not even buy a sari with their own income without the permission of their husbands? Do women not deserve even Eid gifts from their husbands because of their earning capacities?

According to maintenance law, a husband cannot force his wife to use money for family expenditures. What is the point of joining the paid labour force and taking on a double burden if wives cannot control their own income and it is appropriated or controlled by their husbands or in-laws? Is this not a new form of dowry? To prevent appropriation of wives' income, Bangladeshi law should recognize it as a new form of dowry and criminalize the practice of appropriating or controlling it. The dowry system has shifted as a result of women's increasing paid labour force activities and the Dowry Prohibition Act 1980 must be amended to take this into account. Despite women's participation in the paid labour force, we cannot expect any major changes in the status of women if appropriation of wives' income by husbands or in-laws continues. If women cannot control their income, paid employment will only give them a 'double burden' instead of benefit and this will further strengthen patriarchy. I suggest the following recommendations for the amendment of the Dowry Prohibition Act 1980:

1. Appropriation of wives' income or attempting to appropriate wives' income should be considered as receiving or attempting to receive dowry. 'Appropriation of a wife's income' should be defined to include any practice or activity that interferes with working wives' discretion in relation to the use of their income.
2. A husband or any member of his family should not require a working wife to maintain the family or spend money for family expenditures directly or indirectly. A husband should not be permitted to withdraw financial support for the family and thereby accumulate wealth as well as enhance his own living standards. It should be at the wife's discretion whether or not she contributes financially to the family and this should be recognized.
3. A husband or any member of his family should not prevent a wife from taking care of her parental family financially. This should also be considered as appropriation of a wife's income or attempting to appropriate a wife's income.
4. A husband or any member of his family should not prevent a wife from giving to charity. Preventing a wife from giving to charity by a husband or any of his family members should be considered appropriation of a wife's income or attempting to appropriate a wife's income.
5. It should be a criminal offence to be a dowry taker or an abettor to the practice.
6. Psychological abuse for dowry should be criminalized.
7. The law should recognize that presents given to the bride should be under her control and presents given to the groom should be under his control.
8. Any advertisement in a newspaper or any other media offering or demanding dowry directly or indirectly should be banned.

Notes

1 Convention on the Elimination of All Forms of Discrimination Against Women (CEDAW), 1 March 1980, UNTS I-20378, UN Division for the Advancement of Women, Department of Economic and Social Affairs, available at www.un.org/womenwatch/daw/cedaw/text/econvention.htm [accessed 25 July 2016].

2 Article 2, CEDAW. State parties condemn discrimination against women in all its forms and agree to pursue by all appropriate means and without delay a policy of eliminating discrimination against women and, to this end, undertake:

[a] To embody the principle of the equality of men and women in their national constitutions or other appropriate legislation if not yet incorporated therein and to ensure, through law and other appropriate means, the practical realization of this principle;
[b] To adopt appropriate legislative and other measures, including sanctions where appropriate, prohibiting all discrimination against women;
[c] To establish legal protection of the rights of women on an equal basis with men and to ensure through competent national tribunals and other public institutions the effective protection of women against any act of discrimination;
[d] To refrain from engaging in any act or practice of discrimination against women and to ensure that public authorities and institutions shall act in conformity with this obligation;
[e] To take all appropriate measures to eliminate discrimination against women by any person, organization or enterprise;
[f] To take all appropriate measures, including legislation, to modify or abolish existing laws, regulations, customs and practices which constitute discrimination against women;
[g] To repeal all national penal provisions which constitute discrimination against women.

Article16[c], CEDAW. The same rights and responsibilities during marriage and at its dissolution.

3 Article 1, CEDAW.

References

Abdullah, T. A. and Zeidenstein, S. (1980). *Village Women of Bangladesh: Prospects for Change*, Oxford: Pergamon Press.

Abusulayman, A. A. (2003). *Marital Discord: Recapturing the Full Islamic Spirit of Human Dignity*, London: The International Institute of Islamic Thought.

Adnan, S. (1989). '"Birds in a Cage": Institutional Change and Women's Position in Bangladesh', *The Journal of Social Studies*, 46, pp. 1–34.

Afsar, R. (2003). 'Internal Migration and the Development Nexus: The Case of Bangladesh', Paper presented at the Regional Conference on Migration, Development and Pro-Poor Policy Choices in Asia, 22–24 June 2003, Dhaka, Bangladesh.

Ahmed, H. S. (2009). 'National Child Rights Week: Girlhood Interrupted', *Star Weekend Magazine, Daily Star*, 9 October 2009, available at http://archive.thedailystar.net/magazine/2009/10/02/human_rights.htm [accessed 25 July 2016].

Ahmed, N. (2003). 'From Monopoly to Competition: Party Politics in the Bangladesh Parliament (1973–2001)', *Pacific Affairs*, 76(1), pp. 55–77.

Ahmed, R. and Naher, M. S. (1987). *Brides and the Demand System in Bangladesh: A Study*, Dhaka: Centre for Social Studies.

Ahmed, S., Khanum, P. A. and Islam, A. (1998). *Maternal Morbidity in Rural Bangladesh: Where Do Women Go for Care?*, B Working Paper No.113, Dhaka: International Centre for Diarrhoeal Disease Research.

Ahsan, S. (2005). 'Left in the Lurch', cover story, *Star Weekend Magazine, Daily Star*, 6 May 2005.

Akhter, F. (2006). 'Working Women vs Powerful Women', *New Age. Third Anniversary Special.*

Akhter, F. (2013). *The 13 Point Demands of Hefazat-e-Islam and the Middle Ages Controversy*, available at www.kaagoj.com/details?id=199 [accessed 16 July 2016].

Alam, K., Blanch, L. and Smith, Anna (2011). *Stitched Up, Women Workers in the Bangladeshi Garment Sector*, London: War on Want, available at www.waronwant.org/sites/default/files/Stitched%20Up.pdf [accessed 16 July 2016].

Alamgir, M. (2016). 'Women's Participation in Workforce Drops', *New Age*, 12 March 2016.

al-Hibri, A. (1997). 'Islam, Law and Custom: Redefining Muslim Women's Rights', *American University International Law Review*, 12(1), pp. 1–44.

al-Hibri, A. Y. (2003). 'An Islamic Perspective on Domestic Violence', *Fordham International Law Journal*, 27, pp. 195–224.

Al-Mahmud, S. Z., Karim, E., Kamol, E. and Hossain, A. (2010). 'Breaking the Glass Ceiling', *The Star, Daily Star*, 5 March 2010.

Ali, K. (2003). 'Progressive Muslims and Islamic Jurisprudence: The Necessity for Critical Engagement With Marriage and Divorce Law', in O. Safi (ed.), *Progressive Muslims On Justice, Gender and Pluralism*, Oxford: Oneworld Publications, pp. 163–189.

Ali, S. S. (n.d.). *Conceptualizing Islamic Law, CEDAW and Women's Human's Rights in Plural Settings: A Comparative Analysis of Application of CEDAW in Bangladesh, India, and Pakistan*, available at http://asiapacific.unwomen.org/~/media/field%20office%20eseasia/docs/publications/southasia/report studies/05_human%20rights/complete-study%20pdf.ashx [accessed 18 July 2016].

Ali, S. S. (2000). *Gender and Human Rights in Islam and International Law: Equal Before Allah, Unequal Before Man?*, Boston, MA: Kluwer Law International.

Ali, S. S. and Mullally, S. (1992). 'Women's Rights and Human Rights in Islamic Countries: A Case Study', in H. Hinds, A. Phoenix and J. Stacey (eds), *Working Out: New Directions for Women's Studies*, London: The Falmer Press, pp. 113–123.

Ali, T. S., Árnadóttir, G. and Kulane, A. (2013). 'Dowry Practices and Their Negative Consequences from a Female Perspective in Karachi, Pakistan – A Qualitative Study', *Health*, 5(7A4), pp. 84–91.

Ameen, N. (2005). *Wife Abuse in Bangladesh: An Unrecognized Offence*, Dhaka: The University Press Limited.

Amin, S. and Cain, M. (1997). 'The Rise of Dowry in Bangladesh', in G. W. Jones (eds), *The Continuing Demographic Transition*, Oxford: Oxford University Press, pp. 290–306.

Amin, S. and Chandrasekhar, S. (2009). *Looking Beyond Universal Primary Education: Gender Differences in Time Use Among Children in Rural Bangladesh*, Working Paper No. 17, New York: Population Council.

Amin, S. and Huq, L. (2008). *Marriage Considerations in Sending Girls to School in Bangladesh: Some Qualitative Evidence*, Working Paper No. 12, New York: Population Council.

Amin, S., Diamond, I., Naved, R. T. and Newby, M. (1998). 'Transition to Adulthood of Female Garment-Factory Workers in Bangladesh', *Studies in Family Planning*, 29(2), pp. 185–200.

An-Na'im, A. (1987). 'The Rights of Women and International Law in the Muslim Context', *Whittier Law Review*, 9, pp. 491–516.

An-Na'im, A. (1990a). *Toward an Islamic Reformation: Civil Liberties, Human Rights, and International Law*, Syracuse, NY: Syracuse University Press.

An-Na'im, A. (1990b). 'Human Rights in the Muslim World: Socio-political Conditions and Scriptural Imperatives – a Preliminary Inquiry', *Harvard Human Rights Journal*, 3, pp. 13–52.

An-Na'im, A. (1994). 'State Responsibility Under International Human Rights Law to Change Religious and Customary Laws', in R. J. Cook (ed.), *Human Rights of Women: National and International Perspectives*, Philadelphia, PA: University of Pennsylvania Press, pp. 167–188.

An-Na'im, A. (2000). 'Islam and Human Rights: Beyond the Universality Debate', ASIL Proc. 94, pp. 95–101.

Anderson, S. (2000). *The Economics of Dowry Payments in Pakistan*, Tilburg, Netherlands: Tilburg University, Center for Economic Research.

Anwar, Z. (2005). 'Sisters in Islam and the Struggle for Women's Rights', in F. Nouraie-Simone (ed.), *On Shifting Ground: Muslim Women in the Global Era*, New York: The Feminist Press at the City University of New York.

Anwari, A. K. M. F. R. (2002). *Maksudul Mumin*, Dhaka: Abed Art Press.

Archampong, E. (2006). 'Reforming Ghana's Matrimonial Property Law to Achieve Greater Gender Equality Upon Marriage Breakdown', PhD thesis, Osgoode Hall Law School, York University, Toronto, Ontario, Canada. [Unpublished].

Arends-Kuenning, M. and Amin, S. (2001). 'Women's Capabilities and Right to Education in Bangladesh', *International Journal of Politics, Culture and Society*, 15(1), pp. 125–142.

Arens, J. (2014). *Women, Land and Power in Bangladesh: Jhagrapur Revisited*, Dhaka: The University Press Limited.

Asian Development Bank (2010). *Country Gender Assessment: Bangladesh*, Mandaluyong City, Philippines.

Aziz, K. M. A. and Maloney, C. (1985). *Life Stages, Gender and Fertility in Bangladesh*, Dhaka: ICDDRB.

Babul, P. (2010). 'Women in Media', *Daily Star*, 8 August 2010.

Badawi, G. A. (1977). 'Women in Islam', in K. Ahmed (ed.), *Islam: Its Meaning and Message*, Delhi: Ambika Publications, pp. 131–145.

Badawi, J. (n.d.). *Gender Equity in Islam: Basic Principles*, New Delhi: Millat Book Centre.

Baillie, N. B. E. (1965). *A Digest of Moohummdan Law*, 4th ed., Lahore: Premier Book House.

Baines, B. (2007). 'Polygamy's Challenge: Women, Religion and the Post-Liberal State', *Les Ateliers De L'ethique*, 2(1), available at https://papyrus.bib.umontreal.ca/xmlui/bitstream/handle/1866/2503/baines.pdf?sequence=1&isAllowed=y [accessed 18 July 2016].

Bangladesh Awami League (2008). *Election Manifesto*, Dhaka: Bangladesh Awami League, available at www.albd.org/autoalbd/index.php?option=com_content&task=view&id=357&Itemid=1 [accessed 11 July 2016].

Bangladesh Awami League (2014). *Election Manifesto*, Dhaka: Bangladesh Awami League.

Bangladesh Bureau of Statistics (2013). *Statistical Yearbook Bangladesh 2012*, Dhaka: Bangladesh Bureau of Statistics.

Bangladesh Bureau of Statistics (2015). *Labour Force Survey Bangladesh 2013*, Dhaka: Bangladesh Bureau of Statistics.

Barlas, A. (2002). *'Believing Women' in Islam: Unreading Patriarchal Interpretations of the Qur'an*, Austin, TX: University of Texas Press.

Barman, T. (2009). '" Patri Chi" Biggapone Patrir Joggotaboli', *Prothom Alo*, 1 April 2009.

Bartlett, K. T. (1999). 'Perspectives in Feminist Jurisprudence', in B. Taylor, S. Rush and R. J. Munro (eds), *Feminist Jurisprudence, Women and the Law: Critical Essays, Research Agenda, and Bibliography*, New York: Fred B. Rothman Publications, pp. 3–21.

Baxter, C. (1992). 'Bangladesh in 1991: A Parliamentary System', *Asian Survey*, 32(2), pp. 162–167.

Becker, M. E. (1987). 'Prince Charming: Abstract Equality', *The Supreme Ct. Rev.*, pp. 201–247.

Becker, M. E. (1993). 'Prince Charming: Abstract Equality', in D. Kelley Weisberg (ed.), *Feminist Legal Theory Foundations*, Philadelphia, PA: Temple University Press, pp. 221–236.

Begum, A. (2004). 'Protection of Women's Rights in Bangladesh: A Legal Study in an International and Comparative Perspective', PhD thesis, University of Wollongong. [Unpublished].

Begum, M. (2006) *Joutuker Sangskriti* [in Bengali], Dhaka: The University Press Limited.

Bhat, P. N. M. and Halli, S. S. (1999). 'Demography of Brideprice and Dowry: Causes and Consequences of the Indian Marriage Squeeze', *Population Studies*, 53(2), pp. 129–148.

Bhuiyan, R. (2007). 'The Personal Laws of Muslim and Hindu Women in Marriage and Divorce in Bangladesh: Addressing the Critical Issues from a Feminist Perspective', PhD thesis, Cornell University. [Unpublished].

Bhuiyan, R. (2010). *Gender and Tradition in Marriage and Divorce: An Analysis of Personal Laws of Muslim and Hindu Women in Bangladesh*, Dhaka: UNESCO.

Bhutto, B. (1988). *Daughter of the East*, London: Hamish Hamilton.

Bhuyan, M. O. U. (2013). '98pc of Women Working Abroad Are Maids: Study', *New Age*, 21 June 2013.

Billig, M. S. (1991). 'The Marriage Squeeze on High-Caste Rajasthani Women', *The Journal of Asian Studies*, 50(2), pp. 341–360.

Biplob, B. H. (2013). 'Female Workers Abroad: Low Pay, Hostile Environment', *Daily Star*, 13 July 2013.

Blenkhorn, L. E. (2002). 'Islamic Marriage Contracts in American Courts: Interpreting Mahr Agreements as Prenuptials and Their Effect on Muslim Women', *Southern California Law Review*, 76, pp. 189–243.

Bose, C. E. (1985). *Jobs and Gender: A Study of Occupational Prestige*, New York: Praeger Publishers.

Brooks, R. E. (2002). 'Feminism and International Law: An Opportunity for Transformation', *Yale Journal of Law and Feminism*, 14, pp. 345–361.

Cain, M. et al. (1979). 'Class, Patriarchy and Women's Work in Bangladesh', *Population and Development Review*, 5(3), pp. 405–438.

Caldwell, J. C., Reddy, P. H. and Caldwell, P. (1983). 'The Causes of Marriage Change in South India', *Population Studies*, 37(3), pp. 343–361.

Chamallas, M. (2003). *Introduction to Feminist Legal Theory*, New York: Aspen Publishers.

Charlesworth, H. (1994). 'What Are "Women's International Human Rights?"', in R. J. Cook (ed.), *Human Rights of Women National and International Perspectives*, Philadelphia, PA: University of Pennsylvania Press, pp. 58–84.

Charlesworth, H. and Chinkin, C. (2000). *The Boundaries of International Law: A Feminist Analysis*, Manchester: Manchester University Press.

Charlesworth, H., Chinkin, C. and Wright, S. (1991). 'Feminist Approaches to International Law', *The American Journal of International Law*, 85(4), pp. 613–645.

Chaudhury, R. H. (1979). 'Marriage, Urban Women, and the Labour Force: The Bangladesh Case', *Signs*, 5(1), pp. 154–163.

Chichilnisky, G. (2008). 'The Gender Gap', *Review of Development Economics*, 12(4), pp. 828–844.

Chinkin, C. and Freeman, M. A. (2012). 'Introduction', in M. A. Freeman, C. Chinkin and B. Rudulf (eds), *The UN Convention on the Elimination of All Forms of Discrimination against Women: A Commentary*, Oxford: Oxford University Press, pp. 2–33.

Choudhury, D. (2005). *Sexual Harassment of Bangladeshi Women at Workplace*, Dhaka: Forum on Women in Security and International Affairs.

Chowdhury, F. D. (2002). 'English Language Problems Among Female Students of Rajshahi University: An Empirical Study', *Journal of the Asiatic Society of Bangladesh*, 47(1), pp. 183–192.

Chowdhury, F. D. (2004). 'The Socio-cultural Context of Child Marriage in a Bangladeshi Village', *International Journal of Social Welfare*, 13, pp. 244–253.

Chowdhury, F. D. (2007) *Middle Class Married Women's Income in Bangladesh: Who Controls It and How?*, Major research paper, Department of Political Science, York University, Toronto, Ontario, Canada. [Unpublished].

Chowdhury, F. D. (2009a). 'Problems of Women's Participation in Bangladesh Politics', *The Round Table*, 98(404), pp. 555–567.

Chowdhury, F. D. (2009b). 'Theorizing Patriarchy: The Bangladesh Context', *Asian Journal of Social Science*, 37(4), pp. 599–622.

Chowdhury, F. D. (2010a). 'Dowry, Women and Law in Bangladesh', *International Journal of Law, Policy and the Family*, 24(2), pp. 198–221.

Chowdhury, F. D. (2010b). 'Middle Class Married Women's Income in Bangladesh: Who Controls It and How?', *African and Asian Studies*, 9, pp. 1–30.

Chowdhury, F. D. (2013a). *Muslim Family Law in Bangladesh: Resistance to Secularization*, in M. Maclean and J. Eekelaar (eds), *Managing Family Justice in Diverse Societies*, Oxford and Portland, OR: Hart Publishing Limited, pp. 263–269.

Chowdhury, F. D. (2013b). *Problems of Women's Political Participation in Bangladesh: An Empirical Study*, Dhaka: The University Press Limited.

Connors, J. (1996). 'The Women's Convention in the Muslim World', in M. Yamani (ed.), *Feminism and Islam: Legal and Literary Perspectives*, New York: New York University Press, pp. 351–371.

Cook, R. J. and Howard, S. (2007). 'Accommodating Women's Differences Under the Women's Anti-Discrimination Convention', *Emory Law Journal*, 56(4), pp. 1039–1091.

Dannecker, P. (2002). *Between Conformity and Resistance: Women Garment Workers in Bangladesh*, Dhaka: The University Press Limited.

Dannecker, P. (2005). 'Transnational Migration and the Transformation of Gender Relations: The Case of Bangladeshi Labour Migrants', *Current Sociology*, 53(4), pp. 655–674.

Das, T. K. (2016). 'Shortage of Day Care Facilities: Working Mothers Forced to Quit Jobs', *New Age*, 10 January 2016.

Doi, A. R. I. (1984). *Shari'ah: The Islamic Law*, London: Ta Ha Publishers.

Eberts, M. (1985). 'Sex-Based Discrimination and the Charter', in A. F. Bayefsky and M. Eberts (eds), *Equality Rights and the Canadian Charter of Rights and Freedoms*, Toronto: Carswell, pp. 183–229.

Edlund, L. (2006). 'The Price of Marriage: Net vs. Gross Flows and the South Asian Dowry Debate', *Journal of the European Economic Association*, 4(2/3), pp. 542–551.

Emon, A. M. (2013). 'The Paradox of Equality and the Politics of Difference: Gender Equality, Islamic Law, and the Modern Muslim State', in Z. Mir-Hosseini, Kari Vogr, Lena Larsen and Christian Moe (eds), *Gender and Equality in Muslim Family Law: Justice and Ethics in the Islamic Legal Tradition*, London: IB Tauris, pp. 237–258.

Epstein, C. F. (1988). *Deceptive Distinctions: Sex, Gender, and the Social Order*, New Haven, CT: Yale University Press.

Epstein, T. S. (1973). *South India: Yesterday, Today and Tomorrow. Mysore Villages Revisited*, New York: Holmes & Meier Publishers.

Ericksen, J. A., Yancey, W. L. and Ericksen, E. P. (1979) 'The Division of Family Roles', *Journal of Marriage and the Family*, 41(2), pp. 301–313.

Esposito, J. L. and DeLong-Bas, N. J. (2001). *Women in Muslim Family Law* New York: Syracuse University Press.

Esposito, J. L. and Mogahed, D. (2008). *Who Speaks for Islam? What a Billion Muslims Really Think*, New York: Gallup Press.

Fadl, K. A. E. (2001). *Speaking in God's Name: Islamic Law, Authority, and Women*, Oxford: Oneworld Publications.

Faraizi, A., Rahman, T. and McAllister, J. (2011). *Microcredit and Women's Empowerment: A Case Study of Bangladesh*, London: Routledge.

Fatima, K. (2016). 'Lot More Needs to be Done for Women's Economic Empowerment', *Independent*, 8 March 2016.

Feldman, S. (2001). 'Theories of Patriarchy: A Perspective from Contemporary Bangladesh', *Signs: Journal of Women in Culture and Society*, 26(4), pp. 1097–1127.

Feldmann S. and McCarthy, F. E. (1983). 'Purdah and Changing Patterns of Social Control Among Rural Women in Bangladesh', *Journal of Marriage and the Family*, 45, pp. 949–959.

Fineman, M. A. (1983). 'Implementing Equality: Ideology, Contradiction and Social Change. A Study of Rhetoric and Results in the Regulation of the Consequences of Divorce', *Wisconsin Law Review*, 4, pp. 789–886.

Fineman, M. A. (1991). *The Illusion of Equality: The Rhetoric and Reality of Divorce Reform*, Chicago, IL: The University of Chicago Press.

Fineman, M. A. (2009). 'Evolving Images of Gender and Equality: A Feminist Journey', *New England Law Review*, 43, pp. 437–460.

Fredman, S. (1997). *Women and the Law*, Oxford: Clarendon Press.

Gardner, K. (1994). 'Purdah, Female Power and Cultural Change: A Sylheti Example', *The Journal of Social Studies*, 65, pp. 1–24.

Gaulin, S. J. C. and Boster, J. S. (1990). 'Dowry as Female Competition', *American Anthropologist*, 92(4), pp. 994–1005.

Geirbo, H. C. and Imam, N. (2006). *The Motivation Behind Giving and Taking Dowry*, Research Monograph Series No. 28, Dhaka: BRAC, Research and Evaluation Division.

Ghosh, I. (2016). 'The Secret Life of a "Working Girl"', *New Age*, 4 March 2016.

Gibson, S., Mahmud, S., Toufique, K. and Turtonic, K. (eds) (2004). *Breaking New Ground: Livelihood Choices, Opportunities and Tradeoffs for Women and Girls in Rural Bangladesh*, Dhaka: The IDL Group.

Goode, W. J. (1964). *The Family*, Englewood Cliffs, NJ: Prentice-Hall.

Goody, J. (1973). 'Bridewealth and Dowry in Africa and Eurasia', in J. Goody and S. J. Tambiah (eds), *Bridewealth and Dowry*, Cambridge: Cambridge University Press, pp. 1–58.

Gove, W. R. (1972). 'The Relationship Between Sex Roles, Mental Illness, and Marital Status', *Social Forces*, 51(1), pp. 34–44.

Gove, W. R. and Tudor, J. F. (1973). 'Adult Sex Roles and Mental Illness', *American Journal of Sociology*, 78(4), pp. 812–835.

Government of India (1974). *Towards Equality*. Report of the Committee on the Status of Women in India, New Delhi: Government of India.

Government of the People's Republic of Bangladesh (1980). Dowry Prohibition Act 1980 (Act No. XXXV of 1980), available at http://bdlaws.minlaw.gov.bd/print_sections_all.php?id=607 [accessed 8 July 2016].

Government of the People's Republic of Bangladesh (2005). *Opinion on the Study Report for Marriage, Inheritance and Family Laws in Bangladesh Towards a Common Family Code*, Dhaka: Law Commission, available at www.lawcommissionbangladesh.org/reports/69.pdf [accessed 15 July 2016].

Government of the People's Republic of Bangladesh (2013). Parents Maintenance Act 2013 (Act No. 49 of 2013), available at http://bdlaws.minlaw.gov.bd/bangla_all_sections.php?id=1132 [accessed 12 July 2016].

Greenberg, J. (2003). 'Criminalizing Dowry Deaths: The Indian Experience', *American University Journal of Gender, Social Policy & Law*, 11(2), pp. 801–845.

Griffiths, A. (2001). 'Gendering Culture: Towards a Plural Perspective on Kwena Women's Rights', in J. K. Cowan, M. B. Dembour and R. A. Wilson (eds), *Culture and Rights: Anthropological Perspectives*, Cambridge: Cambridge University Press, pp. 102–126.

Haddad, T. (2007). *Imra 'tuna fi 'l-sharia wa 'l-mujtama*, trans. with introduction as *Muslim Women in Law and Society* by R. Husni and D. L. Newman (eds), London: Routledge.

Haider R. and Akhtar, R. (1999). 'The Role of NGO and Women's Perception of Empowerment: An Anthropological Study in a Village', *Empowerment*, 6, pp. 57–68.

Haider, Z. (1999). 'Role of Military in the Politics of Bangladesh: Mujib, Zia, and Ershad Regimes (1972–1990)', *Journal of South Asian and Middle Eastern Studies*, 22(3), pp. 57–82.

Haider, Z. (2006). *The Changing Pattern of Bangladesh Foreign Policy: A Comparative Study of the Mujib and Zia Regimes*, Dhaka: The University Press Limited.

Hakim, M. A. and Haque, A. S. (1995). 'Governmental Change and Constitutional Amendments in Bangladesh', *South Asian Survey*, 2(2), pp. 255–270.

Halder, R. and Akhter, R. (1999). 'The Role of NGO and Women's Perception of Empowerment: An Anthropological Study in a Village', *Empowerment*, 6, pp. 57–68.

Hamid, A. G. (2006). 'Reservations to CEDAW and the Implementation of Islamic Family Law: Issues and Challenges', *Asian Journal of International Law*, 1, pp. 121–155.

Hashmi, T. I. (2000). *Women and Islam in Bangladesh: Beyond Subjugation and Tyranny*, London: Macmillan Press Ltd.

Hassan, R. (1999). 'Feminism in Islam', in A. Sharma and K. K. Young (eds), *Feminism and World Religions*, Albany, NY: State University of New York Press, pp. 248–278.

Hoodfar, H. (1988). 'Household Budgeting and Financial Management in a Lower-Income Cairo Neighborhood', in D. Dwyer and J. Bruce (eds), *A Home Divided: Women and Income in the Third World*, Stanford: Stanford University Press, pp. 120–142.

Hogg, P. W. (2009). *Constitutional Law of Canada*, Toronto: Carswell.

Hoque, R. and Khan, M. M. (2007). 'Judicial Activism and Islamic Family Law: A Socio-Legal Evaluation of Recent Trends in Bangladesh', *Islamic Law and Society*, 14(2), pp. 204–239.

Hossain, R. (2008). 'What Has Changed?' *Forum*, *Daily Star*, 3(1), January 2008.

Huda, S. (1999). 'Perspectives on Sexual Harassment in Bangladesh: Acknowledging its Existence', *Empowerment*, 6, pp. 19–28.

Huda, S. (2003). 'Sexual Harrasment and Professional Women in Bangladesh', *Asia-Pacific Journal on Human Rights and the Law*, 2, pp. 52–69.

Huda, S. (2006). 'Dowry in Bangladesh: Compromising Women's Rights', *South Asia Research*, 26(3), pp. 249–268.

Huffman, S. L., Chowdhury, A. K. M. A., Chakraborty, J. and Simpson, N. K. (1980). 'Breast-Feeding Patterns in Rural Bangladesh', *The American Journal of Clinical Nutrition*, 33(1), pp. 144–154.

Human Rights Watch (2015). 'Whoever Raises Their Head Suffers the Most: Workers' Rights in Bangladesh's Garment Factories', available at www.hrw.org/report/2015/04/22/whoever-raises-their-head-suffers-most/workers-rights-bangladeshs-garment [accessed 25 July 2016].

Hunter, R. (2008). 'Introduction: Feminism and Equality', in R. Hunter (ed.), *Rethinking Equality Projects in Law Feminist Challenges*, Oxford: Hart Publishing, pp. 1–10.

Huque, A. S. and Akhter, M. Y. (1987). 'The Ubiquity of Islam: Religion and Society in Bangladesh', *Pacific Affairs*, 60(2), pp. 200–225.

Hussain, A. (2006). 'Nothing to Lose But Their Chains', *Star Weekend Magazine*, *Daily Star*, 8 April 2006.

Imam, M. (2013). 'Alarming Violence Against Women', *The Daily Star*, 18 March 2013.

International Labour Organization (2012). *Global Employment Trends for Women*, Geneva: ILO.

International Labour Organization (2016). *Women at Work: Trends 2016*, available at www.ilo.org/wcmsp5/groups/public/—dgreports/—dcomm/—publ/documents/publication/wcms_457317.pdf [accessed 20 July 2016].

Islam, K. S. (2010). 'Nowhere to Turn', *Star Weekend Magazine*, *Daily Star*, 29 January 2010.

Islam, M. (n.d.). *CEDAW and Bangladesh: A Study to Explore the Possibilities of Full Implementation of CEDAW in Bangladesh*, available at http://asiapacific.unwomen.org/~/media/field%20office%20

eseasia/docs/publications/southasia/reportstudies/05_human%20rights/complete-study%20pdf.ashx [accessed 18 July 2016].

Islam, N. (2013). *Future Uncertain for Bangladesh Factory Collapse Victims*, available at http://nimithu.wordpress.com/2013/08/12/future-uncertain-for-bangladesh-factory-collapse-victims/ [accessed 20 July 2016].

Ismail, S. (n.d.). *Asian University for Women*, available at www.asianuniversity.org/profiles/shakina.htm [accessed 11 July 2016].

Jahan, R. (1975). 'Women in Bangladesh', in *Women For Women: Bangladesh 1975*, Dhaka: The University Press Limited, pp. 1–30.

Jahan, R. (1980). *Bangladesh Politics: Problems and Issues*, Dhaka: The University Press Limited.

Jahan, R. (1987). *Bangladesh Politics: Problems and Issues*, Dhaka: The University Press Limited.

Jahan, R. (1995). 'Men in Seclusion, Women in Public: Rokeya's Dream and Women's Struggles in Bangladesh', in A. Basu (ed.), *The Challenge of Local Feminisms: Women's Movements in Global Perspective*, San Francisco, CA: Westview Press, Inc., pp. 87–109.

Jahan, M. (2007). 'Gender Mainstreaming in Bangladesh Civil Service: Prospects and Constraints', *Asian Affairs*, 29(1), pp. 41–72.

Jephcott, P., Seear, N. and Smith, J. (1962). *Married Women Working*, London: Allen & Unwin.

Jhappan, R. (1998). 'The Equality Pit or the Rehabilitation of Justice', *Canadian Journal of Women and the Law*, 10(1), pp. 60–107.

Jhutti, J. (1998). 'Dowry Among Sikhs in Britain', in W. Menski (ed.), *South Asians and the Dowry Problem*, London: Trentham Books Limited, pp. 175–198.

Kabeer, N. (1997). 'Women, Wages, and Intra-household Power Relations in Urban Bangladesh', *Development and Change*, 28, pp. 261–302.

Kabeer, N. and Mahmud, S. (2004). 'Globalization, Gender and Poverty: Bangladeshi Women Workers in Export and Local Markets', *Journal of International Development*, 16(1), pp. 93–109.

Kabir, B. M. (1995). 'Politico-economic Limitations and the Fall of the Military-Authoritarian Government in Bangladesh', *Armed Forces & Society*, 21(4), pp. 553–572.

Kabir, Z. N., Szebehely, M., Tishelman, C., Chowdhury, A. M. R., Höjer, B. and Winblad, B. (1998). 'Aging Trends – Making an Invisible Population Visible: The Elderly in Bangladesh', *Journal of Cross-Cultural Gerontology*, 13, pp. 361–378.

Kamal, S. (n.d.). *Law for Muslim Women in Bangladesh*, available at www.globalwebpost.com/farooqm/study_res/bangladesh/kamal_law_women.pdf [accessed 7 July 2016].

Kandiyoti, D. (1988). 'Bargaining With Patriarchy', *Gender & Society*, 2(3), pp. 274–290.

Kapur, R. (2012). 'Un-veiling Equality: Disciplining the "Other" Women Through Human Rights Discourse', in M. A. Emon, M. Ellis and B. Glahn (eds), *Islamic Law and International Human Rights Law*, Oxford: Oxford University Press, pp. 265–290.

Karim, A. K. N. (1980). *The Dynamics of Bangladesh Society*, New Delhi: Vikas Publishing House Pvt. Ltd.

Karim, E. (2009). 'Making It More Endurable', *Star Weekend Magazine, Daily Star*, 1 May 2009.

Karim, E. (2010). 'The Working Woman's Dilemma', *The Star*, 9(18), available at http://archive.thedailystar.net/magazine/2010/04/05/human_rights.htm [accessed 25 July 2016].

Karim, L. (2011). *Microfinance and Its Discontents: Women in Debt in Bangladesh*, London: University of Minnesota Press.

Karlekar, M. (1982). *Poverty and Women's Work: A Study of Sweeper Women in Delhi*, New Delhi: Shakti Books.

Kay, H. H. (1993). 'Equality and Difference: The Case of Pregnancy', in D. K. Weisberg (ed.), *Feminist Legal Theory Foundations*, Philadelphia, PA: Temple University Press, pp. 180–189.

Kealey, L. (1979). 'Introduction', in L. Kealey (ed.), *A Not Unreasonable Claim: Women and Reform in Canada 1880s–1920s*, Toronto: The Women's Press, pp. 1–14.

Khan, M. S. (2014). 'Working Women Wilt Under Double Burden', *New Age*, 27 January 2014.

Khan, N. (2016). 'Sad State of Domestic Workers in Bangladesh', *The Independent*, 21 March 2016.

Khan, S. (1993). *The Fifty Percent Women in Development and Policy in Bangladesh*, Dhaka: The University Press Limited.

Khan, Z. R. (1992). *Women, Work and Values: Contradictions in the Prevailing Notions and the Realities of Women's Lives in Rural Bangladesh*, Dhaka: Centre For Social Studies.

Khatun, F. (2009). 'A Woman's Worth', *Forum*, *Daily Star*, March 2009.

Khundker, N. (2006). *Perpetuation of Dowry as a Social Practice in Bangladesh*, Dhaka: Research Initiatives, Bangladesh.

Kibria, N. (1995). 'Culture, Social Class, and Income Control in the Lives of Women Garment Workers in Bangladesh', *Gender & Society*, Vol. 9, No. 3, pp. 289–309.

Kim, N. (1993). 'Toward a Feminist Theory of Human Rights: Straddling the Fence Between Western Imperialism and Uncritical Absolutism', *Columbia Human Rights Law Review*, 25, pp. 49–105.

Kishwar, M. (1986). 'Dowry: To Ensure Her Happiness or to Disinherit Her?', *Manushi*, 34, pp. 2–13.

Kishwar, M. (1988). 'Rethinking Dowry Boycott', *Manushi*, 48, pp. 10–13.

Kotalova, J. (1996). *Belonging to Others: Cultural Construction of Womanhood in a Village in Bangladesh*, Dhaka: The University Press Limited.

Krieger, L. J. and Cooney, P. N. (1983). 'The Miller-Wohl Controversy: Equal Treatment, Positive Action and the Meaning of Women's Equality', *Golden Gate University Law Review*, 13, pp. 513–572.

Krivenko, E. Y. (2009). *Women, Islam and International Law Within the Context of the Convention on the Elimination of All Forms of Discrimination Against Women*, Boston, MA: Martinus Nijhoff Publishers.

Kumari, R. (1989). *Brides Are Not For Burning: Dowry Victims in India*, New Delhi: Radiant Publishers.

Lindenbaum, S. (1981). 'Implications for Women of Changing Marriage Transactions in Bangladesh', *Studies in Family Planning*, 12(11), pp. 394–401.

MacKinnon, C. A. (1989). *Toward a Feminist Theory of the State*, Cambridge, MA: Harvard University Press.

Mahr, K. (2013). *Bangladesh Factory Collapse: Uncertain Future for Rana Plaza Survivors*, available at http://world.time.com/2013/06/10/bangladesh-factory-collapse-uncertain-future-for-rana-plaza-survivors/ [accessed 20 July 2016].

Majumder, P. P. (2000). 'Violence and Hazards Suffered by Women in Wage Employment: A Case of Women Working in the Export-Oriented Garment Industry of Bangladesh', *Empowerment*, 7, pp. 1–30.

Majury, D. (2002). 'The Charter, Equality Rights and Women: Equivocation and Celebration', *Osgoode Hall Law Journal*, 40(3–4), pp. 297–336.

Makino, M. (2014). *Dowry and Women's Status in Rural Pakistan*, Interim Report for Institutional Roles of Marriage in the Developing World: Empirical Studies from the Perspectives of Gender Empowerment, Chiba, Japan: IDE-JETRO.

Maloney, C., Aziz, K. M. A. and Sarker, P. C. (1981). *Beliefs and Fertility in Bangladesh*, Monograph No. 2, Dhaka: International Centre for Diarrhoeal Disease Research.

Manik, J. A. (2009). 'The Trial We Are Still Waiting For', *Forum*, *Daily Star*, December.

Maniruzzaman, T. (1990). 'Bangladesh Politics: Secular and Islamic Trends', in R. Ahmed (ed.), *Religion, Nationalism and Politics in Bangladesh*, New Delhi: South Asian Publishers, pp. 63–93.

McLachlin, Beverley, the Right Honourable (2001). 'Equality: The Most Difficult Right', 14 S.C.L.R. (2d).

Mencher, J. P. (1988). 'Women's Work and Poverty: Women's Contribution to Household Maintenance in South India', in D. Dwyer and J. Bruce (eds), *A Home Divided: Women and Income in the Third World*, Stanford: Stanford University Press, pp. 99–119.

Menski, W. (1998). 'Legal Strategies for Curbing the Dowry Problem', in W. Menski (ed.), *South Asians and the Dowry Problem*, London: Trentham Books Limited, pp. 97–149.

Menski, W. (2002). *Dowry and Violence Against Women in South Asia: Prevention, Protection and Provision*, Paper presented at the International Conference on Dowry: Realities and Strategies for Intervention. Working Together for Change in the 21st Century, Dhaka, 30–31 January 2002.

Menski, W. (2011). 'Flying Kites: Managing Family Laws and Gender Issues in Bangladesh', *Stamford Journal of Law*, 2(1), pp. 109–134.

Merry, S. E. (2006). *Human Rights and Gender Violence: Translating International Law into Local Justice*, Chicago, IL: The University of Chicago Press.

Mies, M. (1986). *Patriarchy and Accumulation on a World Scale: Women in the International Division of Labour*, London: Zed Books.

Miles, A. R. (1985–1986). 'Feminism, Equality, and Liberation', *Canadian Journal of Women and Law*, 1, pp. 42–68.

Mill, J. S. (1869). *The Subjugation of Women*, New York: D. Appleton Co.

Ministry of Education (2014). *Education Statistics*, available at www.moedu.gov.bd/index.php?option=com_content&task=view&id=300&Itemid=301 [accessed 25 July 2016].

Mir-Hossaini, Z. (2009). 'Towards Gender Equality: Muslim Family Laws and the *Sharia*', in Z. Anwar (ed.), *Wanted Equality and Justice in the Muslim Family*, Selangor, Malaysia: Musawah, pp. 23–64.

Moin, J. (2002). 'Sexual Exploitation of the Rural Working Women: A Field Level Observation', *Empowerment*, 9, pp. 75–84.

Monsoor, T. (1999). *From Patriarchy to Gender Equity: Family Law and Its Impact on Women in Bangladesh*, Dhaka: The University Press Limited.

Monsoor, T. (2003). 'Dower and Dowry: Its Effect on the Empowerment of Muslim Women', *Daily Star, Star Law Analysis*, 27 July 2003.

Monsoor, T. (2008). *Gender Equity and Economic Empowerment: Family Law and Women in Bangladesh*, Dhaka: British Council EWLR.

Mossman, M. J. (1994). 'Running Hard to Stand Still: The Paradox of Family Law Reform', *Dalhousie Law Journal*, 17(1), pp. 5–34.

Muhammad, A. (2011). 'Wealth and Deprivation: Ready-Made Garments Industry in Bangladesh', *Economic & Political Weekly*, 46(34), pp. 123–161.

Murickan, J. (1975). 'Women in Kerala: Changing Socio-economic Status and Self-Image', in A. D. Souza (ed.), *Women in Contemporary India: Traditional Images and Changing Roles*, Delhi Manohar Book Service, pp. 73–95.

Musawah (2011). *CEDAW and Muslim Family Laws in Search of Common Ground*, Selangor, Malaysia: Muswah.

Nasir, J. J. (1990). *The Islamic Law of Personal Status*, Boston, MA: Kluwer Law International.

Nasrin, S. (2011). 'Crime or Custom? Motivations Behind Dowry Practice in Rural Bangladesh', *Indian Journal of Gender Studies*, 18(1), pp. 27–50.

Naved, R. T. and Persson, L. A. (2010). 'Dowry and Spousal Physical Violence Against Women in Bangladesh', *Journal of Family Issues*, 31(6), pp. 830–856.

Naved, R. T., Newby, M. and Amin, S. (2001). 'The Effects of Migration and Work on Marriage of Female Garment Workers in Bangladesh', *International Journal of Population Geography*, 7(2), pp. 91–104.

Nazneen, S. (2013). 'Men Aboard? Movement for a Uniform Family Code in Bangladesh', in M. A. Sharmani (ed.), *Feminist Activism, Women's Rights and Legal Reform*, London: Zed Books, pp. 101–124.

Niaz, U. (2004). 'Women's Mental Health in Pakistan', *World Psychiatry*, 3(1), pp. 60–62.

Odhikar (2014). *Human Rights Report: On Bangladesh*, Dhaka: Odhikar.

Okin, S. M. (1989). *Justice, Gender, and the Family*, New York: Basic Books, Inc.

Oldenburg, V. T. (2002). *Dowry Murder: The Imperial Origins of a Cultural Crime*, Oxford: Oxford University Press.

Olmsted, J. C. (2005). 'Is Paid Work the (Only) Answer? Neoliberalism, Arab Women's Well-Being, and the Social Contract', *Journal of Middle East Women's Studies*, 1, pp. 112–139.

Pahl, J. (1980). 'Patterns of Money Management Within Marriage', *Journal of Social Policy*, 9(3), pp. 313–335.

Parker, K. and Wang, W. (2013). 'Modern Parenthood Roles of Moms and Dads Converge as They Balance Work and Family', Pew Research Centre, available at www.pewsocialtrends.org/2013/03/14/modern-parenthood-roles-of-moms-and-dads-converge-as-they-balance-work-and-family/ [accessed 25 July 2016].

Parveen, S. (2014). 'Rana Plaza Factory Collapse Survivors Struggle One Year On', BBC, 23 April 2014, available at www.bbc.com/news/world-asia-27107860 [accessed 20 July 2016].

Paul-Majumder, P. P. (1997). 'Sramajibi Mohilader Daridrer Bibhinna Matra', in R. I. Rahman (ed.), *Daridra O Unnayan: Prekkhapot Bangladesh* [in Bengali], Dhaka: Bangladesh Institute of Development Studies, pp. 123–161.

Paull, G. (2008). 'Children and Women's Hours of Work', *The Economic Journal*, 118(526), pp. F8–F27.

Pereira, F. (2002). *The Fractured Scales: The Search for a Uniform Personal Code*, Delhi: STREE.

Perveen, R. (2014). 'Social Injustice Behind the Practice of Dowry', *Scoop Independent News*, 11 January 2014.

Perveen, R., Hadi, R. and Mooni, Z. (2011). *Forgotten. Dowry: A Socially Endorsed Form of Violence in Pakistan*, Islamabad: Sachet Pakistan/UN Women Pakistan.

Phillips, A. (1987). 'Introduction', in A. Phillips (ed.), *Feminism and Equality*, Oxford: Basil Blackwell, pp. 1–23.

Preetha, S. S. (2012). 'The Working Mother', *The Star*, 11(15), available at http://archive.thedailystar.net/magazine/2010/04/05/human_rights.htm [accessed 25 July 2016].

Quraishi, A. (2011). 'What if *Sharia* Weren't the Enemy? Rethinking International Women's Right Advocacy on Islamic Law', *Columbia Journal of Gender and Law*, 25(5), pp. 173–249.

Rahman, F. (1982). 'The Status of Women in Islam: A Modernist Interpretation', in H. Papanek and G. Minault (eds), *Separate Worlds: Studies of Purdah in South Asia*, Columbia: South Asia Books, pp. 285–310.

Rahman, M. M. G. (1984). *Maksudul Momeneen*, Dhaka: Ratan Art Press.

Rahman, R. I. and Islam, R. (2013). *Female Labour Force Participation in Bangladesh: Trends, Drivers and Barriers*, Asia-Pacific Working Paper Series, Geneva, ILO.

Ram, K. (1991). *Mukkuvar Women: Gender, Hegemony and Capitalist Transformation in a South Indian Fishing Community*, London: Allen & Unwin Pty Ltd.

Ramadan, T. (2009). *Radical Reform: Islamic Ethics and Liberation*, Oxford: Oxford University Press.

Rao, N. (2012). 'Breadwinners and Homemakers: Migration and Changing Conjugal Expectations in Rural Bangladesh', *The Journal of Development Studies*, 48(1), pp. 26–40.

Rao, V. (1993). 'The Rising Price of Husbands: A Hedonic Analysis of Dowry Increases in Rural India', *Journal of Political Economy*, 101(4), pp. 666–677.

Rao, V. V. P. and Rao, V. N. (1980). 'The Dowry System in Indian Marriages: Attitudes, Expectations and Practices', *International Journal of Sociology of the Family*, 10, pp. 99–113.

Rashid, S. F. (2006). 'Emerging Changes in Reproductive Behaviour Among Married Adolescent Girls in an Urban Slum in Dhaka, Bangladesh', *Reproductive Health Matters*, 14(27), pp. 151–159.

Rashiduzzaman, M. (2002). 'Bangladesh in 2001: The Election and a New Political Reality?', *Asian Survey*, 42(1), pp. 183–191.

Rastogi, M. and Therly, P. (2006). 'Dowry and Its Link to Violence Against Women in India: Feminist Psychological Perspectives', *Trauma, Violence, & Abuse*, 7(1), pp. 66–77.

Raynor, J. (2005). 'Educating Girls in Bangladesh: Watering a Neighbor's Tree', in S. Aikman and E. Unterhalter (eds), *Beyond Access: Transforming Policy and Practice for Gender Equality in Education*, Oxford: Oxfam, pp. 83–105.

Rozario, S. (1992). *Purity and Communal Boundaries: Women and Social Change in a Bangladeshi Village*, London: Allen & Unwin.

Rozario, S. (1998). 'Disjunctions and Continuities: Dowry and the Position of Single Women in Bangladesh', in C. Risseeuw and K. Ganesh (eds), *Negotiation and Social Space: A Gendered Analysis of Changing Kin and Security Networks in South Asia and Sub-Saharan Africa*, London: AltaMira Press, pp. 259–275.

Rozario, S. (2002). 'Grameen Bank-Style Microcredit: Impact on Dowry and Women's Solidarity', *Development Bulletin*, 57, pp. 67–70.

Rozario, S. (2004). *Building Solidarity Against Patriarchy*, Dhaka: CARE Bangladesh.

Rozario, S. (2009). 'Dowry in Rural Bangladesh: An Intractable Problem?', in T. Bradley, E. Tomalin and M. Subramaniam (eds), *Bridging the Gap between Theory and Practice*, London: Zed Books, pp. 29–58.

Roy, S. D. (2014). 'No End Yet to Wage Discrimination', *Daily Star*, 9 March 2014.

Rudd, J. (2001). 'Dowry-Murder: An Example of Violence Against Women', *Women's Studies International Forum*, 24(5), pp. 513–522.

Salehin, M. M. (2016). *Islamic NGOs in Bangladesh: Development, Piety and Neoliberal Governmentality*, London: Routledge.

Salway, S., Jesmin, S. and Rahman, S. (2005). 'Women's Employment in Urban Bangladesh: A Challenge to Gender Identity', *Development and Change*, 36, pp. 317–349.

Samuel, E. (2002). 'Dowry and Dowry Harassment in India: An Assessment Based on Modified Capitalist Patriarchy', *African and Asian Studies*, 1(3), pp. 187–229.

Sangari, K. (2002). *Politics of the Possible: Essays on Gender, History, Narratives, Colonial English*, London: Anthem Press.

Scales, A. (1981). 'Towards a Feminist Jurisprudence', *Indiana Law Journal*, 56, pp. 375–444.

Schuler, S. R., Hashemi, S. M., Riley, A. P. and Akhter, S. (1996). 'Credit Programs, Patriarchy and Men's Violence Against Women in Rural Bangladesh', *Social Science Medicine*, 43(12), pp. 1729–1742.

Self, S. and Grabowski, R. (2009). 'Modernization, Inter-caste Marriage, and Dowry: An Analytical Perspective', *Journal of Asian Economics*, 20(1), pp. 69–76.

Serajuddin, A. M. (2001). *Shari'a Law and Society: Tradition and Change in South Asia*, Karachi: Oxford University Press.

Shah, N. A. (2006). 'Women's Human Rights in the Koran: An Interpretive Approach', *Human Rights Quarterly*, 28(4), pp. 868–903.

Sharma, U. (1993). 'Dowry in North India: Its Consequences for Women', in P. Uberoi (ed.), *Family, Kinship and Marriage in India*, Delhi: Oxford University Press, pp. 341–356.

Shehabuddin, E. (2008a). 'Jamaat-i-Islami in Bangladesh: Women, Democracy and the Transformation of Islamic Politics', *Modern Asian Studies*, 42(2–3), pp. 577–603.

Shehabuddin, E. (2008b). *Reshaping the Holy Democracy: Development, and Muslim Women in Bangladesh*, New York: Columbia University Press.

Siddiqi, D. (2003). *The Sexual Harassment of Industrial Workers: Strategies for Intervention in the Workplace and Beyond*, Paper 26, Dhaka: Centre for Policy Dialogue.

Siddiqua, R. (2010). 'Domestic Helps: Are They Protected?', *Law and Our Rights, Daily Star*, 9 January 2010.

Sohrab, J. A. (1993). 'Avoiding the "Exquisite Trap": A Critical Look at the Equal Treatment/Special Treatment Debate in Law', *Feminist Legal Studies*, 1(2), pp. 141–162.

Srinivas, M. N. (1984). *Some Reflections on Dowry*, Oxford: Oxford University Press.

Srinivasan, P. and Lee, G. R. (2004). 'The Dowry System in Northern India: Women's Attitudes and Social Change', *Journal of Marriage and Family*, 66(5), pp. 1108–1117.

Srinivasan, S. (2005). 'Daughters or Dowries? The Changing Nature of Dowry Practices in South India', *World Development*, 33(4), pp. 593–615.

Stone, L. and James, C. (1995). 'Dowry, Bride-Burning, and Female Power in India', *Women's Studies International Forum*, 18(2), pp. 125–134.

Sultan, R. (n.d.). *Divorce in Islam*, available at www.zawaj.com/articles/divorce_reem_sultan.html [accessed 16 July 2016].

Sultana, A. M. (2010). 'Socio-cultural Dimensions of Women's Discriminations in Rural Communities', *Ozean Journal of Social Sciences*, 3(1), pp. 31–38.

Sultana, M. (2016). 'Facilities for Female Staff: Commercial Banks' Performance Improves, Says BB Reports', *Financial Express*, 8 March 2016, available at www.thefinancialexpress-bd.com/2016/03/08/19953/Commercial-banks'-performance-improves,-say-BB-reports [accessed 25 July 2016].

Suran, L., Amin, S., Huq, L. and Chowdury, K. (2004). *Does Dowry Improve Life for Brides? A Test of the Bequest Theory of Dowry in Rural Bangladesh*, No. 195, New York, Population Council, available at www.eldis.org/vfile/upload/1/document/0708/DOC19221.pdf [accessed 19 July 2015].

Taher, M. A. and Jamaluddin, S. Z. (2015). 'Reluctance of Seeking Legal Remedy in Dowry Violence Cases in Bangladesh: An Analysis of Influencing Factors', *Women's Studies International Forum*, 53, pp. 83–89.

Tamanna, N. (2008). 'Personal Status Laws in Morocco and Tunisia: A Comparative Exploration of the Possibilities for Equality-Enhancing Reform in Bangladesh', *Feminist Legal Studies*, 16, pp. 323–343.

Tamanna, N. (2013). 'Recognition of "Difference" in Shari'a: A Feminist Scrutiny Through the Lens of Substantive Equality', *Journal of Social Welfare and Family Law*, 35(3), pp. 329–345.

Tamanna, N. (2014). 'The "Welfare of the Child" in Shari'a Law: An Analysis of Child Custody Law and Practices in Bangladesh from a Feminist Perspective', *Child and Family Law Quarterly*, 26(3), pp. 283–300.

Tambiah, S. J. (1973). 'Dowry and Bridewealth and the Property Rights of Women in South Asia', in J. Goody and S. J. Tambiah (eds), *Bridewealth and Dowry*, Cambridge: Cambridge University Press, pp. 59–169.

Thanwi, M. A. A. (n.d.). *Bihishti Zewar*, Vol. 2, Dhaka: Emdadia Library.

Thanwi, M. A. F. (1990). *Bihishti Zewar*, trans. with commentary as *Perfecting Women: Maulana Ashraf Ali Thanwi's Bihishti Zewar* by B. D. Metcalf, Berkeley, CA: University of California Press.

The Women in Public Service Project (2014). *Women Leading Public Service and Political Participation in South Asia: New and Emerging Developments*, Washington, DC: The Woodrow Wilson International Center for Scholars.

Uddin, A. K. M. Z. (2015). 'Female Staff Percentage Drops Alarmingly in Banking Sector', *New Age*, 9 September 2015.

Uddin, M. J. (2015). *The Micro-politics of Microcredit Gender and Neoliberal Development*, London: Routledge.

Uddin, S. and Hopper, T. (2003). 'Accounting for Privatization in Bangladesh: Testing World Bank Claims', *Critical Perspectives on Accounting*, 14(7), pp. 739–774.

Upadhya, C. B. (1990). 'Dowry and Women's Property in Coastal Andhra Pradesh', *Contributions to Indian Sociology*, 24(1), pp. 29–59.

Urmee, F. (2011). 'Women Development Policy Forward Looking But Not Flawless', *The Star*, 12 March 2011.

van der Veen, K. W. (1971). *I Give Thee My Daughter: A Study of Marriage and Hierarchy Among the Anavil Brahmans of South Gujarat*, Assen, Netherlands: Van Gorcum.

Venkatesan, R. (2013). 'Clothing Garment Workers in Safety: The Case of Bangladesh', *Economic and Political Weekly*, 48(28), available at www.epw.in/journal/2013/28/web-exclusives/clothing-garment-workers-safety-case-bangladesh.html# [accessed 25 July 2016].

Venkatraman, B. A. (1995). 'Islamic States and the United Nations Convention of All Forms of Discrimination Against Women: Are the *Sharia* and the Convention Compatible?', *American University Law Review*, 44(5), pp. 1949–2027.

Wadud, A. (1999). *Qur'an and Women Rereading the Sacred Text from a Woman's Perspective*, Oxford: Oxford University Press.

Wallace, B. J., Ahsan, R. M., Hussain, S. H. and Ahsan, E. (1987). *The Invisible Resource: Women and Work in Rural Bangladesh*, Boulder, CO and London: Westview Press.

Weisberg, D. K. (1993). 'Introduction', in D. K. Weisberg (ed.), *Feminist Legal Theory Foundations*, Philadelphia, PA: Temple University Press, pp. 121–127.

Weitzman, L. J. (1981). 'Economics of Divorce: Social and Economic Consequences of Property, Alimony and Child Support Awards', *UCLA Law Review*, 28, pp. 1125–1180.

Weitzman, L. J. (1985). *The Divorce Revolution: The Unexpected Social and Economic Consequences for Women and Children in America*, New York: The Free Press.

Wentholt, K. (1999). 'Formal and Substantive Equal Treatment: The Limitations and the Potential of the Legal Concept of Equality', in T. Loenen and P. R. Rodrigues (eds), *Non-Discrimination Law: Comparative Perspective*, London: Kluwer Law International, pp. 53–64.

White, S. C. (1992). *Arguing with the Crocodile Gender and Class in Bangladesh*, London: Zed Books.

White, S. C. (2010). 'Domains of Contestation: Women's Empowerment and Islam in Bangladesh', *Women's Studies International Forum*, 33, pp. 334–344.

White, S. C. (2013). *Patriarchal Investments: Marriage, Dowry and Economic Change in Rural Bangladesh*, Bath Papers in International Development and Well-Being, Working Paper No. 19, Bath: University of Bath.

Whitehead, A. (1981). '"I'm Hungry, Mum": The Politics of Domestic Budgeting', in K. Young, C. Wolkowitz and R. McCullagh (eds), *Of Marriage and the Market: Women's Subordination in International Perspective*, London: CSE Books, pp. 88–111.

Winkvist, A. and Akhtar, H. Z. (2000). 'God Should Give Daughters to Rich Families Only: Attitudes Towards Childbearing Among Low-Income Women in Punjab, Pakistan', *Social Science & Medicine*, 51, pp. 73–81.

Wolgast, E. H. (1980). *Equality and the Rights of Women*, London: Cornell University Press.

World Bank (2014a), available at http://data.worldbank.org/indicator/SL.TLF.CACT.FE.ZS [accessed 16 July 2016].

World Bank (2014b), available at http://data.worldbank.org/indicator/SL.TLF.CACT.MA.ZS [accessed 16 July 2016].

World Health Organization (2015a). 'Why Do So Many Women Still Die in Pregnancy and Childbirth', 12 November 2015, available at www.who.int/features/qa/12/en/ [accessed 20 July 2016].

World Health Organization (2015b). *Trends in Maternal Mortality: 1990 to 2015. Estimates by WHO, UNICEF, UNFPA, World Bank Group and the United Nations Population Division*, Geneva: World Health Organization.

Wright, S. (1988). 'Economic Rights and Social Justice: A Feminist Analysis of Some International Human Rights Conventions', in *12 Australian Yearbook of International Law*, pp. 241–264.

Zafarullah, H. (2011). 'Dissecting Public Sector Corruption in Bangladesh: Issues and Problems of Control', *Public Organization Review: A Global Journal*, 1, pp. 465–486.

Zaman, H. (1996). *Women and Work in a Bangladesh Village*, Dhaka: Narigrantha Prabantana.

Cases

Abul Basher Howlader v. *The State and another* (1994) 46 DLR (AD) 169 [Bangladesh].

Begum Hamida v. *Abdul Hamid* (1974) 26 D.L.R. S.C. 26 [Bangladesh].

Bliss v. *Attorney General of Canada* (1979) 1 S.C.R. 183.

Geduldig v. *Aiello* (1974) 417 US 484.

General Electric Co. v. *Gilbert* (1976) 429 US 125.

Hayes v. *Malleable Men's Working Club and Institute* (1985) ICR 703.

Hefzur Rahman v. *Shamsunahar Begum* (1995) 47 D.L.R. HCD. 54 [Bangladesh].

Hefzur Rahman v. *Shamsunahar Begum* (1999) 51 D.L.R. HCD. 172 [Bangladesh].

Hosne Ara Begum v. *Md. Rezaul Karim and others* (1991) 43 D.L.R. 543 [Bangladesh].

Jamila Khatun v. *Rustom Ali* (1996) 48 D.L. R. 110 [Bangladesh].

Md. Abu Bakar Siddique v. *S.M.A. Bakar and others* (1986) 38 DLR, AD 106 [Bangladesh].

Moge v. *Moge* (1992) 3 S.C.R. 813.

Mollick v. *State* (1996) 48 DLR 329 [Bangladesh].

Mst. Amena Khatun v. *Sherajuddin* (1965) 17 D. L. R. 687 [Bangladesh].

Poddar v. *Saha* (1985) 37 DLR 227 [Bangladesh].

Rezaul Karim v. *Mst. Taslima Begum* (1988) 40 DLR 360 [Bangladesh].

Rustom Ali v. *Jamila Khatun* (1991) 43 D. L. R. HCD 301 [Bangladesh].

Index

For Product Safety Concerns and Information please contact our EU representative GPSR@taylorandfrancis.com Taylor & Francis Verlag GmbH, Kaufingerstraße 24, 80331 München, Germany

Batch number: 10726294

Printed by Printforce, the Netherlands